The Order of Rome

Imperium Romanum

Charlemagne and the
Holy Roman Empire

Empires

Their Rise and Fall

The Order of Rome

Imperium Romanum

Charlemagne and the
Holy Roman Empire

Jack Holland

Imperium Romanum

John Monroe

Charlemagne and the Holy Roman Empire

Preface by M. Gwyn Morgan,
Professor of Classics and History
The University of Texas at Austin

Boston Publishing Company, Inc.
Boston, Massachusetts

Empires: Their Rise and Fall is published in the United States by Boston Publishing Company, Inc., and distributed by Field Publications.

Authors: Jack Holland, John Monroe
Picture Researcher, Janet Adams
Assistant Picture Researcher, Noreen O'Gara
Historical Consultant, Judith Hanhisalo
Project Consultant, Valerie Hopkins
Design Implementation, Designworks

Boston Publishing Company, Inc.

President, Robert J. George
Editor-In-Chief, Robert Manning
Managing Editor, Paul Dreyfus
Marketing Director, Jeanne Gibson

Field Publications

President, Bruce H. Seide
Publisher, Marilyn Black
Marketing Director, Kathleen E. Long

Rizzoli Editore

Authors of the Italian Edition:
    Introduction: Professor Ovidio Dallera
    Imperial Rome: Dr. Flavio Conti
    Holy Roman Empire: Dr. Alfredo Bosisio
    Maps: Fernando Russo
Idea and Realization, Harry C. Lindinger
Graphic Design, Gerry Valsecchi
General Editorial Supervisor, Ovidio Dallera

© 1986 by Rizzoli Editore
Printed in Italy.

Library of Congress Catalog Card Number: 79-2507
ISBN: 0-15-004026-1

Field Publications offers handsome bookends and other decorative desk items. For information, write to:
Field Publications, P.O. Box 16617, Columbus, Ohio 43216.

Contents

Preface

Rome and the Romans still exercise a powerful hold on the popular imagination. Two questions arise time and again: How could the inhabitants of one small village on the banks of the Tiber River have conquered first Italy, then the entire Mediterranean world? And how could this empire, in some respects the greatest history has ever seen, have disintegrated as completely as it did?

However intriguing, these questions tend to obscure the significance of Rome's accomplishment. Rome's real achievement was neither winning nor losing territory but running an empire successfully for several centuries and, in the process, civilizing much of Europe. Without benefit of courses in business management or public administration, but rather on the basis of a certain innate pragmatism and tolerance, the Romans absorbed a world and governed it under law.

The Holy Roman Empire, which originated more than three hundred years after the fall of Rome, was a deliberate attempt to re create in Europe the unity, the stability, and the culture of Rome under a new, Christian God. The ambitiousness of this attempt and the failure to achieve it become clear when we compare the two empires. The Roman Empire saw more than its share of civil wars and internecine strife but managed until its last days to hold together as a single unit. The Holy Roman Empire, by contrast, pursued the ideal of unity in vain. What was needed, but seldom achieved, was a balancing act between emperors, popes, barons, independent city-states, and dissident religious leaders—not to mention enemies beyond the frontiers. Far from unifying Europe under a single Christian ruler, the Holy Roman Empire remained a fragmented conglomeration, lasting as long as it did because it was weak, a counter in a power struggle played out on a larger board.

The same striking contrast between the two empires shows up in the cultural sphere. Putting Greek theories into practice (something the ancient Greeks often found difficult to do), the Romans regarded the city as the hallmark of their civilization and founded cities with all the appropriate physical amenities: temples, marketplaces, theaters, amphitheaters, circuses for chariot racing, aqueducts, sewers, public baths, even public latrines. In intellectual matters, however, Rome's highly cultured ruling classes left their subjects more or less to their own devices; the resources were there, but the aristocracy's concern was socialization rather than education.

In the case of the Holy Roman Empire, the theme of public building is practically exhausted once the castles and cathedrals have been described, but intellectual activity flourished. At first, education was rare even among the elite (Charlemagne himself, we are told, could read but not write) and so was sponsored enthusiastically by church and state alike. Later, the very disunity that plagued the empire encouraged the exchange of opinions by pen as well as by sword, spreading education through a wider segment of the population and leading to the foundation of the first universities. So Europe was readied for the influx of knowledge that came to the West after Constantinople fell to the Turks in 1453. And from Europe this knowledge, old and new, was spread still farther afield, to a certain rebellious colony where the Founding Fathers considered Roman practices a serviceable guide when they set about drafting a constitution for their infant republic.

In these respects the Roman Empire and the Holy Roman Empire resemble two sides of a single coin, both essential to the evolution of Western civilization but different in many ways. Yet the dissimilarities should not obscure underlying similarities, similarities of the human condition that tied these cultures to each other—and link them to us. In both worlds, the bulk of the population—peasants in the fields or workers in the towns—lived behind a veil of anonymity that is stripped away only occasionally by discoveries like those in Pompeii and Herculaneum. But we can still form a fair idea of what people sought, thought, and experienced by taking an attentive look at their history and cultural achievements. Their accomplishments reflect the hopes and aspirations of those distant times and yet speak directly to us across the intervening centuries. For these were people whose ideas and actions, wants and needs, all fed into the heritage that has made us what we are today.

M. GWYN MORGAN
Professor of Classics and History
The University of Texas at Austin

Imperium Romanum

Rome challenges and haunts the mind of Western man. On the one hand, it recalls images of the relentless drive to mastery, the thrill of triumph, and the dream of universal order. On the other, it confirms the unsettling ambiguity of imperialism as it inevitably succumbs to the malaise of decline. The sheer expanse of the territory Rome held under its sway has for centuries been a source of wonderment. By the beginning of the second century A.D., when Rome reached its greatest extent, the borders of the empire stretched from the Atlantic Ocean in the west to the Euphrates River in the east, from the vast African deserts in the south to the misty highlands of Britain and the thick German oak forests in the north. Altogether, the empire covered an area of about two million square miles, and its population totaled fifty million or more.

Upon the diverse peoples of the empire Rome im-

9

Fanciful legends were created to exalt Rome's beginnings. This Pompeian fresco (above left) depicts Mars, the god of war, and the royal princess Rhea Silvia, who bore the god twin sons, Romulus and Remus. The princess' uncle, the king, ordered the baby boys set afloat on the Tiber to drown (below left), but the river brought the twins safely to the city that Romulus was to found and give his name to. There a she-wolf suckled the two. This sculpture of the she-wolf (right) dates from Etruscan times. The twins were added during the Renaissance.

posed its legal system, culture, and language. Yet the empire was flexible enough to change and adapt as it absorbed. The Romans, however brutal, were not as a rule genocidal, nor did they attempt to construct a form of monolithic elitism—racial, cultural, or otherwise. Although no empire can be built on liberal principles, the Romans were never oblivious to the moral demands of the Roman good faith (*fides Romana*). From the earliest days, they were amenable to compromise, often enfranchising conquered peoples and bringing them into Roman society. By the second century A.D., the provinces were providing the capital with the emperors themselves.

The origins of Rome are enshrined in legends that have become part of Western culture. The best known tells how Rhea Silvia, the daughter of King Numitor of Alba, was made pregnant by Mars, the god of war, and gave birth to the twins Romulus and Remus. The twins' wicked granduncle Amulius, who had deposed Numitor, set the infants on the Tiber in a basket to drown. The river carried the twins safely, however, to the future site of Rome, where a she-wolf suckled them. Years later, after killing Amulius and restoring their grandfather Numitor to his throne, Romulus and Remus returned to the place where they were nursed by the she-wolf to found a city. The

legend tells that each brother chose a hilltop and waited for a sign from heaven. Remus saw six birds from the Aventine Hill, but Romulus counted twelve from the Palatine. Romulus thus built the city, gave it his name, and became its first king. Tradition dates the founding of the city to 753 B.C.

The origin of such tales can only be surmised. But archaeology has shown that the earliest settlers at the site of Rome lived not only on the Palatine but also on the Quirinal and Esquiline hills from about the tenth century B.C. Their forefathers were part of the great Indo-European migration that had begun over a millennium before and had populated western

Europe with, among others, the ancestral tribes of the Germans, the Italians, and the Celts.

Rome's site was a natural crossroads by water and land. Navigation from the sea up the Tiber ended at Rome, halted by shallows and an island; these barriers afforded the first natural crossing above the river mouth. Here, an ancient salt road from the sea intersected the north-south route between Etruria and the rich plains of Campania. The crossing was surrounded by steep and defensible bluffs and mesas—the so-called hills of Rome—that water had carved from the volcanic sediments of the plain.

The first settlers inhabited only the hilltops, leav-

ing the low ground for burial of their dead. These early inhabitants formed cults, joining with other Latin tribes that had settled in the region. One cult center was the Alban Mount, the volcano that had formed the plain. This religious unity eventually led to the establishment of the Latin League, over which Rome eventually gained hegemony. But in the early sixth century B.C., Rome fell under the domination of its Etruscan neighbors from the north, who transmitted Greek culture and instituted public works. The Forum, established at this time, served as a market and as a place for political assemblies, unifying the communities of the hills.

During the seventh and sixth centuries B.C., Rome was ruled by kings: Numa Pompilius, Tullus Hostilius, Ancus Marcius, Tarquinius Priscus, Servius Tullius, and Tarquinius Superbus (Tarquin the Haughty). The name Pompilius points to a mingling of Sabine neighbors with the Latin stock of Rome and Tarquinius and the dominion of the Etruscans from across the Tiber.

The Etruscans, unlike the Romans, did not speak an Indo-European language; legend and linguistic evidence associate them with the East. But both the Etruscans and the Italic tribes shared the Iron Age culture of central Italy and experienced Greek influence from the eighth century on. By that time, the

These black stones (top) near the heart of the Roman Forum marked, according to legend, the "tomb of Romulus." An archaic inscription found nearby contains the word "king." After the warrior-king Romulus, legend provided Rome with the priest-king Numa Pompilius, shown on this coin (immediately above) of the first century B.C. As Romulus was a military founder, so Numa was the founder of religious customs and the ways of peace. The so-called Walls of Servius (near right), credited to Rome's sixth king, made Rome by far the largest enclosed city in Italy and provide early evidence of work by Greek masters in Rome.

Rome drove out its seventh and last king, Tarquin the Haughty, at the close of the sixth century B.C. When Tarquin attempted a countercoup, one Horatius Cocles held him off until the bridge over the Tiber could be dismantled. He then swam the river (right). Below right and bottom right, a striped agate seal with its print: two priests of Mars, the Salii (leapers), bearing the shields sacred to the god. The Salii danced in procession on the fifteenth of Mars' month (the Ides of March).

Etruscans had come to dominate the areas of Umbria and Tuscany and, in the late seventh century, parts of Latium and Campania. They also pushed north as far as the valley of the Po. In the sixth century, a Greek, one of many who had been assimilated in Etruria, established the Etruscan dynasty at Rome.

The legacy that the Etruscans left to Rome is incalculable. From them, for example, the Romans acquired the Greek alphabet. The Etruscan dynasty gave the city its first urban development, not only establishing the Forum but erecting the massive temple of Jupiter on the Capitoline Hill that symbolized the city's power. One tradition also relates that the sixth king, Servius Tullius, was Etruscan and that he gave the Romans their class structure.

This system was based on each citizen's ability to furnish certain necessities for military service. The richest class, the knights, was composed of those who could afford to furnish a horse and armor. Next in rank came those of moderate wealth, who were able to fit themselves out as heavily armed foot soldiers, with breastplate, shield, and spear. The poorest citi-

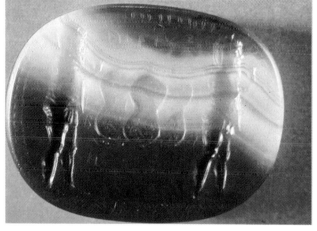

zens formed the auxiliaries, who were lightly equipped.

To carry out the assessment for military service, Servius instituted the so-called centuriate assembly, which met on the Field of Mars (Campus Martius) outside Rome. This assembly was later used for voting purposes and was organized to insure that the voting groups of the wealthy would always outweigh those of the poor. Servius is also said to have been responsible for dividing Rome into four tribes and for building its first fortification, the Walls of Servius, which made Rome the largest enclosed area in Italy, if not the world.

At the end of the sixth century, King Tarquin the Haughty was expelled from Rome. According to legend, his son had raped Lucretia, the wife of a noble. This outrage was the culmination of what came to be depicted as a classic tyranny in the Greek mold. For the Etruscans, the loss of Rome was followed by a series of setbacks from which they never really recovered. Having never coalesced to form a nation, they instead remained a loose association of highly individual states. In the end, this lack of national identity and institutions made them an easy target for the Romans, who seized the Etruscan cities one by one. By the end of the third century, the Etruscans were

The Etruscans were a major influence in Rome's development. Relics of their culture include this bronze statuette (far left) and this once richly plumed helmet (near left), with its elegant curled beard and curved horns. Above, the gate of Ferentino, one of the main cities of the Hernici, an Italic tribe that eventually was absorbed by Rome's expanding power. The helmet (right) of another Italic tribe, the Apuli, was decorated with a cross.

almost completely absorbed by their erstwhile Roman subjects.

After expelling its last king, Rome became a republic. In the new oligarchical constitution, the monarch was replaced by two consuls, who were elected annually by the centuriate assembly. Theirs was the *imperium,* or power of civil and military rule over the state. Other civil and religious offices gradually developed: praetor, dictator, quaestor, censor, pontifex, augur, aedile. Nevertheless, the consulship, the most powerful of the offices apart from dictatorship, remained the province of the founding families, the patricians, even after it was technically opened to a wider circle of the lower class, or plebs, in 367 B.C.

After the republican constitution came into effect, Rome scored a series of successes in asserting influence over its nearest neighbors. Expansion faltered briefly with the invasion of the Gauls, who sacked Rome in 387 B.C., but the young republic quickly showed recuperative powers. Within a generation, it had reestablished its position in Latium, reformed its army, and rebuilt its great ring of fortifying walls.

This was the age of the soldier-farmer, a time when, as the Greek antiquarian Plutarch was to write, "that pure and golden race of men was still in possession of the Forum." Self-possessed, frugal, self-sacrificing, and courageous, these men of Rome's semilegendary heroic age are typified by Cincinnatus. Summoned from his farm duties and appointed dictator in 458 B.C. to rescue a trapped Roman army, Cincinnatus

simply performed the required task and returned to his plow. His story would be retold with bitter emphasis when the dictatorship later came to be abused as a tool of autocratic power.

From the Gallic invasion of the fourth century B.C. emerged one of Rome's first historical heroes—the general Camillus, who was credited with reforming the Roman army. Camillus succeeded in having the army abandon its old Greek-Etruscan phalanx for-

mation in favor of a more flexible organization. The legion was now drawn up in three lines instead of one, each line made up of smaller units, or maniples. Now that its army was more effective, the Roman Republic won most of the wars it fought during the next two centuries.

As Rome expanded, it adopted a flexible policy toward its closest neighbors and kinsmen, the Latin tribes. By 381 B.C., for instance, Rome had already granted citizens' rights to the conquered city of Tusculum. When most other Latin cities finally came under its sway in 338 B.C., Rome pursued this policy selectively, admitting some to full rights and others to the less-than-total "Latin rights." The cities in return were obligated to supply Rome with soldiers and to subordinate their foreign policy to Rome's.

Rome next reached beyond the Latins, south into the fertile plains of Campania and into central

Of bread and circuses

Bread, like so much else at Rome, followed sharp divisions by class. There were three grades: "plebeian," which was black and was baked from barely sifted flour; "second," slightly refined; and "white," destined for the tables of the rich.

Bread was first made in Rome in the second century B.C., even though grains had been grown since the earliest times. Private ovens produced bread in the wealthier single-family homes, with bakeries serving the great numbers of apartment dwellers. On the march, the legionary carried an issue of wheat, which he ground with a hand mill and made into a rough whole-wheat bread.

Since grain was so vital to both the civilian and military diet and since Italy was not self-sufficient, the *annona*, or annual supply, came under public control by the third century B.C. From the end of the second century B.C., it caused persistent political strife. Grain for the poor was progressively subsidized until, finally, for the urban proletariat it was distributed free of charge. Only a bold leader could cut back these ancient welfare rolls.

The annona was a key to power—as well as a dangerous burden. When an opponent blockaded the grain shipments, popular discontent forced Augustus to launch a naval campaign (36 B.C.). Remembering this, Augustus kept the breadbasket, Egypt, as his private domain when he reorganized the empire. In a sense, the dole was a secret of imperial rule. As the satirist Juvenal wrote a century after Augustus: "The people, that once bestowed commands, consulships, legions, and all else now ... long eagerly for just two things: bread and circuses."

Above left, grain jars of the second century A.D. These great earthenware jars, sunk into the ground, were used to store wheat at Ostia, just south of Rome. By the mid-first century A.D., Ostia had become a thriving commercial hub and the main center for the shipment of oil, wine, and grain for the capital. The port boasted many mills (top center) and bakeries. This tomb relief (center right) shows a baker with a long paddle placing bread in an oven.

Bottom, the whole chain of the "annual supply," from tilling the field (top left, proceeding clockwise) to sowing, harvesting, threshing, transporting, milling, and finally baking in the characteristic domed oven. The baked bread itself appears in this Pompeian wall painting (right), with round, puffy loaves like some that have been discovered at Pompeii. The picture may have advertised the owner's trade, or perhaps the central figure is an official seeking popularity by distributing free bread.

Italy—an expansion motivated in part by the pressures of the class struggle at home. The plebeians, who were landless, could be placated with farms formed from territory won by conquest. For its part, the patrician upper class sought the prestige of command. As early as 396 B.C., when Rome destroyed the neighboring Etruscan town of Veii, thousands of citizens settled on the town's lands. This active colonization policy was to continue during the third century, spurred by the increasing political power of the plebeians and growing patrician ambitions. In 328 B.C., the Romans established a military colony at Fregellae, which commanded the inland route to Campania, in flagrant violation of a treaty. In 312 B.C., they built the Appian Way, the famous military road south through the lowlands and along the sea.

Expansion southward brought the Romans into conflict not only with the Italic Samnites but with the Greeks, who had been settling along the southern coasts since the eighth century. In 282 B.C., the Romans became embroiled in a conflict with the Greek colony of Tarentum, in southeastern Italy. Tarentum asked for assistance from Pyrrhus, the prince of Epirus in northwestern Greece and a relative of Alexander the Great. An able and ambitious commander, Pyrrhus landed in Italy in 280 B.C. with

Rome extended its dominion in Italy through the resilience of its citizen armies and the energy of consuls like C. Flaminius, who pushed the main road northeast to the Adriatic. The bridge at Rimini (above) was rebuilt by Augustus in A.D. 14. To the southeast, two other main roads met at Egnatia (above right); to the northwest, the great Aurelian road passed Libarna (below).

Territory controlled by Rome after Samnite War (290 B.C.)
Territory controlled by Rome and its allies during the First Punic War (264 B.C.)
Territory acquired by Rome after the Second Punic War (201 B.C.)

Pass of Little St. Bernard
Montgenevre Pass
Massilia
Ticinus X GAUL
Cremona
Trebia X
Piacenza
CISPADANIA
Lucca
Rimini
Pisa
Metaurus X
Lake Trasimenus X
Perugia
ETRURIA
CORSICA
Aleria
LATIUM
Rome
CAMPANIA
Olbia
Capua
Cannae X
Naples
Taranto
SARDINIA
LUCANIA
Cagliari
BRUTTIUM Croton
Mylae (Milazzo)
Trapani
Palermo
X
Marsala
SICILY Messina
Rhegium
Carthage
Agrigentum
Syracuse
Zama X
Ecnomus X
Malta

X battles

20

an army modeled on Alexander's phalanx system: Pike men, ranked twelve deep, were supported by a small cavalry force and a herd of twenty elephants. Pyrrhus' forces proved a formidable war instrument that took the Romans completely by surprise. In an initial engagement, the cavalry defeated the Romans, although it paid dearly for the victory.

Pyrrhus was so impressed with the Roman legions he had faced that he offered Rome a peace treaty, but his ambassador returned with a rejection. Another battle the following year also ended inconclusively. As the prince dryly remarked: "One more victory like this and we are lost." Pyrrhus decided to withdraw to

Sicily. He made one more foray into Italy in 275 B.C. but was defeated at Maleventum. After this he left, never to return. On departing, he is said to have commented with ironic foresight: "O what a battle-field I am leaving for Carthage and Rome."

Rome was now a major city. The repulse of Pyrrhus had secured its position as the dominant power in central and southern Italy. Rome's most menacing new rival was Carthage, a city on the coast of North Africa. Founded by traders from Sidon and Tyre—the Phoenicians—Carthage was the heart of an emerging maritime empire. By the mid-third century,

A bas-relief (right) shows travel in a Gallic petorritum *(four-wheeler) decorated in barbaric splendor. Although Rome created the first efficient road system, roads were designed primarily for military purposes. Shipping by land was almost prohibitively expensive. In the late empire, for example, carting wheat fifty miles could increase the price by one third to two fifths. Whenever possible, the Roman road (below) was built in a straight line, usually twenty feet wide. A surface of hard stone was laid over layers of stones in mortar, which in turn rested on a foundation of rubble. Below right, a chariot wheel. Because of the din and the danger, Julius Caesar banned all wheeled vehicles from city streets during certain hours.*

The early guilds

In the days of Numa, Rome's second king, only eight craft guilds were at work in Rome: the flutists, goldsmiths, wood-workers, dyers, cobblers, tanners, potters, and coppersmiths. At the height of imperial power, the number had grown to more than 125. There were, of course, those engaged in the shipping and building trades: rope makers, caulkers, cabinet makers, brick makers, ironsmiths, and so on. Imperial Rome also demanded the services of barbers, tailors, itinerant scholars, poets, physicians, pimps, perfumers, and purveyors of rare fish, spices, silks, and pearls. Yet wealth did not generate large industry or mass production. Slave labor kept working rates low and free artisans often went unemployed. Burial inscriptions suggest that only ten percent of the artisans in Imperial Rome were of free birth. Many were freed men working under patronage of their former masters.

Reliefs from two sarcophagi: a cobbler working on a paneled cabinet (above left) and a wood-worker plying his trade (above right). In Roman pottery shops (right), the most prized pottery came from Etruria, Greece, and Asia. In Augustan Rome the market in fine pottery was captured by the Etruscan town of Arretium, where most of the potters seem to have been slaves.

Various examples of commercial art from the thriving port of Ostia have survived intact. A shop sign (top right) offers poultry, rabbits, and vegetables as in any Mediterranean town today. On the counter are two monkeys—if not for sale, then perhaps to catch the eye. Behind the counter is a saleswoman, a common sight in ancient Rome. Although businesses and trades belonged for the most part to men, as the evidence of funerary inscription shows, women were employed in almost every type of retail selling and in the working of wool, which was traditionally a female domain. Often, especially among the lowest classes, women were forced to trade on their sex. This advertisement for a butcher (center right) shows the butcher with cleaver in hand. Cuts of meat—a head, a heart, and lungs—can be seen on a rack. Immediately below, a monument to two cutlers, with daggers, knives, and sickles on display.

Left, a stonecutter at work. In Rome, as in medieval cities, workers in the same craft tended to gather in the same street or quarter. Even though the competition represented by slave labor created widespread urban unemployment, cities swarmed with small artisans and vendors who made, repaired, and sold anything and everything. The working day in summer was about seven hours —in winter, about five. Immediately above, a bread and pastry shop.

Above, part of the entourage of a Roman magistrate: two trumpeters and lictors. Lictors, who were of lower-class origin, cleared a way through crowds and bore on their left shoulders the rods that served for punishment in early times.

the Carthaginians were established in Spain, Sardinia, and western Sicily, and their mercenary armies exacted tribute from the desert tribes of Africa. By 264 B.C., the distance between the spheres of influence of Carthage the sea power and Rome the land power had shrunk to the width of the narrow Strait of Messina, which separates Italy from Sicily. Once again, the immediate cause of the clash was a political initiative of the plebs, who voted to send two legions to help the little town of Messina ward off Carthaginian advances. Their success began a struggle that was to prove both long and debilitating, with consequences no one could have foreseen.

The First Punic War (264–241 B.C) began with a series of Roman victories, including, remarkably enough for a state of soldier-farmers, victories over the Carthaginian fleet. With characteristic pragmatism, the Romans devised grappling hooks to grab onto enemy ships, allowing the legionaries to board and clear the decks. In this way, sea battles became a

kind of infantry engagement. These early successes were followed by disastrous setbacks, among them a defeat in a sea battle near Sicily in 249 B.C. But the Romans finally emerged victorious after crushing Carthage off western Sicily in 241 B.C. Rome promptly annexed the island, thus acquiring its first province. Loss of revenue led the mercenaries of Carthage to rebel, and Rome took the opportunity to annex Sardinia in 239 B.C.

The loss of so many territories made defeat all the more unsavory for Carthage and set the scene for the outbreak of a second and far graver war. The protagonist of the Second Punic War was Hannibal, one of history's great generals. Even two hundred years later, the Roman historian Livy would call the war "the most memorable ever waged" and speak of Hannibal as the stuff of legend: "Bold to the extreme in incurring peril, perfectly cool in its presence. No toil could weary his body or conquer his spirit. Heat and cold he bore with equal endurance; the cravings of nature, not the pleasure of the palate, determined the measure of his food and drink." At the age of twenty-six, this formidable leader took command of the Carthaginian army in Spain, where his father, Hamilcar, had been reestablishing Carthage's position after the losses of the First Punic War. Those defeats Hannibal was sworn to revenge.

Women

Women in Rome's founding myths serve essentially as means: Princesses were kept virgin for dynastic ends and the wives and daughters of the Sabines were unceremoniously snatched to give progeny and solace to Romulus' rough crew. Yet the Sabine women took the lead in arranging peace, and the queens of Rome emerge as equal if not superior to men: resolute, fierce, politically astute.

In ordinary life, males and females grew up together and were separated only at puberty. While the males studied military arts and grammar, the females learned how to administer a household. Marriage took place early and gave the woman considerable independence, although the male was master of the house and had power of life and death over the children. In time, women not only gained control over their own property but also over their own lives. This continued until the late empire, before Christianity changed the status of women. Matrimony then became recognized as a sacrament rather than a loose bond, abortion and infanticide were checked, and male supremacy grew. But Rome stands as the ancient society in which women played the most varied and active roles.

Above, a marriage ceremony of the oldest and most formal kind, restricted to patricians. The bride and groom sit on sheepskin spread over joined seats; they touch the ritual cake of spelt.

A literary education in Greek and Latin was available to women who could afford it (below).

The Roman girl required a dowry. Plautus' play The Pot of Gold *tells of a girl cursed with a stingy father. To help her, the lar (left), a god whose shrine appeared in every home, revealed a buried treasure: "The girl prays to me every day. She brings me wine, incense, flowers, and other gifts. For her piety, I'll reveal the gold."*

Immediately above, a midwife helping a woman give birth. The mortality rate in Rome was high. Early marriages and large families replenished Republican legions; in the empire, birthrates declined.

Hannibal soon found a pretext for launching his campaign. He captured Saguntum, a small town on the eastern coast of Spain that was a Roman ally, though within the Carthaginian sphere of influence. Shortly thereafter war was declared, and Hannibal disappeared across the Pyrenees with his army. Seven months later, in December 218 B.C., he emerged from the Alps into the valley of the Po, having completed one of the most extraordinary military feats of ancient times. Though the crossing of the Alps in winter had cost his army severe losses, it gave him the element of surprise—the Romans were caught with one of their armies on its way to Spain, and another in Sicily, preparing to invade Africa.

Hannibal assumed that he would be able to win the local Gallic tribes to his side when he appeared on the northern border of Italy. He knew that from 232 B.C. there had been trouble between these tribes and the Romans, who had annexed considerable land in the Po valley—under pressure, once again, from the plebs. Likewise, he hoped that by defeating the Romans in battle, he could win over their Italian allies, bringing about a collapse of Rome's support in Italy.

Hannibal, who spoke Greek fluently, had studied Hellenistic warfare closely. Above all, he knew the value of mobility. His first two encounters with the Roman legions, at Trebia (December 218 B.C.) and Lake Trasimene (spring 217 B.C.), showed that the Romans did not. On both occasions, the legions were outflanked and surrounded. In spite of these defeats they met Hannibal again, at Cannae on the Adriatic coast of Italy, in August 216 B.C. Though his army was inferior numerically, Hannibal was able to encircle and annihilate the Roman force by a spectacular outflanking maneuver.

Rome had suffered one of the worst defeats in its history, but the Romans reacted coolly. Varro, the general responsible for the decision to engage Hannibal in battle, was welcomed back to Rome by the people because, it was said, he "had not despaired of the commonwealth." Plutarch later wrote with awe about the Roman response to Cannae, amazed that a nation could show such fortitude at so great a loss.

In dire straits, the Romans made Quintus Fabius Maximus dictator and settled down to conduct a war of avoidance and attrition in Italy—a war of the sort the astute Fabius had advocated all along. The Romans had at last perceived that the war might well be won not in Italy, where some of their allies had deserted after Cannae, but in Spain, where the legions were more successful. Spain was an important source of mineral wealth for Carthage and a recruiting ground for its armies. Since Rome now controlled

Above, a Carthaginian coin depicting Tanit, a lunar and fertility goddess of North Africa that the Phoenicians, who settled Carthage, identified with their own god Baal. The coin's style shows how Greek arts influenced other Mediterranean peoples besides the Romans. Below, a soldier of Carthage. For the most part, the Punic armies comprised mercenaries recruited from Gaul, Spain, the Balearic Islands, and Africa. African cavalry was crucial to the successes of the greatest Punic general, Hannibal. Its absence at the battle of Zama (202 B.C.) gave Rome the victory in the Second Punic War.

When Rome expanded beyond Italy, a clash with Carthage became inevitable. As the most important sea power in the western Mediterranean, Carthage challenged Rome to learn to fight on sea as well as land (below center). Anchors and beaked prows from captured ships adorn the monument (below) to Rome's victory at Mylae (260 B.C.). Rome finally destroyed Carthage but later resettled the site with its own colony (left).

the sea, Spain was the only base from which Hannibal could expect supplies and reinforcments. Though Rome's forces at first suffered reverses in Spain under Publius Cornelius Scipio—a precocious young commander who was sent there in 210 B.C.—the Carthaginians were eventually expelled. A Carthaginian army did manage to slip past Scipio in an attempt to reinforce Hannibal, but it was annihilated before it could get to Italy. The news was vividly relayed to Hannibal, who was the recipient of the head of the defeated general—his brother.

Hannibal, meanwhile, had been frustrated by an enemy that would not stand and fight. Reduced to fighting inconclusive skirmishes, he was finally trapped in the heel of Italy. Scipio, on his return from Spain, determined to strike at Carthage by invading Africa. Despite opposition from the cautious Fabius,

whose defensive policy had kept Hannibal at bay for so long, Scipio landed northwest of Carthage in 204 B.C. Shortly aferward, Hannibal, after fifteen years in Italy, was forced to go back to defend his homeland. Ironically, the man he was about to engage in battle had gained his victories in Spain by using Hannibal's own tactics.

Scipio was not only a brilliant commander—"greater than Napoleon" one military historian has called him—but a Roman of a new breed. Steeped in Greek culture, unorthodox, impatient with traditional Roman attitudes, and something of a mystic, Scipio broke the rules that had previously applied to Roman generals. Not only was he young—he was only twenty-five when he went to Spain in 210 B.C.—but he was not even of consular rank, the usual prerequisite for assuming military command. In addition, he held supreme command for ten years, breaking the custom

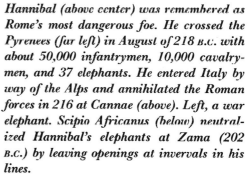

Hannibal (above center) was remembered as Rome's most dangerous foe. He crossed the Pyrenees (far left) in August of 218 B.C. with about 50,000 infantrymen, 10,000 cavalrymen, and 37 elephants. He entered Italy by way of the Alps and annihilated the Roman forces in 216 at Cannae (above). Left, a war elephant. Scipio Africanus (below) neutralized Hannibal's elephants at Zama (202 B.C.) by leaving openings at intervals in his lines.

Left, a coin depicting a Roman galley. Above, a coin showing Romans voting in special saepta (pens). The political system emerged weakened from the Punic Wars. Below, Perseus, the last king of Macedon, who challenged the expansion of Roman power to the Greek east but was defeated in 168 B.C.

of annual replacement: No one before him had wielded such power.

In 202 B.C., the master met his pupil in battle at Zama, a town on the plains some five-day march from Carthage. Hannibal was deprived of his most important striking arm, the Numidian cavalry, which had joined the Romans. Disorder in the ranks of his army led to internal fighting at the height of the battle. At first, Hannibal's old guard stood by him, but, outflanked by the Numidian horsemen, the troops fled the field. The pupil had beaten the master, and the Second Punic War was over.

Rome was now the chief power in the western Mediterranean. Its next challenge came from the east. As early as 216 B.C., after Hannibal's massacre of the legions at Cannae, Philip V of Macedon had declared war on Rome. The Romans countered by brewing trouble on Philip's home front. A brief peace followed, but, with Carthage humbled, Rome turned toward Macedon on the pretext of championing several small Greek states that were protesting Macedonian aggression. After defeating the Macedonian phalanx at the battle of Cynoscephalae in 197 B.C., the Roman general Flamininus proclaimed the liberty of Greece, which had for over a century been under Macedonian sway. Flamininus—like Scipio an admirer of all things Greek—soon realized that it was easier to get involved in the internal affairs of Greece than it was to disengage. Subsequent quarrels among the Greeks soon brought the Romans into a war against the Greek king Antiochus of Syria. He was overthrown in 190 B.C. at the battle of Magnesia, Rome's first major conflict in the Near East.

Right, a fresco of Bacchus enthroned. The god of wine holds a cup in his right hand and a sacred wand tipped with a pine cone in his left. In the wake of conquest and increasing contact with Greece in the third and second centuries B.C., new cults were brought from the East. That of Bacchus, most of whose followers were women, brought orgiastic rites and spread disorders throughout Italy, with the result that the Senate voted a ban in 186 B.C. In this period Rome also imported the cult of the Great Mother from Phrygia. The priests of this cult castrated themselves; Roman citizens were forbidden to serve.

In 146 B.C., a die-hard aristocratic faction in Rome led by Cato the Elder found an excuse to go to war with Carthage for a third time, razing it to the ground and forming the province of Africa. The eastern Aegean seaboard subsequently became the province of Asia when King Attalus III bequeathed the kingdom of Pergamum to Rome. Rome was thus building an empire.

The Second Punic War and the wars that followed had momentous consequences for Roman society. During the exhausting struggle with Hannibal, the legions had been maintained in the field for fifteen years and more. Most of the soldiers were small farmers, whose farms fell into disuse. In addition, the conquests brought increasing numbers of slaves to Rome. Both developments tended to impoverish the Roman yeomanry, which had for so long carried the weight of Roman arms. Lacking both employment and land, the poor moved to urban areas in increasing numbers. Their anger grew as the landowners established great estates all over Italy and exploited them with slave labor. By the middle of the second century B.C., massive social upheaval was impending. When it finally came, it was precipitated by the growing power of the plebeian tribunes, officials who, since the fifth century B.C., had been elected annually to protect the legal rights of the poor. The tribunes became the spokesmen for the discontent that would inspire the so-called Roman Revolution, which would ultimately undermine the republic.

The most powerful of the tribunes were the brothers Gracchi, Tiberius and Gaius, relatives of the great Scipio. Their legislative proposals outraged the wealthy landowners. In 133 B.C., Tiberius proposed that the state-owned lands—which, though public,

were in fact left at the disposal of the rich—be divided up into small holdings. Though his legislation was passed, he was killed the same year in a riot between his supporters and a senatorial faction. In 122 B.C., Gaius tried to win the support of the urban proletarians by proposing that they receive an allowance of cheap grain. He also courted the increasingly influential commercial interests, particularly the tax collectors, by proposing that they be allowed five-year contracts to collect taxes in the recently acquired and very rich province of Asia. A hostile faction of the Senate clashed with his followers, and Gaius committed suicide when the fighting went against him. In the witch hunt that ensued, three thousand of his supporters were killed. Nevertheless, the Gracchi had ex-

Feasting as the Romans did

"Lucullan feasts," "dinners like Trimalchios'"—the culinary preferences of Rome's grandees, real and imaginary, have become proverbial. The menu might have included "a huge lobster, garnished with asparagus, . . . a mullet from Corsica, . . . the finest lamprey the Straits of Sicily can purvey, . . . a goose's liver, a capon as big as a house, a boar piping hot, . . . truffles and delicious mushrooms. . . ." Thus did the satirist Juvenal describe a banquet of the first century A.D.

Earlier Romans had been more frugal, proud of what they grew at home. Turnips were a national food and remained a favorite at all periods. The one main meal (*cena*) took place toward evening, although a glutton like the emperor Nero sat down for a cena at noon. The Romans ate while reclining on sloping couches arranged around a square table. Not having forks, they used their fingers in addition to spoons, ladles, and knives. A full-scale banquet might consist of at least seven courses: the hors d'oeuvres, three entrées, two roasts, and the dessert. Eggs and honey mixed with wine always opened the dinner, and wine mixed with water accompanied every course. The dessert included spicy foods meant to stimulate the desire for drink. There was a taste for imaginative dishes—one meat disguised to resemble another, game stuffed with game of different sorts, mushrooms steeped in honey, fish with pulped fruit. It was proper for guests to eat until about to burst, then to induce vomiting and start again.

Above left, Roman kitchen utensils made of bronze. Left, fish and squid. The Romans were fond of seafood of all kinds, much of which came from nearby areas of the Mediterranean. Oysters were especially prized, above all those from the eastern coast of Britain, near Colchester. Above, a Pompeian trompe l'oeil fresco showing pomegranates, apples, figs, and grapes in a realistic transparent glass bowl.

Left, a Pompeian fresco from the house of Julius Felix depicting a death scene from the third century B.C. Reclining on a sloping couch similar to the triclinium on which the wealthier Romans dined is the African princess Sophonisba. The princess was the daughter of Hasdrubal Gisgo and the wife of Syphax, an African ally of Carthage. After Syphax's defeat at the battle of the Great Plains in Africa in 204 B.C., she was captured by Rome's ally Masinissa, who fell in love with her and married her on the spot. The Romans, embarrassed by this, asked him to divorce her. Rather than comply, he sent her a cup of poison, which she drank—apparently, gladly. Below, a glass vessel from Imperial Rome, used for drinking wine.

Left, glass bottles from the Imperial period, when glass production was stimulated by a decline in the quality of pottery. After the Roman conquest of Egypt at the end of the first century B.C., glass was exported to Rome in ever-increasing quantities. This cup in thrown metal (above) from the Imperial age shows Odysseus addressing Philoctetes on the island of Lemnos.

posed the deep divisions within Roman society, divisions that led to the rise of men like Gaius Marius and Julius Caesar, whose popular support would no longer rest on the votes of the plebs but on the swords of the legions. What these men learned from the fate of the Gracchi was that anyone who challenged the powerful conservative factions within the Senate could succeed only with an army at his back.

The century after the deaths of the Gracchi was dominated more by internal than by external wars. For the most part, these were fought between loose factions representing the two political tendencies: the *populares,* appealing more explicitly to broad popular support and championing the cause of the plebs; and the *optimates,* favoring older political customs and the historic, unquestioned leadership of the Senate. Gaius Marius, born the son of poor parents in 157 B.C., belonged by birth and inclination to the people's faction. He rose through the ranks of the army, became a tribune, and won the command of the legions in Africa against Jugurtha, a rebel prince. Jugurtha was finally bested, but only by the machinations of the man who became Marius' deadly enemy—Cornelius Sulla. Marius, however, won the adulation of Rome by defeating two armies of Germans who had been threatening Italy during the last years of the second

century B.C. In the process, he revolutionized the Roman army by drafting into it for the first time the very poor, without reference to property qualifications. He thus gave the Roman state the ambiguous benefit of a thoroughly professional army.

At the same time, Marius was elected to the consulship six times—a record. His rivals decided to make sure that this upstart was taught a lesson. When Marius attempted to reward his veterans with land grants, he was opposed by optimates in the Senate. In the violence that followed, a candidate for the consulship was killed by supporters of Marius, whose domination of politics in the city thus ended. Hoping to open new opportunities for himself in the East, he departed—angry, unforgiving, and bitter.

Marius was recalled to defend Rome once again during the so-called Social Wars, which were fought over Rome's policies toward its allies. Proposals to extend full citizenship to Rome's allies in Italy had been championed since the time of Gaius Gracchus. In 91 B.C., a tribune at Rome, Marcus Livius Drusus, was assassinated while pressing the Italian's case. His death sparked a fierce rebellion that was not brought under control until Rome granted the rights it had withheld. Old age and sickness kept Marius from playing an important role in the Social Wars and the glory went instead to Sulla, his archrival and the

Pompey's brilliant antagonist and conqueror was Julius Caesar (right), who claimed descent from Romulus himself. One of the most extraordinary men of all time, Caesar was a first-class orator, daring general, and consummate politician, as well as an accomplished prose writer, pamphleteer, and poet. His energy appeared boundless. While on his way to Spain during the Civil War, he composed a pamphlet, a poem describing his trip, and part of his famous account of the war. Though he pursued power indefatigably, the Roman biographer Suetonius says: "The resentment he entertained against anyone was never so implacable that he did not willingly renounce it when the chance came." Below, the Rubicon River. On January 11, 49 B.C., Caesar crossed the river into Italy, thus inviting the Civil War.

The Gallic Wars

First relentless war—then veterans owning land and settling in strong towns, a need for intermarriage, and the proliferation of trade and administrative ties between Rome and the provinces. In this way, Rome's expanding power brought acculturation. Most fateful for the shape of modern Europe were Julius Caesar's campaigns in Gaul. Caesar subdued the Belgae, Aquitanes, and Celts in the area from the Mediterranean to the English Channel, and from the Atlantic to to the Rhine. (He could not, however, establish an enduring presence across the Rhine, and the Germans were never Romanized.) On the pretext that migration by the Helvetii from Switzerland into Gaul threatened Rome's interests, Caesar moved in 58 B.C.

The following year, when campaigning against the Belgae in the north, he met with an ambush and near massacre of his legions. Characteristically, his own presence of mind and the discipline of his men eventually saved the day. Rome's expeditions across the Rhine and English Channel provoked the Gauls, who united in revolt against the Roman invaders. The leader of the resistance, Vercingetorix, was defeated at Alesia, where the French have commemorated his valor with a colossal statue that broods over the land. The vanquished chief was put on display in Rome and then strangled in a dungeon at the foot of the Capitoline Hill. Despite a spirited resistance, Gaul eventually succumbed to imperial discipline. In time, the land became Latinized, conserving and transmitting imperial values to the West.

Far left, a statue of Caesar the conqueror, believed to have been carved in his lifetime. This Roman view of Gaul (facing page, below right), with its walled towns, is from an eleventh-century copy of an imperial map that showed all military roads from Britain to the Euphrates. Above, a coin showing Vercingetorix, Caesar's vigorous but unlucky adversary. When Caesar was besieging him at Alesia, the Romans dug and held twenty-five miles of trenches.

Above center, a relief from the mausoleum of the Julii at St.-Rémy-de-Provence depicting a battle between the Romans and the Gauls. The ordinary Gallic warrior thought it unmanly to wear armor, apart from a helmet (below). Left, a Gallic prisoner. Many prisoners were displayed in chains when Caesar finally celebrated his triumph over the Gauls in 46 B.C. Romanization brought improved technology: right, a Roman bridge at Voison. Below right, a Roman helmet found near the battleground of Alesia.

Julius Caesar succumbed to the charms of Egypt's queen Cleopatra, as did his bluff lieutenant and military heir, Mark Antony (left). Not so Octavian, Caesar's great-nephew. When Octavian defeated Antony, Cleopatra committed suicide (above).

INDONESIAN MOSLEMS chat in the street *(opposite)* near their small, unadorned mosque. Their black velvet hats are traditional with the islands' Mohammedan majority.

PHILIPPINE CATHOLICS attend Mass in one of the country's many churches. Brought by the Spanish, Roman Catholicism claims 83 per cent of the islands' population.

Below, a Pompeian fresco depicting a naval battle. The decisive struggle for power between Julius Caesar's successors took place at Actium in 31 B.C. The East, under Antony and Cleopatra, lost to the West, under Octavian. A new Caesar, soon to be called Augustus, became master of the Roman world. After nearly five centuries of the Republic, Rome became a monarchy again—in fact if not in name. Another five centuries were to pass before the last emperor ruled in the city.

Senate's champion. As the wars neared their end, Sulla was given command of the eastern province of Asia, which had been invaded by Mithridates, the king of the Black Sea kingdom of Pontus. But before Sulla could leave, a tribune of the people's party transferred the command of the army to Marius. Sulla's response stunned Rome: He marched on the city.

Marius fled, abandoning his supporters, and for a year Rome's former savior led the life of a vagabond and criminal. When Sulla left in pursuit of Mithridates, however, Marius returned to Rome and entered his seventh consulship. He rode through the city streets, old, haggard, decrepit, and bent on revenge—which he quickly inflicted on those who had previously opposed him. Employing a gang of cutthroats, he murdered all those he even remotely suspected as threats. "When maimed and headless carcasses were now frequently thrown about and trampled upon the streets, people were not so much moved with compassion at the sight, as struck into a kind of horror and consternation," wrote Plutarch of the butchery. Finally, Sertorius, a member of the people's faction and a capable young general, moved against the gang and had them exterminated at night in their barracks. Shortly afterward, Marius died of natural causes. Rome heaved a sigh of relief—prematurely, as it turned out. Sulla was still to have his day.

By 81 B.C., Sulla was back in Rome, after defeating the forces of the people's faction throughout Italy and crushing an uprising of the Samnite tribes. On being elected dictator, he embarked on a purge of his opponents. First, he massacred six thousand Samnite prisoners in the circus. He was addressing the Senate nearby when the screams of the victims began to distract his listeners. Sulla told the Senators not to pay attention to the noise, that it was merely some "offenders being chastised." This done, Sulla drew up a list of one hundred Senators and one thousand knights and had these individuals executed on the pretext of their support for Marius. His real aim, as often as not, was to get his hands on the victims' wealth, which he confiscated and awarded to his henchmen. Sulla then set out to destroy the political power of the plebeian assembly and its tribunes. When he had finished his task, cold-bloodedly and thoroughly, he resigned his dictatorship and abandoned himself to a debauched life. He died shortly afterward. One hostile tradition had it that a vile disease left his body consumed by worms.

Sulla had checked the impetus of the people and restored the Senate to its former prominence. But this measure was merely a stopgap—the republican oligarchy was doomed. Two forces were now uniting to end it: the interests of the legions, which now enrolled the landless, and the ambitions of their generals. The stage was set for Pompey and Caesar.

When Sulla died, Caesar was still a young man, exiled because Marius had been his uncle by marriage. Other men—supporters of Sulla—were the

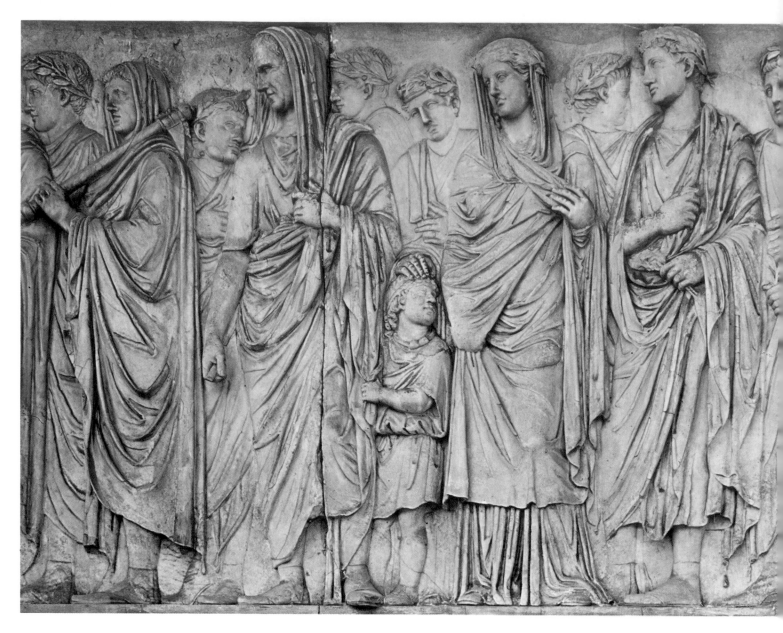

dominant leaders in Rome: Lucius Lucullus, Licinius Crassus (who had become enormously wealthy during the Sullan purges), and Gnaeus Pompey, the young general whom his troops had hailed as *Magnus,* "the Great." But Pompey's reputation as a soldier and commander owed less to actual performance than to flattery, to which he readily succumbed. A man of scant political judgment, Pompey was too easily manipulated.

Pompey's first important commission after the death of Sulla was to quell a rebellion of the people's faction led by Sertorius. After Marius' death, Sertorius had fled to Spain and organized Spanish tribesmen into a guerrilla army that had continually outsmarted the Roman armies sent against it. Pompey at first fared no better than the others before him, but he was eventually able to exhaust the Spanish tribes' willingness to fight as well as their loyalty to Sertorius. Sertorius was assassinated and his movement soon collapsed.

Pompey then returned to Italy just in time to take

part in crushing the slave revolt led by the gladiator Spartacus (73–71 B.C.). The uprising—the most serious of many in that period—had been brought under control by Crassus by the time Pompey finally arrived. Yet even reflected glory glittered: Pompey and Crassus were elected consuls for the year 70 B.C. Three years later, Pompey was voted extraordinary powers to suppress the pirates who reigned unchecked throughout the Mediterranean, a task he executed with great efficiency. Further glory was bestowed on him when he was sent to the East to relieve Lucullus, who had been fighting a drawn-out but successful campaign against the still active Mithridates.

In 62 B.C., having put Rome's presence in the East on a new, more solid footing, Pompey came back to Rome laden with spoils and evoking comparisons to Alexander the Great. In the meantime, the young Caesar had shown himself to be a brilliant demagogue. Imprudently disbanding his army, Pompey was forced to align himself with Caesar and Crassus—by now the wealthiest man in Rome—when

Octavian's victory at Actium ushered in a welcome period of peace. The Altar of Augustan Peace, decreed by the Senate, depicts leaders of the Senate and the family of Augustus (left), as well as Augustus' legendary ancestors Romulus and Aeneas. Augustus himself had commemorated his war on the assassins of Julius Caesar by building the great temple to Avenging Mars that dominated the new Forum in the heart of Rome (below left). This statue of Augustus (below), in heroic Greek attitude, is an idealized representation depicting the emperor as a god.

The expansion of the empire

Originally an insignificant town on the banks of the Tiber, Rome grew to become the center of one of the most powerful and vast empires the world has ever known. By the beginning of the second century A.D., the Roman Empire had reached its greatest extent, encompassing an enormous variety of peoples, cultures, and religions.

Through a series of wars and conquests, Rome gained more and more territory. The peak of this expansion occurred during the reign of Trajan. Under his rule, the province of Dacia, which stretched approximately from the lower Danube to the Black Sea, was brought under Roman sway. Trajan also created the provinces of Assyria and Mesopotamia after capturing the Parthian capital of Ctesiphon in A.D. 114. Administrative exigencies later forced the division of the empire into eastern and western sections.

Augustus

By force, political acumen, and administrative foresight, Augustus (below) turned the heritage of Julius Caesar into a monarchy that could endure. His Julio-Claudian dynasty failed to penetrate Germany but succeeded in annexing Britain.

The Flavians

Under the Flavians, the area between the upper Rhine and Danube was subdued and the Danube fortified.

The Antonines

The dynasty of the Antonines brought the empire of Rome to its peak. Under Trajan (A.D. 98–117) the empire reached its greatest extent, coming to embrace the provinces of Dacia, Arabia, Armenia, Mesopotamia, and Assyria. Trajan's successors generally followed a policy of retrenchment. With Commodus (below), the Antonine line ended.

X battles

Conquests of Trajan

46

Commodus

The reign of Commodus, according to Gibbon, marked the beginning of the empire's decline and fall. Commodus' assassination was followed by a year of anarchy that ended when the first emperor from Africa, Septimius Severus (A.D. 193–211), came to the throne and founded the dynasty of the Severi. The imperial borders remained fairly static during this period, which produced no really able emperors apart from Septimius himself. He contested with several rivals for the throne and grappled with serious economic problems that were to plague the empire until its collapse. Because of the need to buy off his troops during the Civil War, Septimius depreciated the currency drastically. In the following decades, this practice led to chronic inflation and a weakening of the already ailing imperial economy. Septimius also faced recurrent troubles with the Parthians and in Britain. He was succeeded by his son Caracalla (A.D. 211–217), who inherited his father's inflationary practices. Like his father, Caracalla increased the legionaries' pay. His extravagant wars on the Danube forced a further devaluation of the currency. It was during his reign that Roman citizenship was extended to all people of the empire—making them liable to an inheritance tax. His successor was Elagabalus (below), a priest of the sun god Ela-Gabal in Syria who claimed to be Caracalla's bastard son. A transvestite, Elagabalus worshiped the sun god in the form of a black phallic meteorite. He attempted to introduce this bizarre cult in Rome but was assassinated. He was succeeded by his cousin, Alexander Severus (A.D. 222–235), a thirteen-year-old boy with whom the dynasty ended.

Constantine

The dynasty of Constantine (below) lasted nearly sixty years. By this time, the empire's borders had already begun to shrink. In A.D. 273, Dacia had been abandoned to the barbarians, who kept up unrelenting pressure on the empire for the next two centuries. Constantine made Christianity the official religion and moved the capital of the empire from Rome to a site on the Bosporus. Financing the new capital, Constantinople, further debilitated the already weakened imperial finances. Constantine was succeeded by his sons before his nephew Julian became sole emperor in A.D. 361. The most able of Constantine's successors, Julian had little time to exercise his abilities.

Flavius Honorius

The emperor Flavius Honorius (below) ruled in the Latin West of the empire (A.D. 393–423) as a nominal head of state. From the security of the marshes around Ravenna, Honorius watched Spain fall to the Vandals, Rome being sacked by the Goths, and Britain evacuated by the Romans: He could do nothing to stem the barbarian tide. Until A.D. 408, the German mercenery Stilicho had acted with vigor in the imperial cause, but he was murdered at the instigation of Honorius. When Honorius died in A.D. 423, his sister Galla Placidia ruled in the West through her infant son.

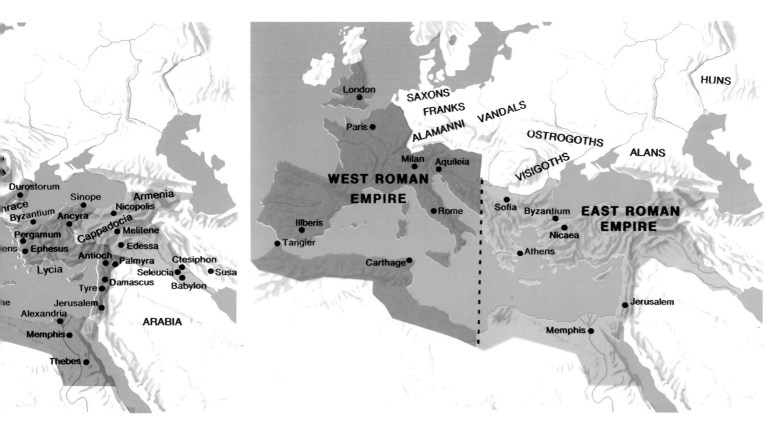

the Senate proved stubborn about ratifying his Eastern settlements and even balked at sanctioning land allotments to his veterans. On Caesar's initiative, Pompey and Crassus joined Caesar in a commission of three—the first triumvirate—to manage public affairs. They supported Caesar's candidacy for the consulship of 59 B.C. The consul in turn saw to it that Pompey's Eastern settlements were ratified and that the interests of the tax collectors, Crassus' friends, were protected. After his consulship ended, Caesar was given the governorship of Transalpine Gaul. Rome's great master thus gained command of the legions that in the not-too-distant future he would forge into the instrument of absolute rule.

In an age of exceptional men, Gaius Julius Caesar stood out. His family was patrician, although obscure in recent generations. But it proudly traced its line to Romulus and even to his heroic forebear, the legendary Trojan Aeneas, son of Venus. Many years before, Sulla had warned someone who scoffed at the young Caesar's apparent vanity and idleness: "That man contains many Mariuses." One of Rome's greatest modern historians, Theodor Mommsen, described him as "the perfect man." No one can contest Caesar's abilities as orator, politician, and general. Bold in strategy and tactics and incredibly quick in action,

Above, a bust of Marcus Vipsanius Agrippa. After the death of Julius Caesar, Agrippa—a man of obscure origins—had a profound effect on the fortunes of Octavian, who was Caesar's heir and the future emperor. An outstanding general, Agrippa successfully quelled an uprising in Gaul, crossed the Rhine, and resettled a Germanic tribe from Gaul—the Ubii—in Germany. When Octavian's control in Italy was threatened by a blockade of the grain supply, he routed the fleet of Pompey's son off the coast of Sicily. In addition, he organized and directed the final victory over Antony and Cleopatra at Actium. For the last ten years of his life, he became part of Augustus' dynastic schemes, fathering five children by Augustus' daughter, Julia. His sons, however, died prematurely; the last one was killed by Tiberius, the second emperor.

he was no less bold and quick to change plans when necessity required. Generous to his men, he relied on their skill and loyalty in the ensuing contest for mastery of the state. Not least, he wrote his own history so well that his reputation with posterity has been largely of his own design.

Caesar's conquest of Gaul took ten years (58–49 B.C.). Success made him seem more menacing than ever to the conservatives, who now sought to use Pompey as their stalking horse. The bonds that joined the first triumvirate had dissolved. Earlier, as part of the settlement, Pompey had married Caesar's daughter Julia. But she died in 54 B.C., ending what seems to have been, in spite of the appearance of expediency, a loving relationship. One year later, Crassus, the third partner, was killed and his army annihilated by Parthians at the battle of Carrhae near the Euphrates. Pompey and Caesar now squared off.

The Senate tried to persuade Caesar to give up his command in Gaul, claiming that his term had expired. Caesar refused. In Rome, two tribunes loyal to Caesar, Mark Antony and Dolabella, tried to argue his case, but at the instigation of the consuls, both optimates, they were driven out. Caesar, who was not about to put himself unarmed at the mercy of his senatorial enemies, had now found the pretext for

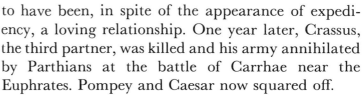

Left, a barbarian submitting to Romans. Such was the ideal in political art, but the new monarchy of Augustus inherited, in fact, an empire that had not successfully subdued vast numbers of Germanic tribes from the Rhine, on the borders of the Gallic province, to the Ukraine. Efforts to extend the frontier from the Rhine to the Elbe failed when, in A.D. 9, a Roman army was annihilated by the German chieftain Arminius. More than a mere setback, it meant the Germans would remain un-Romanized.

Above, the stage and backdrop of a Roman theater in Orange, France. Everywhere that Roman rule extended, provincial culture emulated that of the capital. Local grandees eagerly sought the prestige that building for the public had always conferred at Rome. Left and below, Roman tickets for entrance to the theater.

invading Italy: The sacred personages of the tribunes had been violated. On January 11, 49 B.C., he marched to the Rubicon, a small river that divided Roman Italy from Gaul. As he crossed the stream, he uttered in Greek: "The die is cast."

The civil war that followed lasted almost five years. Pompey vacillated, drawn this way and that by contending factions within his own camp. From the outset, when he inadvisedly abandoned Italy to base himself in Greece, he clearly demonstrated his limitations. After repeated offers to negotiate, Caesar finally brought him to battle at Pharsalus in Thessaly in 48 B.C. and defeated him. Pompey fled, eventually arriving in Egypt, where he was murdered by those wanting to curry favor with Caesar. That was not Caesar's style with a former ally and respected foe: He later had the assassins executed. Neither a Marius nor a Sulla, Caesar intended to reconcile rather than extirpate the opposition. But the intransigent aristocrats were to keep him at war for three more years.

By 45 B.C., Caesar was sole master of the Roman world. Even so, his soldiers felt familiar enough with him to sing as they marched in triumph through the streets of Rome: "Home we bring our bald whoremonger/ Romans, lock your wives away/ All the bags of gold you lent him/ Went his Gallic tarts to pay." Caesar's love of women had not gone unnoticed. Indeed it nearly cost him everything in 48–47 B.C., when his affair with Cleopatra kept him in Alexandria, where he was trapped and nearly killed by her brother's troops.

In 47 B.C., Caesar had been elected dictator. Two years later, he was proclaimed dictator for life and granted absolute military power in all provinces of the empire. Though the annual elections continued, only Caesar's hand-picked candidates could run. Meanwhile, Caesar instigated ambitious projects for settling veterans on land and schemes to untangle the city's traffic. He also readied himself for a campaign against the Parthians to avenge the debacle of Crassus.

It will never be known for certain whether Caesar

Romanization meant roads, theaters, and monumental arches— but also aqueducts, water closets, and baths. More than a means to cleanliness, the Roman bath was a health club and social center, growing to comprise libraries, halls for recitation, grounds for running and wrestling. Here was everything for the "sound mind in a sound body" that Juvenal praised under the early empire. Open to all at a modest fee, public baths were often lavishly appointed and were sometimes immense. The baths of Caracalla, for example, covered twenty-seven acres. Left, a cold-water basin at the end of the caldarium, or hot room, from the modest baths by the road to Stabia in Pompeii.

Leisure pursuits

A large proportion of Rome's one million or so inhabitants had plenty of free time on their hands, either because they were un-employed or because they were wealthy enough to own slaves. But even the workers and businessmen of ancient Rome finished work by noon or early afternoon. Then they might sojourn to the baths, where they would play *trigon*, a catch-ball game for three; or a form of handball, like that still played in Ireland and the Basque country; or *harpastum*, a kind of rugby. Women often played a game of *trochus*, which involved rolling a metal hoop with a tiny key. For the more sedentary, games of "petty-thieves" were always on in the public gardens, played on boards with counters of different values. Also popular was a form of backgammon. More perilous, and ubiquitous, were dice games.

Top, a tavern scene from a Pompeian fresco. Roman bars were often fronts for illegal gambling and brothels. Since "licensed" brothels were forced to remain closed until the ninth hour—about 1:00 P.M. in winter and 2:00 P.M. in summer—taverns, which remained open at all hours, frequently employed prostitutes as barmaids, with gambling rooms in the rear of the bar. Immediately above, a mosaic showing a cock-fight—a bloody and popular pastime. Above left, dice, both six-sided tesserae *and four-sided* tali. *The best throw was "Venus," the worst, "dog." Loaded dice were not infrequent. Left, boys playing ball.*

planned to become king. Three times he spurned a proffered crown. But a group of Senators, who sought a return to the free oligarchy of Republican Rome, pieced together enough evidence to convince themselves that he did. The assassination of Caesar—instigated by Brutus, Cassius, Cinna, among others—brought down the man whom many considered the greatest of the Romans and provoked another bloody civil war (44–42 B.C.).

The defeat of Caesar's assassins left three men in power, a second triumvirate: Octavian, who had been adopted by his granduncle Julius; Mark Antony, Caesar's follower and lieutenant; and Aemilius Lepidus, one of Caesar's generals, who proved of little consequence in what became a two-way struggle between Octavian and Antony.

The contrast between Octavian and Mark Antony could hardly have been greater. Octavian was cold, efficient, able to suppress all desires in pursuit of power; Antony was sensual, erratic, eager for glory but easily distracted—a man who, though first and foremost a soldier, eventually achieved fame through one of history's great affairs of the heart.

The Egyptian temptress Cleopatra proved to be Antony's undoing. Antony preferred Cleopatra to his wife, Octavian's sister, and formally married her in 32 B.C. Octavian promptly accused Antony of planning to make Cleopatra queen of Rome. When the Senate declared war on the Egyptian queen, Antony responded by invading Greece. He and Cleopatra were defeated at the battle of Actium in 31 B.C.; vanquished, they committed suicide. With Antony's death, all possibility of effective opposition ceased. The Roman republic was spent.

When Octavian returned in triumph, he set about reorganizing Rome's political structure into a military autocracy, a transformation he took great pains to disguise. Indeed, he initially proposed that he resign the powers he already had. The Senate instead voted to increase his powers. He was accordingly granted control over the provinces of Gaul, Nearer Spain, Syria, and Egypt for another ten years—somewhat on the model of Caesar's Gallic command. The Senate also handed him the epithet Augustus, ("awesome," "sacred"), a title never before bestowed on a human being. Later, he was granted the powers and immunities of a tribune for life.

Though Augustus, like Caesar, continued the annual elections for the magistracies, he hand picked many of the candidates. He also gradually assumed control of the various branches of civic administration that the magistrates had overseen until, like the consuls, they were reduced to holding merely formal titles. The consulship, on the other hand, remained important as a first step to governing in the provinces, a few of which were still farmed out to members of the Senate. But Augustus kept the volatile frontier provinces of Gaul and Syria under his special jurisdiction, for that was where the majority of Rome's legions—reduced from sixty to twenty-eight after the Civil War—were based. Egypt, which was crucial for the supply of grain that placated the urban plebs, was kept under direct control.

Augustus' interests extended beyond power. Not gifted to be his own historian like Caesar, yet as mindful of posterity, he inaugurated a cultural renaissance. He sponsored the building of a theater in memory of his favorite nephew, Marcellus, and built magnificent new temples to Mars and Apollo. He also claimed to have restored eighty-two other temples that had fallen into disrepair. His general Agrippa was responsible for building the first Pantheon and for enlarging the water supply. His friend, the Etrus-

Augustus' preferred successors died in rapid succession—an unparalleled run of bad luck—leaving only Tiberius Claudius Nero (left), the eldest son of Augustus' steely wife. Tiberius reached the throne with solid military achievements to his credit and proved a capable ruler. He was never loved, however, in part because he retired morosely to his splendid villa (above) on the island of Capri, leaving the administration of the empire to Sejanus, head of the Praetorian Guard. Gossip about his sexual perversions was rife in Rome. Much of it has been recorded by Suetonius, who relates that Tiberius had boys and girls trained to perform sexual acts for him in threes. One woman whom he forced to his bed called him a "filthy-mouthed, hairy, stinking old beast." Right, the emperor Claudius, Tiberius' nephew, and his second wife, Agrippina.

Gods from afar

The earliest Romans were farmers and fighters who worshiped local, practical gods, with names like "Wheat Rust," "Inner House," "Begetter," and "Sex." The Romans also adopted the more anthropomorphic deities of the Greeks: Mars took on the character of Ares, Venus of Aphrodite, Jupiter of Zeus. But Olympian religion was aristocratic and offered scant solace to the nameless poor. The lower classes rallied to Liber, the token of Liberty, and then to his Greek counterpart, Bacchus, whose orgiastic cult was viewed with displeasure by an aristocratic Republican Senate. The urban proletariat and new professional military class, on the other hand, found meaning in gods from the East. One of these, the Persian Mithras, was closely associated with Helios, the sun god. The emperor Aurelian built a splendid temple for the sun god, whose festival fell on December 25. In the end it was another Eastern cult, Christianity, that gained the imperial nod.

Right, an altar dedicated to the worship of Isis. Because serpents were sacred to the deity Isis, Cleopatra—who saw herself as the goddess incarnate—employed asps for her suicide. Below, a bas-relief showing a procession in honor of Isis.

ISIDI·SACR

Left, a statue of Serapis enthroned. A Hellenized version of the Egyptian god Osiris, the mate of Isis, Serapis was worshiped in many of the goddess' temples. Above, Mithras slaying a bull. This act of the Persian god of light was symbolic: Taurine blood indicated life, and the slaying of the bull signified the promise of life after death. The rites of the devotees were secret and conducted in underground rooms and caves. Below left, a Pompeian fresco depicting Helios the sun god. Below, the goddess Cybele, whose cult required self-castration.

Left, a coin of the emperor Galba, Nero's successor. After Nero, dynastic legitimacy vanished as a basis for power. The northern legions hailed Vitellius (below left) as emperor, but the eastern legions replaced him with their own choice, Vespasian.

can grandee Maecenas, became a byword for literary patronage. Virgil and Livy celebrated in verse and prose the glory of the empire, its heroes and its history. Horace, Propertius, and Ovid entertained the privileged with uplifting lyrics, passionately learned elegies, and witty tales of weighty loves.

Less successfully, Augustus encouraged a religious revival, refurbishing various cults and priesthoods as well as shrines. He attempted a moral crusade among the nobility, whose birthrate was declining, to encourage large families and limit sumptuous display. The women of his house continued to spin and weave according to the old aristocratic custom.

The closing years of his long reign were darkened by the scandal of his daughter Julia's alleged promiscuity, the difficulty of determining the succession, and the problems of Rome's borders. Attempts to extend the Roman frontier across the Rhine to the Elbe and consolidate Roman power in Germany came to a disastrous halt in A.D. 9, when three Roman legions under Quintilius Varus were ambushed by Germanic tribes in the gloom of the Teutoburg Forest. Years later, when the Romans visited the scene of the massacre, they found bones tangled among the dense foliage and skulls nailed to tree trunks. The German tribes remained un-Romanized —a constant source of antagonism—and eventually

Nero (above) was the last heir of Augustus. He came to power when his mother, Agrippina the Younger, poisoned her husband, the emperor Claudius, in A.D. 54. Left, the Praetorian Guard, which Augustus made his elite bodyguard in 27 B.C. The power of the Praetorians increased under Tiberius, and soon they were choosing emperors.

took part in the great barbarian invasions of the fourth century A.D. Augustus never forgot that catastrophe in Germany. For the last five years of his life, he is said to have repeated time and again, "Varus, Varus, give me back my legions."

The problem of the succession proved equally intractable. His original heirs, the sons of his daughter Julia, both died young. Augustus, who never had a son, eventually adopted his stepson Tiberius, the son of Augustus' second wife, Livia, by her former husband, Claudius Nero. Tiberius was a gloomy, dour character, and relations between him and Augustus were strained. But in A.D. 13, Augustus invested him with military authority equal to his own. When Augustus died in A.D. 14, Tiberius became emperor, the first of the Julio-Claudian dynasty.

Though Augustus found the question of succession vexing, the history of the next four hundred years shows that the well-being of the empire never really depended on the character and abilities of the emperor, whose deficiencies Rome long managed to survive. Tiberius, in spite of a promising background as a general and administrator, spent nearly half his reign as a recluse on the island of Capri. An imperial bodyguard, the Praetorians, based at Rome, had been formed by Augustus. In the absence of Tiberius, it was their captain, Sejanus, who ran affairs—for his own benefit and that of his friends, as it turned out—until he was finally checked. Meanwhile, the Parthians, those dexterous mounted archers who had annihilated Crassus' forces in 54 B.C., renewed their threats to the eastern borders. Trouble also arose on the Rhine, but still the emperor did not stir from Capri.

When Tiberius died in A.D. 37, his successor demonstrated the worst defect of dynastic succession: failure to guarantee that a man of ability would ascend the throne. Tiberius' grandnephew Caligula was a psychopath, warped no doubt by the atmosphere of intrigue and by aristocratic inbreeding. An incestuous, demented megalomaniac who spent his nights wandering the palace corridors imploring day to dawn, he ruled ineffectively for four years. According to Suetonius, Rome's gossipy historian, his only "military" exploit was to march his legions to the Atlantic coast of Gaul, where he ordered them to line up along the beach. "Gather seashells," came the instruction. The soldiers, with helmets full of shells, were marched back to Rome. Caligula then declared a great victory over Neptune, the god of the sea. His sexual whimsies so angered those around him that he was murdered by guards in A.D. 41.

Caligula was succeeded by his bald, stuttering, and middle-aged uncle Claudius. Against all expectation, he proved perhaps the most competent of Augustus' dynastic successors. Not only did he add the new province of Britain to the empire, but he admitted Gauls to the Senate, something that only Caesar before him had tried. This was a momentous step toward political integration. Behind the scenes, however, Claudius had troubles—mainly with his young

Right, Titus Flavius Vespasian. By the sole authority of his troops, Vespasian founded a new dynasty—the Flavian. Born in the hills north of Rome, he proved an able and frugal ruler. During his reign, supreme power passed from old Roman nobles to the Italian bourgeoisie. In the tradition of monumental public works, he began an amphitheater (below), dedicated in A.D. 80. Later known as the Colosseum, it became Rome's most famous structure, a symbol of the city itself.

Facing page, two contrasting views of Palestine: the arid Qumran region, near the Dead Sea (top), and the fertile region of Galilee (bottom). In A.D. 66, an outbreak of Jewish nationalism led to the massacre of the Roman garrison in Jerusalem. Vespasian and his son Titus took charge of the war against the rebels. The Jews fought tenaciously and were not finally broken until A.D. 70, when Jerusalem was captured and destroyed by Titus; the Diaspora of the Jews had begun. The Jews were generally tolerated by the Romans and suffered little persecution in the empire until Christianity came into power.

wife, Messalina. Thirty-four years his junior, she created her own state within a state, a sort of pornocracy, in which her lovers were promoted and her enemies executed. Gossip—this time from the satirist Juvenal and the letter writer Pliny—tells how she spent her evenings in a brothel, indulging her wildest sexual fantasies. Her uninhibited pastimes were eventually discovered by Claudius, who had her stabbed to death. His next wife, Agrippina, was an even more unfortunate choice: She plotted to bring Nero—her son by a previous marriage—to the throne. Her hope was realized in A.D. 54, when Claudius died—poisoned, it is said, by Agrippina.

With Nero, the period of relative sanity under Claudius gave way to a black comedy of intrigue, assassination, incest, and sexual perversion. Nero's artistic pretentions added a note of farce. He fancied himself a poet but was so insecure about his gift that he locked the gates of the auditorium during his recitals. His reign was marked by an uprising in Britain and by new Parthian invasions in the East. It ended

Gladiators

The brutality of the ancient world is perhaps seen at its worst in the gladiatorial games. Originally part of the great public funerals that enhanced the prestige of the rich, they were first produced at state expense in 104 B.C. Successful politicians and generals would reward the Roman plebs with lavish spectacles in which hundreds of gladiators and thousands of animals might die. At the beginning of the second century A.D., a spectacle was held in which 4,941 pairs of gladiators fought. When Titus opened the Colosseum in A.D. 80, the gladiatorial combats resulted in the deaths—in one day—of five thousand beasts. This insatiable need for bloodshed led to the disappearance of many wild animals from North Africa and parts of the Near East.

The main training schools for gladiators were in Capua, south of Rome. It was here that Spartacus began the great slave rebellion in 73 B.C., with a small force of seventy escaped gladiators. The combatants were characterized according to their arms, and emperors liked to pit different types against each other. Sometimes freak fights were staged: In A.D. 90, the emperor Domitian had a dwarf gladiator fight with a woman. With the triumph of Christianity, the bloody spectacle was abolished.

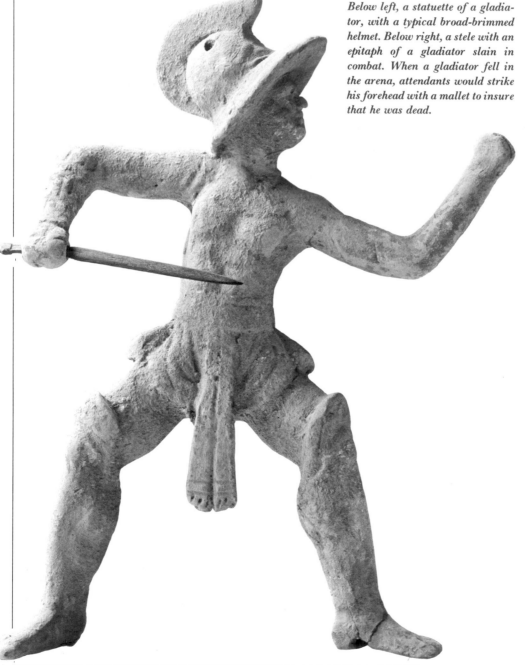

Below left, a statuette of a gladiator, with a typical broad-brimmed helmet. Below right, a stele with an epitaph of a gladiator slain in combat. When a gladiator fell in the arena, attendants would strike his forehead with a mallet to insure that he was dead.

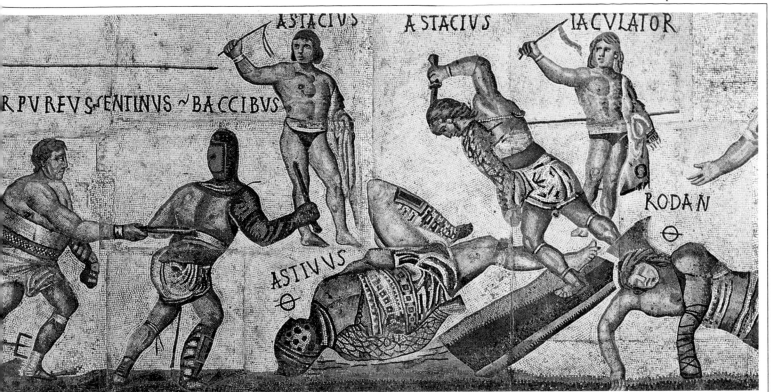

Above, gladiators fighting. The Roman taste for matches between different types of armament shows clearly. Right, a venatio, or battle between man and beast. The Romans also used beasts to dispose of condemned criminals, who were thrown into the arena with hungry lions, a spectacle devised by Augustus. The scene of many such blood baths was the Colosseum (below), which could hold ninety thousand spectators. Here thousands of Christians met martyrdom—a memory honored by the cross in the foreground.

Immediately above, a gladiator's helmet decorated with scenes from the story of Troy. This was part of the full armor worn by the so-called Samnite, who carried a large shield and a sword. Other conventional types were the Thracian, who bore a round buckler and a dagger; the "net man," who carried a trident; and the "myrmillon," who had a helmet crest in the shape of a fish and was pitted against the net man. To vary the spectacle, mounted gladiators or charioteers were sometimes pitted against each other in the arena.

Above, spoils from the temple in Jerusalem being carried off by victorious Roman troops. This relief on the arch between the Colosseum and Forum commemorates the triumph of Titus over the Jews in A.D. 70. Vespasian's son proved popular during his brief reign. Suetonius later called him "the pleasure of the human race."

when, in A.D. 68, the legions in Spain and elsewhere proclaimed their own emperors. Nero, at this news, killed himself. Dying, he exclaimed, "O what an artist dies in me!"

The dynasty of patrician nobles had thus whimpered to an end. A year of anarchy followed, during which four emperors attained the throne. None of the first three—Galba, Otho, and Vitellius, all of whom commanded only factional support—lasted more than

a few months. Power came to rest on the shoulders of Vespasian, the first member of the Italian middle class to become emperor. Neither Senator nor noble, he was a soldier chosen by soldiers. Vespasian had served in Britain and, with his son Titus, had helped crush a Jewish rebellion in Palestine that broke out in A.D. 66.

Vespasian's reign, which began in A.D. 69, was that of a practical, no-nonsense bourgeois. He replenished the treasury, emptied by Nero, by inventing new taxes, including one on the use of urine from the city toilets for industrial purposes. He further advanced the integration of the empire by enfranchising provincials on a large scale.

Vespasian ruled for ten years—a period of comparative stability. Two of his sons eventually succeeded him: Titus and then Domitian (A.D. 81–96). The latter spent a large part of his reign on the Danube

Above, stele of the Good Shepherd. Under Domitian, Titus' successor, Christians were forced to pay homage to the emperor or die. When Domitian discovered Christians within his own family circle, he dealt with them severely, executing Titus Flavius Clemens and banishing Flavia Domitilla. Below, remains of ornamental fountains in Domitian's great new palace. Following pages, Pompeii, buried by the eruption of Vesuvius in A.D. 79.

frontier quelling rebellious tribes. He gathered about him at Rome a motley collection of advisers who formed a council of state. Having bypassed the Senate in these affairs, he was strongly resented as a vulgar upstart. In fact, the old nobility was becoming increasingly impotent. Nevertheless, it enjoyed a brief resurgence when, upon Domitian's death, the Senate's choice, Nerva, became emperor. Perhaps Nerva's reign (A.D. 96–98) is best remembered for the emperor's choice of a successor: Trajan, whose rule brought the Roman Empire to its apex.

The reign of Trajan began the period of imperial grandeur that lasted until the death of Marcus Aurelius nearly a century later. Gibbon, Rome's most famous modern historian, wrote of this time: "In the second century of the Christian era, the Empire of Rome comprehended the fairest part of the earth, and the most civilized portion of mankind. The fron-

Pompeii

In the reign of the good Titus, vines and olives graced the slopes of Mount Vesuvius, much as they do today. Then about noontime on August 24, A.D. 79, Vesuvius struck. When the volcanic eruption was over, two cities had completely disappeared: Pompeii, the local seaport and commercial center, and Herculaneum, a more fashionable resort, both set on the Bay of Naples. At the juncture of south and north in Italy, Pompeii had Italic origins with some Greek and Samnite influences. Herculaneum, as its name suggests, was more Greek, though, like Pompeii, it had been harshly Romanized.

The hot mud that engulfed Herculaneum solidified, making future excavation difficult. The lighter layers of ash and cinder that sifted over Pompeii, however, left the city easier to uncover. Pompeii thus became the byword for a museum-city—all the banalities of everyday life were abruptly immortalized in volcanic ash. Much of what we know of ordinary Romans derives from Pompeii: houses, urban organization, arts and trades, brothels, gardens, even the shape of a loaf of bread.

At the time of its premature burial, Pompeii had a population of about twenty thousand. Many Pompeians appear to have been caught in hot ash, which later hardened. The organic matter decayed and left cavities. The figures that appear when the cavities are filled with plaster (far left) vividly recall the struggle and fear of Pompeii's doomed inhabitants. Near left, one of the main streets, with shops opening directly onto the narrow sidewalks. Steppingstones sheltered pedestrians from the grime of the street but allowed wagons to pass. Below left and far left, houses in Herculaneum.

Top right, a peristyle—an inner court lined with columns in the Greek fashion. Top left, a view into the garden of a house. The atrium (immediately above), the central hall of the Italic house, was lined with bedrooms and lighted by the narrow impluvium. Right, frescoes giving the illusion of spacious architecture.

Right, a statue of the emperor Trajan. Born in Spain in A.D. 53 and Spanish on his mother's side, Trajan was the first Roman emperor of provincial birth. During the reign of this warrior-emperor, the empire reached its greatest extent, coming to include the provinces of Dacia, Armenia, Assyria, Mesopotamia, and Arabia Petraea. From booty acquired in his Dacian wars, the emperor carried out extensive public works projects, such as the forum of Trajan (below). Facing page, a detail of a column describing his campaigns.

tiers of that extensive monarchy were guarded by ancient renown and disciplined valour. The gentle but powerful influence of laws and manners had gradually cemented the union of the provinces. Their peaceful inhabitants enjoyed and abused the advantages of wealth and luxury." Ironically, although he initiated the golden period of Roman peace, Trajan found it necessary to spend most of his reign campaigning on the frontiers. He created the new province of Dacia in an area stretching roughly from the lower Danube to the Black Sea after subduing tribes that had troubled the border for over a decade. He then moved east to confront the Parthians, advancing to the Tigris and capturing the Parthian capital of Ctesiphon in A.D. 114. Subsequently, he created two more provinces: Assyria and Mesopotamia. These marked the limits of Roman expansion eastward.

Trajan had come from the province of Spain. He appointed as his successor his cousin Hadrian, also from the same area. Hadrian's rule (A.D. 117–138) was characterized more by diplomacy than war. He abandoned some of the newly acquired eastern provinces and negotiated a settlement with the Parthian king. He also established the boundary of the province of Britain by constructing a long wall across its northern border.

Hadrian's twenty-one years as emperor were marked by a surge of building projects in the provincial capitals, whose architecture began to rival Rome's own. Hadrian himself rebuilt the Pantheon in its familiar domed form. More liberal attitudes were adopted toward slaves, confirming a trend

Roman aqueducts

Public works bespeak the values of society. Rome stands out not only for its attention to the tools of power but also for its interest in the amenities of civilian life. Fresh water—whether lugged home to tenements by the plebs, piped in to restful peristyles by the rich, siphoned off without payment by the unscrupulous, or enjoyed in the public baths by all—was of prime concern to Romans.

As early as the sixth century B.C., Etruscan engineers drained the Forum and showed the Romans how to channel local water. By the end of the fourth century B.C., the population outgrew the capacity of wells, cisterns, and local springs. Whatever other concerns they may have had, Rome's leaders did not neglect the issue of water supply. Appius Claudius, who built the road of dominion to the south (the Appian Way), also built the first aqueduct. Augustus, who "found Rome adobe and left it marble," nearly doubled the water supply. By the time of Trajan, eight aqueducts brought Rome an estimated 222,237,060 gallons of water daily. Throughout the empire, aqueducts attested to the skill of their engineers and the Roman values of the towns.

Top right, the aqueduct of Tarragona, Spain. During imperial times, many of the finest aqueducts were constructed in the provinces. Their characteristic striding arches were necessary to give a uniform inclination to the conduit that ran along the top. Center right, a detail of an aqueduct in North Africa, clearly showing the water channel. Below, an aqueduct built by Hadrian to supply Rome's colony at Carthage.

Above right, an arcade of the Pont du Gard, in southern France. Built in the first century A.D., this is one of the finest examples of Roman engineering. Its large central arches have a span of 82 feet, and the total height of the structure is 162 feet. The water was carried in a conduit above the third tier of arches. Below, a detail of the conduit of the Pont du Gard, showing the accumulation of calcium deposits.

Above, terra-cotta piping from Pompeii. Terra-cotta or lead pipes brought water from the aqueducts to public fountains, private houses, and baths. The vast majority of the population, however, had no direct water supply at home and was forced to rely on water carriers. The cost of building and maintaining aqueducts was enormous, yet no attempt was made to relate user fees to capital needs or even running expenses. For this reason, water—like bread and circuses—became yet another imperial obligation to the people.

71

A provincial from Spain, Hadrian (left) reduced still further the domination of Italy. Adopted by Trajan on his deathbed but already proven in public service, he spent half his reign (A.D. 117–138) in travel, consolidating and unifying his domain. Hadrian was imbued with the culture of Greece, and the Greek East hailed him as a new Panhellenic Zeus. Among the Athenians, he earned the name of "Olympian." Hadrian's temple at Ephesus (below left) was long revered.

begun under Claudius, who had decreed that any master who left a sick slave to die would be tried for murder. Hadrian abolished the master's power over life and death; now, only a magistrate could impose the death penalty on a slave.

Antoninus Pius, hand picked by Hadrian to be his successor, reigned for over twenty uneventful years. Early in his reign, a eulogist had written: "Yours is a universal empire, distinguished herein that your subjects are all free men. The whole world keeps holiday, the age-long curse of the sword has been laid aside. . . . " In spite of the hyperbole, the poet had some reasons for his praise: The empire was not threatened, and Rome, its capital, was a magnificent metropolis. The city had now expanded well beyond the old Servian boundaries, and the head of a pacified world no longer felt the need of walls. Covering an area of about eight square miles, it had a total estimated population of as much as one and a half million. The majority was housed in tenements which numbered perhaps as many as forty-six thousand in all. Some of these tenements were skyscrapers by ancient standards, sixty-five feet high. Many were slums of unimaginable squalor that stood side by side with the palaces of the wealthy and the magnificent monuments erected by the emperors.

Left, a section of Hadrian's Wall, at Cuddy's Crag in Britain. Begun after Hadrian's inspection of Britain in A.D. 122, the wall was designed to secure the northern frontier against the Caledonian barbarians. Generally moderate and successful in provincial administration, the emperor provoked rebellion in Judea by building a shrine to Rome's great father god, Capitoline Jupiter, on the site of the Jewish temple in Jerusalem that Titus had sacked in A.D. 70. In Rome, he built rich and innovative monuments, including the Pantheon, which has become a symbol of the Eternal City. Hadrian's final achievement was the adoption of Antoninus Pius (above) and subsequently Marcus Aurelius as his successors. Hadrian's successors ended the period of "the five good emperors," which began with Nerva and Trajan.

"In wreaths thy golden hair"

What slender Youth bedew'd with liquid odours/ Courts thee on Roses in some pleasant cave;/ Pyrrha, for whom bind'st thou/ In wreaths thy golden hair, Plain in thy neatness? Milton, in the tradition of Horace the Augustan lyricist, celebrates a simple hair style. Yet Ovid, writing several years after Horace, indicates that frippery flourished even in the austere climate fostered by Livia and Augustus: "Easier," Ovid says, "to count an oak's acorns than the new hair styles in a day."

So it was that taste in hair styles followed a whimsical course. In the stern Republic, the hair was parted evenly in front and gathered at the back of the neck in a knot. By Livia's time, however, braids were coming into fashion. Subtle variations in the coiffure depended on the shape of the face, according to Ovid: An elongated face required a part in the middle of the forehead, with the hair delicately framing the cheeks; a round face needed a knot on the top of the head, with the ears uncovered.

In the spirit of the ever-increasing luxury and grandiosity of the empire, the trichotectonic and comoplectic arts outdid themselves. The twisted curls and locks that rose in tiers led the poet Statius to compare a woman's headdress to a stage set. The *ornatrix,* or adorner, was a slave much prized and abused: "One curl of the whole round of hair was astray," writes the epigrammatist Martial, "badly set by a loose pin. This crime was avenged with the telltale mirror and the maid fell stricken because of the cruel locks." The new art in life forced a new liveliness on art. To keep up with the latest fashions, sculptors invented a removable marble wig—a stone worked separately from a sculpted likeness that could be changed according to occasion and style.

Roman women would often affect wigs, which were highly admired and imported en masse: blonde hair from the Germans and red hair from the barbarians in the north. On top of these fancy hairdos women set large pins, diadems, combs of bone or tortoise, ribbons, and even little

Above, Agrippina the Younger, with a comparatively simple hair style (A.D. 50). Below left, Julia Flavia and an example of the tiered style (A.D. 70). Below, Faustina the Elder (A.D. 160s), with a restrained style known in all periods.

vials containing perfume—or poison, according to the aim of the encounter in view. In the later empire, bands bordered or entwined with pearls came into vogue, a custom that we see reflected in the early products of Byzantine art. Nor were dyes lacking, even intense red, black, and ash grey. Yellows and blues were taboo, however, except for courtesans.

Above, curls gathered under a diadem—the iconography of an empress. Depicted here is Poppaea, Nero's mistress and second wife. Left, the empress Julia Domna. This coin, struck by Julia's husband, Septimius Severus, shows an elaborately curled coiffure. Top right, the wife of Trajan, the empress Plotina. Her hair style is of the tiered variety, popular at court from the late first century A.D. onward. Center right, Agrippina the Elder. The daughter of Julia and Agrippa and granddaughter of Augustus displays a curled but simple style that soon went out of fashion. Bottom right, a lady of the late Republic and early empire showing the "classic style."

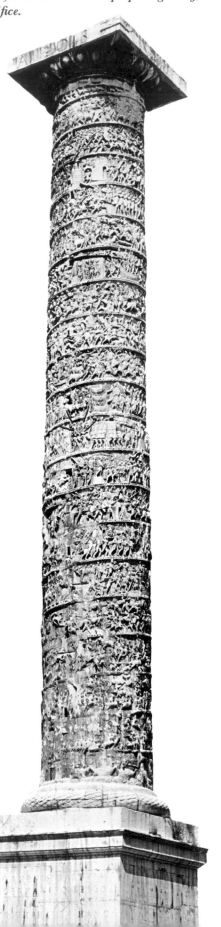

Antoninus Pius was the last emperor who could while away his time in Rome. Barbarian pressure on the borders could no longer be ignored. Marcus Aurelius, his successor (A.D. 161–180), spent nearly his entire reign fending off the wild tribes that were once more threatening Dacia and the Danube. A Stoic by philosophy, a humble man by nature, and a general only by necessity, he was the first emperor to witness the irruption of barbarian tribes as far into the empire as northern Italy itself, which was ravaged briefly by the Marcomanni and the Quadi tribes from central Europe. At the same time, there were losses in the East, and the legions returning from service there

Below, a head of the first African emperor, Septimius Severus (A.D. 193–211). Above, Severus' son Caracalla (A.D. 211–217). Caracalla generally proved to be despotic and cruel, purging all those whom he suspected of being friends with his brother Geta, whom he had murdered. During his reign, the citizenship of Rome was extended to all free males of the empire. Right, a detail of brickwork from the enormous baths begun by Septimius but opened and named by Caracalla. An admirer of the barbarians, Caracalla took his name from a long hooded cloak worn by the Gauls that he introduced to Rome.

brought back with them a plague that decimated the Roman population. Marcus Aurelius drove the barbarians out, but the trouble spots were so numerous that he was not able to concentrate Rome's increasingly inadequate manpower in any one place long enough to achieve decisive results. Marcus died while campaigning near Vindobona (now Vienna), and his son Commodus succeeded him.

It was with the reign of Commodus (A.D. 180–192) that Gibbon chose to begin his account of the Roman Empire's decline. The underlying causes are as complex as the civilization of Rome itself. Increased barbarian pressure had become apparent during the lifetime of Marcus Aurelius. Commodus gave up the effort to quell the Germanic tribes beyond the Danube and instead used bribes to stave them off. At the same time, economic difficulties were manifest. Inflation became so serious—perhaps in part because of the cost of the border wars—that Commodus was forced to introduce a list of maximum prices for various articles. Another crisis added to the growing economic gloom and made the emperor's measures inadequate: Plague struck Rome once again in A.D. 189, killing as many as two thousand people a day.

Commodus was assassinated in A.D. 192. A year of bloody anarchy, like that after Nero's death, brought to the throne Septimius Severus, the first African-

Above, a bust of the emperor Gordian the First (A.D. 238). One of the many emperors nominated by the troops in the chaos following the fall of the Severi, he ruled for twenty-two days, then killed himself.

Below, the Roman amphitheater in Thysdrus. It was here that Gordian the First was proclaimed emperor when he was governor of the province of Africa. The amphitheater was one of the empire's largest.

born emperor. During his reign (A.D. 193–211) and that of his son, Caracalla (A.D. 211–217), inflation increased drastically. Severus responded by devaluing the imperial coinage—the silver denarii. The cost of Caracalla's wars on the Danube and in the Near East led to further devaluation, such that by the middle of the third century, banks in Egypt refused to accept the devalued currency.

Meanwhile, the frontiers were making new military demands. During the reign of Alexander Severus (A.D. 222–235), the nomadic people known as the Goths began raiding the province of Dacia. In A.D. 238, they crossed the Danube and overran the Balkan provinces of the empire, which at this time were in the throes of another civil war of succession. Shortly afterward, the Alemanni, a confederation of Germanic tribes, threatened the whole length of the Rhine frontier. The military situation was further complicated by the emergence on Rome's eastern borders of a new Persian dynasty, which in the years A.D. 223–226 overthrew the declining Parthian Empire, weakened by its centuries of strife with Rome. Between A.D. 242 and 260, the mail-clad cavalry of the Persian king Shapur I laid waste the Roman possessions in Asia Minor, defeating the legions and even carrying off the emperor Valerian.

The empire was saved temporarily by a new series of able emperors, all from the province of Illyria in

Roman agriculture

Agriculture was the social and economic base of Roman society. Small owners—citizen farmers—made the best soldiers in the Republic and were the most frugal citizens. Even at the height of imperial expansion, agriculture accounted for ninety-five percent of the revenue of the state.

From the Punic Wars on, small farmers tended to be displaced by great estates. Purchased with the spoils of conquest and worked by slaves, these estates undermined the traditional yeoman class and obviated the need for improvement in agricultural technology. During the period of relative stability from Augustus to Commodus, this slave economy produced just enough to assure its own subsistence and to supply the needs of the cities with their parasitical upper classes. In the second, third, and fourth centuries, however, the growing costs of the border wars put increasing demands on the rural economy in taxes and manpower requirements for the army. Rome's economic base gradually broke up into the entirely self-sufficient economy of the Middle Ages, the first signs of which appeared with the manor-type estates of the third century A.D.

T·PACONIVS·T·F·COL·CALEDVS·
OCTAVIA·A·L·SALVIA·

Top right, a fourth-century mosaic of a fortified farm. The breakdown of authority in the late empire forced slave and freeman alike to submit to such arrangements for security. Center right, milking and breeding sheep. Above, a sarcophagus depicting a master overseeing laborers in the fields. Left, an olive press. Right, bringing in the vintage, from the Church of St. Constance in Rome. The symbols of Bacchus (Liber), who had been the god of freedom from earthly cares, were easily incorporated into Christian iconography.

Above, a coin of the emperor Aurelian (A.D. 270–275), who was called "the restorer of the world." He saved the empire from impending disintegration after it had suffered a series of humiliating setbacks. The emperor Valerian (right), for one, had bowed to the Persian king Shapur I. Valerian was defeated and captured by the Persians in A.D. 260. Below, the Tetrapylon of Palmyra in Syria. Palmyra, which rebelled against Rome but was recaptured by Aurelian in A.D. 273, supplied Rome with mounted archers.

In the late empire, artists departed from the traditional Greco-Roman classicism. Volume and geometric line came to prevail over realistic representation (right), the new style subserving the imperial ideology. In this realistically executed sculpture done in porphyry, Valerius and Constantius embrace.

northwest Greece. Claudius the Goth (A.D. 268–270), Aurelian (A.D. 270–275), Probus (A.D. 276–282), and Diocletian (A.D. 284–305) beat back the barbarians and patched up the borders. But the fabric of power was torn. The area between the upper Rhine and the upper Danube had to be abandoned, as did Trajan's province of Dacia, the first to fall to barbarians. Economically, this was a serious blow, since Dacia was the source of much-needed gold and silver. Aurelian, who gave up Dacia, also built a new wall around the capital, an ominous sign of insecurity.

Under Diocletian, the empire created a kind of ag-

ricultural system similar to that of medieval Europe. From the time of Marcus Aurelius, increasing numbers of barbarians—defeated or otherwise—had been settling on the land as tenant farmers. Under Diocletian, these tenants became bound to the estates on which they worked. Because money had been devalued almost beyond use, the army was often paid by distribution of goods, which were requisitioned by force from reluctant landowners and peasants. Diocletian reorganized the army and greatly increased its size. He built up a network of garrison forces settled along the far frontiers and supported by strategically

Christianity

As Rome extended its dominions, new peoples submitted not only to its power but also to its gods. By the end of the third century, the cult of the emperor had become the very basis of imperial order. A few recalcitrant Judeans, however, would have none of it. In the eyes of the emperor, Judea was a province troublesome out of all proportion to its importance. Here, Christianity, in one or another sect, had proved contagious. Already in the first century there were pockets of Christians at Ephesus in the Asian province, at Corinth and Philippi in Greece, and even at Rome—enough to provide the emperor Nero with convenient scapegoats after the great fire of A.D. 64. Pliny was similarly perturbed by the Christian settlements that grew up along the Black Sea, where he was governor under Trajan (A.D. 98–117).

A unified and confident empire did not feel unduly threatened by the early Christians. By the second half of the third century, however, with imperial order in crisis, rejection of the emperor cult seemed more dangerously subversive. Harsh and methodical persecutions took place under Decius (A.D. 249–251), Valerian (A.D. 257–258), and finally Diocletian (A.D. 303–311). But martyrs bred still more martyrs, and Christianity refused to yield.

Top, the catacombs of Saint Agnes in Rome. Though early Christians preferred to bury their dead above ground, persistent persecution forced them to construct catacombs—underground passages where they also met and held mass. Left, the catacombs of Domitilla. A distant relation of the emperor Domitian, Domitilla was exiled for being a Christian. Immediately above, the loaf and the fish, Christian symbols. The Greek word for "fish" is the acrostic of Greek words meaning "Jesus Christ God's Son Savior."

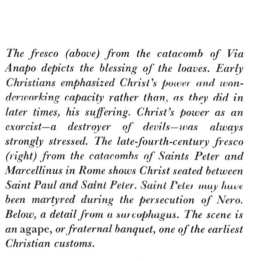

The fresco (above) from the catacomb of Via Anapo depicts the blessing of the loaves. Early Christians emphasized Christ's power and wonderworking capacity rather than, as they did in later times, his suffering. Christ's power as an exorcist—a destroyer of devils—was always strongly stressed. The late-fourth-century fresco (right) from the catacombs of Saints Peter and Marcellinus in Rome shows Christ seated between Saint Paul and Saint Peter. Saint Peter may have been martyred during the persecution of Nero. Below, a detail from a sarcophagus. The scene is an agape, or fraternal banquet, one of the earliest Christian customs.

Above, Constantine the Great (shown here with his family) who became sole ruler of the West by defeating Maxentius at the Milvian Bridge just outside Rome in A.D. 312. Before the battle he is said to have inscribed the chi-rho, a symbol for Christ, on the shields of his troops.

Below, the ruins of the basilica of Maxentius, Constantine's defeated rival for the Western empire. Completed by Constantine, this hall was the largest in the ancient world and was modeled on the Roman baths. Its vaults were over sixty feet in height.

placed mobile strike troops that were ready to race to any emergency. He also proposed legislation to introduce wage and price controls and set out to restructure the empire's administration. As a reorganization measure, he created two blocs, east and west, each with its own "Augustus," or emperor, and "Caesar," or subordinate emperor.

From about A.D. 286 onward, Diocletian ruled as Augustus of the East from Nicomedia, near the Black Sea. His fellow Augustus was Maximian, who ruled in the West. Their rule was blatantly autocratic—a sharp contrast to the appearance assumed by Au-gustus two and a half centuries earlier. Diocletian's court had an elaborate ritualistic character akin to that of an Eastern king, foreshadowing the style of the Byzantine emperors. In A.D. 305, Diocletian and Maximian abdicated, and Diocletian retired to his estate on the Dalmatian coast. To those who importuned him to take up power again, he wrote: "If you could see my cabbages, you would not wish me to abandon this happy life." It is believed that he died in A.D. 316, quietly in his bed.

Unfortunately, Diocletian's reforms failed to provide for a smooth succession, and his abdication was

followed by yet another round of internal conflict. The man who eventually emerged as ruler was Constantine the Great (A.D. 312–337). Though often engaged in warfare—not only with Roman rivals but with Goths, Alemanni, and Franks (German tribes from the middle and lower Rhine)—Constantine managed to institute profound changes in the empire. He abandoned the now almost valueless silver denarii in favor of the gold solidus—setting the stage for financial stability that was to last long after the Western empire had broken up. The solidus became the currency of the Byzantine Empire and the basis of trade throughout the Middle Ages. Other reforms enacted by Constantine heralded the end of the ancient world. At Rome, he abolished the senatorial nobility by merging it with the wealthy bourgeoisie. He also disbanded the Praetorian Guard and banned the bloody gladiatorial contests.

Other initiatives were even more dramatic. Like many of the later emperors, Constantine spent little time in Rome. The emperor's presence was too often needed on the vulnerable frontiers, mainly the lower Danube region and the Near East. Constantine decided to found a new capital on the site of the old Greek colony of Byzantium. It occupied a commanding position and was close to the main theaters of action. In A.D. 324, he began building his new Rome: Constantinople.

What links the age of Constantine most strongly to the following epoch is the triumph of Christianity. By the fourth century A.D., Christianity was well entrenched at all levels of Roman society. Shortly after becoming emperor, in A.D. 313, Constantine proclaimed the official toleration of Christianity throughout the empire, and some ten years later he made it the official religion. His new capital was to be

The last defender of the old Roman gods was Constantine's nephew Julian (left), called the Apostate because he renounced the Christian faith in which he was reared. He sought during his brief reign to reestablish paganism, but his attempts left little impression. Julian saved Gaul from the barbarians in A.D. 360, but he died while fighting the Persians in A.D. 363.

Theodosius (A.D. 378–395) finally abolished the pagan cults. This painted, gold-plated medallion (below) depicts his heirs, Galla Placidia, Valentinian, and Honorius. Its lavish material and other worldly expression typify the art of the age. The empire was by this time disintegrating. It had succumbed to Christianity from the east, and now barbarians (right) assailed it in the west.

a thoroughly Christian city, in which the temple would give way to the church.

Perhaps Constantine had hoped to find in Christianity a force for unity in his realm. Instead, he discovered that the Christians were embroiled in a heated and often bloody series of theological disputes over doctrinal issues. In fact, Christianity introduced into religion an element of sectarian violence that had been largely unknown to the pagan world.

After his death, Constantine's three sons ruled the empire during a quarter century of new internal strife. Unfortunately for Rome, the new dissension coincided with a fresh wave of barbarian invasions,

which were quelled only by the actions of Julian, a gifted young general who became sole emperor in A.D. 361 after the death of Constantius, the last of Constantine's sons. Julian, known to history as "the Apostate" because of his futile attempt to revive paganism, saved Gaul from the Franks and Alemanni and then marched east to deal with the Persians. His death in battle in A.D. 363 was a serious blow to Rome's hopes for survival, for the empire lost not only an able and humane administrator but also a military commander of great energy and skill.

Julian's death triggered off a chain of events that would destroy the empire in the West. Sometime toward the middle of the second century A.D., the Ostrogoths, a Gothic tribe, had established a kingdom north of the Black Sea. In A.D. 370, the kingdom fell to the Huns, nomadic Mongols that had for centuries been migrating from Central Asia. So terrifying were the Huns that the Goths believed them to be the offspring of witches and devils. The westward push of the Mongolians in turn forced the Visigoths, who had settled near the lower Danube, to cross the river. The emperor of the East, Valens, admitted large numbers of the frightened Goths into the empire, but his governors in Thrace foolishly created tension between them and the provincials. This eventually led to the disastrous battle of Adrianople in A.D. 378, which saw the destruction of the Roman army and the death of the emperor himself. As at Cannae and Carrhae, a lack of mobility and a failure to cope with efficient cavalry brought a Roman defeat. This time, however, Rome had no capacity to recuperate. The Western emperor, Gratian (A.D. 367–383), was forced to cede the Balkan provinces to the Goths.

When Gratian was murdered, Theodosius became sole emperor—the last Roman ever to do so. At his death, he was succeeded by his sons Honorius, who ruled in the West, and Arcadius, who became emperor of the East. They proved utterly ineffective, and the empire was left in the capable hands of the German mercenary Stilicho, who saved Italy from a Gothic invasion in A.D. 402. Honorius spent his life in Ravenna, at the head of the Adriatic, surrounded by sycophants and impenetrable marshlands, both of which kept him from knowing of the grim reality of what was happening to the empire. Partly as a result of this environment, Honorius had Stilicho murdered six years later, and so exposed Rome to its crowning humiliation.

In A.D. 405, a vast horde of barbarians crossed the frozen waters of the Rhine, meeting no opposition. That same year the Romans evacuated Britain, and shortly afterward, Spain fell to the Vandals, a powerful Germanic people. The seeds of the future nation-states of Europe were being planted in the fragments of the Roman West.

Rome itself was blockaded by the Gothic king Alaric and his hordes in A.D. 410. The Romans were powerless to prevent the sack of the city, which took place in August of that year. The news that Rome had fallen was shattering; it seemed to presage the end of civilization. On hearing of Alaric's triumph, the Christian scholar Saint Jerome wrote: "The brightest light of the whole world was extinguished. . . . The Roman Empire was deprived of its head. . . . To speak more correctly, the whole world perished in a city." The Dark Ages had begun.

Charlemagne and the Holy Roman Empire

The Holy Roman Empire was one of history's great paradoxes. In 1756, Voltaire caustically remarked that it was "neither holy, nor Roman, nor an Empire," and historians have been arguing with him—and with each other—about the question ever since. In theory, the Holy Roman Empire was a universal secular Christian government that was inaugurated on Christmas Day in A.D. 800, when Pope Leo III crowned Charlemagne *imperator augustus,* "great and peace-making Emperor of the Romans." On paper, the empire survived until the early nineteenth century, when Napoleon systematically dismantled it. Although its boundaries were constantly shifting, the empire at one time or another comprised all or part of

what we now know as France, Germany, Italy, Spain, Austria, Hungary, Poland, the Netherlands, Belgium, and Czechoslovakia.

The Holy Roman Empire was often more idea than reality. At times, there was no emperor at all; at other times, the empire existed only in writing. The disunity that plagued the empire stemmed from chronic political strife: regional and tribal conflicts; inconsistent support from the papacy (weak popes upheld the empire, strong popes tried to undermine it); the retrogressive effects of feudalism; and above all, the simultaneous emergence of Protestantism and nationalism. But even though it was in shambles

much of the time, the Holy Roman Empire endured a thousand years, and it played a crucial role in shaping the culture, politics, and attitudes that would eventually give birth to modern-day Europe.

The territory we now call Europe lay in chaos in 742, the year Charlemagne was born. The Roman Empire had collapsed centuries earlier. In 476, the last emperor of the Western Roman Empire, the timid Romulus Augustulus, had been forced to abdicate by the barbarian general Odoacer, the son of one of Attila the Hun's ministers. Meanwhile, the old empire's northern tier of provinces, which had been under firm Roman control since the days of Julius

Throughout his reign, Charlemagne led his armies in an almost endless series of military adventures. One of his most significant campaigns was against the Lombards. Above, a seal, probably of a Lombard prince. Charlemagne's victory in 774 over Adelchi (left), the son of the Lombard king Desiderius, earned him the decisive support of Pope Adrian I, who met with him afterward in Rome (below).

Caesar, had gradually cut all ties with the Eternal City and reverted to an independent status.

In Rome itself, a new institution—the papacy—slowly began to accrue power. Initially its power owed more to prayer than to the sword, for the popes' only hope of subduing the fierce tribes of the northern provinces rested in converting them to Christianity. The Church did this in miraculous numbers. But even so, many of the converted tribes refused to recognize any universal temporal authority, and they continued to engage each other in an almost endless round of petty wars. Under these conditions, Roman roads, bridges, and aqueducts—to say nothing of

Rome's celebrated social institutions—fell into ruins. Roman law, Roman governmental administration, Roman engineering, Roman arts and letters—all the hallmarks of the great empire's civilization—eroded away.

The barbarous tribes who swept down from the north were a colorful lot. One of the earliest descriptions of them comes from Tacitus, who wrote of the German warriors in the first century: "All have fierce blue eyes, red hair, huge frames." In some tribes, a young man wasn't permitted to grow a beard—the symbol of his manhood—until he had slain a foe. These tribes ultimately evolved into the peoples of

Charlemagne was crowned emperor by Pope Leo III (above) in the Basilica of St. Peter in Rome on Christmas Day in the year 800. The ceremony, said to have come as a surprise to Charlemagne, officially revived the ancient empire of the Caesars in the West. Among some tribes such as the Saxons, however, the emperor's formal authority counted for little, and Charlemagne continually had to subdue them by force. Left, Charlemagne's army on the move.

Europe. As the centuries passed, one tribe came to dominate the European landscape: the Franks, who were known for their boldness and independence (the word "Frank" meant "freeman").

In the fifth century, a Frankish chieftain named Clovis united the various factions of Franks into a single kingdom, and so, in a sense, he became the first king of France. Eighteen subsequent French kings would bear his name ("Louis" is a variant of "Clovis"). Clovis' achievement was short-lived, however. The kingdom promptly fell apart in the less able hands of his descendants. Since most of Clovis' successors preferred debauchery to statesmanship, the real authority passed to the king's chief administrative assistant, the *major domus*, or mayor of the palace.

The most famous of these was Charles Martel (Charles the Hammer), who stopped the Moslem conquest of Europe at Tours in 732 in what has proven to be one of the most decisive battles in history. Although Charles Martel wasn't a king in name, he behaved like one. Before he died in 741, he bequeathed the Frankish lands to his sons. One son, Pepin the Short, ruled as the mayor of the palace, and a year after he took office, his common-law wife, Bertha, gave birth to a son. He was named Charles, after his famous grandfather, but the world would know him as Charles the Great—Charlemagne.

Few eyebrows were raised over young Charles' illegitimacy, for at this time the Franks were regarded as just a shade above pagans. After a visit to Pepin's court, Saint Boniface wrote to the pope that "the Franks are little better than heathen." However, in this period, the Church was beginning to assert its rights over the sacrament of marriage. As a result, Pepin, who needed the pope's support in consolidating his rule over the Franks, eventually had his marriage legitimized. Pepin needed the pope even more when, chafing under the title of mayor of the palace, he decided that he wanted to reign as well as rule. With the pope's help, Pepin deposed the weak Frankish king, Childeric III, and in 751 was crowned king of the Franks by Saint Boniface himself. This elaborate ceremony marked the beginning of the Carolingian line, which would take its name from Pepin's son Charles (Carolus). Pepin, a wise and cautious ruler, died in 768, and Charles, who was then twenty-six, assumed the throne.

The tasks that faced the young king were enormous. To maintain and strengthen his rule, he would lead his armies in more than fifty-three campaigns during his reign, many at the behest of Pope Adrian I, against such heathen peoples as the Moors in Spain, the Slavs, the Bavarians, the Bretons, the Bohemians,

Above, a twelfth-century stained-glass window depicting Charlemagne being received by Constantine VI at the gates of Byzantium, a meeting that never actually occurred. During the Crusades, poetic and pictorial (below) tributes ascribed fictitious heroic deeds to Charlemagne in "battle" against the Saracens, even though he died nearly three hundred years before the First Crusade.

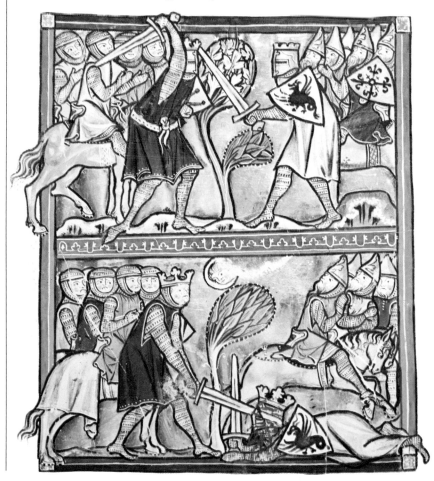

93

Charlemagne

Soon after being crowned emperor on Christmas Day in A.D. 800, Charlemagne began strengthening the Carolingian empire he inherited. Among those peoples he conquered were the Saxons in Bavaria and the Lombards in northern Italy. With these conquests, what was later to be known as the Holy Roman Empire began its period of expansion. This empire, based on the concept that there should be only one political leader in the world, ruling in harmony with the Church, lasted for several centuries.

Maximilian I

As king of Germany (1486–1519) and Holy Roman emperor (1493–1519), Maximilian I created an intricate system of alliances that made him an important figure in all of Europe's politics.

Charles V

Charles V, who was elected emperor in 1519, temporarily united Germany, Spain, and the Netherlands under one ruler. He eventually relinquished control over much of his realm, abdicating in 1556.

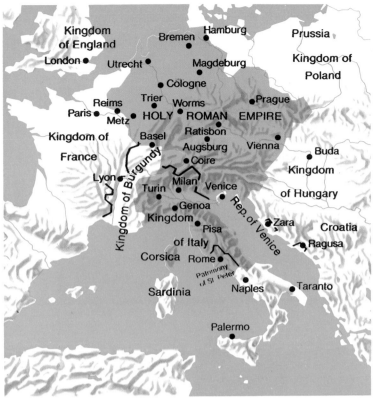

The Ottonians

When Otto I became emperor in 962, he sought to revive the weakened empire. His territory, however, was relatively small, encompassing only Germany and northern and central Italy.

The Hohenstaufens

Frederick Barbarossa was the first of the Hohenstaufen rulers.

During his reign (1152–1190), the papacy-empire conflict was revived, but Frederick's main concern centered on territorial problems in Italy.

The Treaty of Westphalia

The Treaty of Westphalia (1648) marked the end of the Thirty Years' War and formalized the political disunity that had been plaguing the Holy Roman Empire. The treaty recognized the territorial independence of the German princes, according them various rights, including the right to wage war and to negotiate peace, and prevented the Holy Roman emperor from playing a role in governing their lands. This in effect signaled the end of the Holy Roman Empire.

independent territory

95

Imperial insignia

The symbols and trappings of office were of supreme importance to the empire throughout every stage of its thousand-year history. Much of the time, the authority of the emperor—as universal monarch over all of western Christendom—was more symbolic than real, and lavish ceremonies and bejeweled crowns, scepters, and swords were especially necessary to maintain at least the illusions of imperial dignity. The imperial crown (right) was made for the coronation of Otto I in 962. The octagonal shape symbolizes the Heavenly Jerusalem; the bow or arch atop it signifies world dominion. The cross stands for Christ, the emperor of heaven, whose authority on earth is invested in the man who wears the crown.

Charlemagne's sword (below) was probably buried with its owner at Aachen and removed by the emperor Otto III some two centuries later. As emperors also served as rulers of individual kingdoms, Charlemagne was entitled to wear the iron crown of Lombardy (below right), forged, according to legend, from a nail of the True Cross.

Above center, a second-century Roman gem used by Charlemagne as a seal to ratify documents. The seal emphasized the continuity between ancient Rome and the new empire. The imperial orb (above far right), now part of the imperial crown-jewel collection in Vienna, symbolized both the empire's worldly dominion (a globe) and its heavenly charter (the cross). Right, Charlemagne's white marble throne in Aachen cathedral.

and the Saxons. The pagan Saxons, who amused themselves by burning down monasteries and churches, were particularly truculent. Charles had to invade their territory in present-day Bavaria year after year before subduing them at last in 804. He was a ruthless Christian. On one occasion, he had 4,500 Saxons beheaded in a single day.

Another tribe, the Lombards, had occupied northern Italy and was threatening to capture Rome itself. Charles, who initially sought to ally himself with the Lombards, married the daughter of Desiderius, the Lombard king. He soon changed his mind about the alliance, though, and cast his wife aside in the interest of political expediency. At the urging of Pope Adrian, who pleaded with him to subdue the "perfidious, stinking Lombards," he invaded Italy and defeated a force led by his former brother-in-law, Adelchi. The victory made Charles king of the Lombards as well as king of the Franks, and it put the papacy deeply in his debt.

In 796, when Adrian died, Leo III became pope. Pope Leo was despised in Rome, where he was considered a tyrant and a rake, and soon after his accession he was attacked and beaten by a band of armed men during a religious procession. Leo's assailants left him for dead, but the pope somehow recovered and

Charlemagne's empire had no fixed capital. The emperor and his court migrated from city to city, and imperial palaces, cathedrals, and monasteries were built in scattered locations throughout the empire. Above, Trier cathedral, an eleventh- and twelfth-century Franciscan church. Top right, Lorsch gatehouse. Center right, cloister of the monastery at Essen. Bottom right, Porta Nigra, Trier. Far right, Aachen cathedral.

escaped from Rome to seek Charles' protection in the north. The king of the Franks immediately took the disgraced pope under his wing and restored him to power in Rome. When Charles went to Rome in 800, he paid homage to Leo at St. Peter's Basilica on Christmas Day. As Charles knelt before the pontiff, Leo crowned him emperor and deemed him the heir and successor to the empire of the Caesars that had ended 324 years earlier. Though Charles probably planned the coronation himself, contemporaries wrote that he was stunned and embarrassed by the

Charlemagne's chief intellectual advisers were Einhard (above left) and Alcuin of York (pictured with Charlemagne, right). Below, a page from "History of the Lombards," one of the best primary sources of the period. Below right, an initial from Alcuin's Bible. Facing page, left, Turpino and Egmeaux writing Charlemagne's biography; above right, a silver denier; below right, the death of Charlemagne.

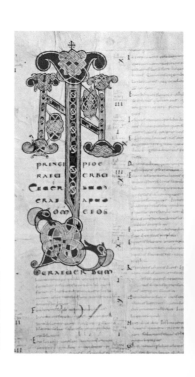

event. Charles claimed later that he would never have entered St. Peter's that day if he had known of the pope's plans.

Whatever his true feelings may have been, Charles was certainly shrewd enough to see that Leo's motives in the affair were far from selfless. By assuming the prerogative of crowning an emperor, the pope had taken for himself the highest temporal power of all—that of a king maker. Nevertheless, the deed was done. People proclaimed everywhere that the glory of the old Roman Empire had been rekindled. Europe was a political entity at last, and Charles was hailed as the new Augustus.

To his subjects, his physical stature alone was awesome. A contemporary wrote that he was "seven times the length of his foot," which meant that he was well over six feet tall at a time when the average man's height was far less than it is today. Though his culinary and sexual appetites were robust (he had five wives and many concubines in the tradition, as he thought, of David and Solomon), Charles abominated drunkenness. According to Einhard, Charles' biographer and one of the scholars in his court, he dressed simply, especially for a king. His wardrobe varied little from that of the common people. He wore a linen shirt and linen breeches under a tunic. In cold weather, he wore a snug coat of otter and marten skins. He always carried a sword.

As outstanding a general as Charles was, he proved to be an equally great administrator and delegator of authority. He saw to it that local governments in his kingdom were ruled by his own selected counts, and he appointed *missi dominici,* or royal messengers, to travel about keeping these officials under control. Charles was horrified by the prevalent illiteracy of the day and was especially scornful of the bad grammar and "unlettered tongues" of some Church officials. He urged all monasteries and cathedrals to establish schools, making no distinction between the "sons of serfs and of freemen, so that they might come and sit on the same benches to study grammar, music, and arithmetic."

Instructions such as these were issued in formal decrees, known as capitularies, or chapters of legislation, that dealt with every aspect of his kingdom—not only education but also agriculture, coinage, taxation, road and bridge maintenance, industry, and even the morals of his subjects. Not all these capitularies were obeyed, or even enforceable, but they did represent, in the words of one modern historian, "a conscientious effort to transform barbarism into civilization." Charles imposed on his many subjects one culture, one liturgy, one legal code, even a single script—Carolingian minuscule.

In his older years, Charles gathered about him the

most brilliant minds of his time. He had a splendid palace constructed for his court at Aachen, his favorite capital (there were also palaces at Ingelheim and Nijmegen), and in it he established the Palace Academy, a sort of royal literary society that met in the king's thermal baths in the palace, where weighty theological and grammatical questions were discussed. Charles brought in the famous scholar Alcuin from York, England, and from the monastery at Monte Cassino, the Lombard historian Paul the Deacon. Charles instructed Alcuin to standardize the Latin mass, and he personally saw to the preservation of many classical Latin works that would otherwise

After Charlemagne's death in 814, the empire was divided up by his son Louis the Pious among Charlemagne's grandsons, who fought each other in a civil war that lasted until 843. Facing page, above left, a coin showing Louis the Pious; below left, a carved ivory relief of a Carolingian warrior; right, Charlemagne's grandson Lothair I. This page, above, Charles the Bald, another of Charlemagne's grandsons, being presented with the Bible. Below right, a twelfth-century book cover showing Christ seated between Charlemagne and his father, Pepin, with an array of heirs beneath them.

Carolingian jewelry

During the renaissance of the Carolingian period, the art of jewelry making and metalwork flourished. The emphasis on jewelry was probably a carry-over from earlier centuries, when migratory tribes first settled Europe. To these barbarians, art meant little more than ornamentation and finery. Works of art had to be portable, and the most prized art was nonrepresentational, abstract jewelry. Gold and precious stones—especially the larger and more ostentatious gems—were highly prized. By Charlemagne's time, craftsmen had rediscovered the possibilities of pale, subdued ivory. The jewelers' artistry was most often shown in small curved boxes called reliquaries, which contained relics of saints. Chalices, crosses, crowns, buckles, rings, and brooches were other common examples. The Cross of Berengar (above), a pectoral cross with a subtle combination of gold and gems, shows how sophisticated the jewelers' art had become by the tenth century.

be lost to us today. Ironically, Charles himself had never learned to write, though he tried to learn in his old age and kept tablets under his pillow so that he could practice at odd hours. He could read Greek, and he spoke Latin exceptionally well.

Charlemagne's chief worry in his last years may have been his son and successor, Louis. Louis had proved himself a fair enough general in his father's wars in Aquitaine, but he was somewhat introspective and sincerely religious—he practiced what his father had often merely preached. Louis—known as Louis the Pious—was so religious, in fact, that Charles felt it necessary to forbid him to become a monk. Despite his reservations about his son's uncompromising piety, Charles had him crowned coemperor at Aachen in 813. Charles died the following year, after a glorious reign of forty-six years.

Now the sole emperor, Louis immediately set a different tone in the palace. He was faithful to his wife. He banished his immoral sisters from the court. He also attempted to reform the monasteries, and he became far more subservient to the pope than his father had been. As a result of his selflessness, he committed a severe political mistake: He divided his empire up among his three sons—Pepin, Lothair, and Ludwig. When his first wife died, Louis remarried and had a fourth son, known to us as Charles the Bald. Having already divided his kingdom three ways, Louis, eager to be fair, tried to redivide it to give his fourth son a share.

The three older sons objected and instigated a rebellion that lasted eight years, culminating in a battle in which Louis' own supporters deserted him. The battleground at Rotfield, near Colmar, was afterward called the Lugenfeld, or Field of Lies. Louis was taken captive, but when his three rebellious sons began to fight among themselves, two of them decided to restore him to power. Pepin, who is said to have gone insane, died in 838. Two years later, when Louis himself died, war broke out once more among the surviving sons. It was several years before an agreement was reached at Verdun. The Treaty of Verdun broke Charlemagne's great empire into three weaker fragments that roughly coincided with the present-day states of France (which went to Charles the Bald, considered the first king of France), Germany (to Ludwig), and Italy (to Lothair).

The fratricidal wars were costly. While the brothers were using their armies to fight each other, the Norse invaded the kingdom and got as far as Paris. Saracens captured Palermo and Bari, and Arabs set fire to Marseille. Amid all the havoc, the power of the kings began to erode. In succeeding generations, kings lost more respect, as the appellations their subjects gave them attest: Louis the Stammerer, Charles the Fat, Charles the Simple, Ludwig the Silent. A new ruling class arose—feudal lords and nobles, who began to act independently of the king and rule their own separate fiefdoms. In France, along with the rise of feudalism came a new, stronger French royal house—the Capetians—and France would never again be a part of the

In the century and a half after Charlemagne's death, the empire had all but ceased to exist, but it was given new life in 962, when Otto I (left), the Saxon king of the Germans, was crowned emperor by the pope. Although Otto lacked Charlemagne's cultural pretensions, he was an astute ruler, managing to unite Germany and Italy under a single monarch. Above, Otto's seal. The letters of his name are aligned in the shape of a cross.

Otto's successors tried to reunite Charlemagne's disjointed legacy, but their attempts failed. Otto II (above) died in his twenties in 983. His son, Otto III (right), shown holding a model of his church, also died young. During this time, the Cluniac order of monks was trying to bring about ecclesiastical reforms. Below, an eleventh-century manuscript showing Saint Hildefonsus, a Cluniac monk.

empire. Although the Carolingian line survived its founder by more than a century and a half, it is fair to say that most of its glory died at Aachen with Charlemagne.

The nobles of Germany, realizing the need for a central national power, gave the German throne to a Franconian duke, Conrad I. Conrad spent most of his seven-year reign battling a Saxon duke, Henry, whom he was nevertheless farsighted and generous enough to name as his successor. Ironically, the very Saxons Charlemagne had fought were now furnishing the king who would begin restoring the empire.

Henry's son, Otto I, who became emperor in 962, was responsible for the resurgence of the empire. Otto, known as Otto the Great, has been called the Charlemagne of Germany. Though he lacked Charlemagne's intellectual and cultural ambition, he was a strong-willed and clever ruler. By a series of shrewd political maneuvers, he succeeded in winning the loyalty of the German feudal barons and fused their separate fiefdoms into a moderately coherent state. With Germany in his grasp, he cast his eye on Italy—a ready target.

Italy's king, Berengar II, was involved in a dispute with the reigning pope, John XII. John, who had become pope at the age of eighteen, was a wastrel. He not only gambled at dice but prayed for the devil's aid while doing so. He appointed a ten-year-old boy as a bishop. He had a deacon castrated. He committed incest with his sisters. Finding himself in need of help in his struggle with the Italian king, John decided to secure an ally by crowning an emperor. Otto, happy to oblige, came to Italy with his army and was made emperor in 962. (Although various pretenders had claimed the imperial throne since the collapse of the Carolingians, none had assumed real power.) Otto now ruled all of Germany and most of Italy. Pope John, for his part, soon began to regret Otto's dominance and complained bitterly of it. Otto simply

Hildesheim in lower Saxony had its golden age under the Ottonians. To counter the growing power of the German nobles, the Ottonian emperors favored the ecclesiastical officials; the bishops of Hildesheim eventually achieved princely status. St. Michael's church (top), considered the most important Ottonian church, was begun by Bishop Bernwald of Hildesheim around A.D. 1000. Goslar (immediately above), founded in 922, was for all practical purposes the capital city of the empire until 1125. At Ottmarsheim in France, the octagonal Convent Church (left) was consecrated by Pope Leo IX in 1049.

107

Agriculture

Agriculture formed the economic basis of medieval society. Nine out of every ten men worked in the fields as peasants. Much of what they produced had to be turned over to the landowner—either a feudal lord or a monastery. The peasant was bound to the soil and could not leave the manor estate without the lord's permission. Those who attempted to escape could be tried and punished, the landlord himself acting as judge. If the landlord sold his fields, the peasant had to build his own dwelling—usually a crude, one-room hut—and make and repair his own tools. The light plows the Romans had used in the Mediterranean area were unsuitable in the less fertile northern lands, and a heavier iron plow was developed which cut a much deeper furrow. A stiff-collared harness was also devised, enabling a horse to pull a plow without choking, which resulted in a remarkable increase in efficiency (a horse could plow three times as much land as an ox). The most revolutionary innovation was the three-field system of crop rotation. The Roman two-field system had left half of the usable land unproductive each year. The medieval peasant discovered that wheat or rye could be sown in the autumn as well as in the spring, thus doubling the annual yield. Under the new system, one area was planted with rye or wheat in the fall and harvested the following summer; a second area planted with barley, oats, and pease was harvested in the spring; a third area was left fallow. Despite the increased yields, the work continued to be as hard and unremitting as ever. The role of the serf in the Middle Ages was purely economic—a forced consumer in times of glut, a producer at other times. His body was, by a legal fiction, capable of being divided and sold to different lords. Whatever he possessed was deemed to have been lent to him for the discharge of his tasks and had to be returned upon his death. The Church, which demanded a tithe, or tenth, of the peasants' crops, provided the only respite: "Our oxen," the peasants said, "know when Sunday comes, and will not work on that day."

Medieval manuscripts give a picture of daily life. Above, the gathering of honey. Fruit trees (right) were systematically cultivated and pruned. The arable farm land on a lord's estate (below) was divided among individual peasants into small strips that were plowed separately. Each peasant might be responsible for two or three of them scattered throughout the estate.

The medieval manor was a self-sufficient economic entity. All food was grown on the estate, and all tools and clothing were made there as well. Except in times of famine, the peasants' diet was for the most part wholesome. Meat, dairy, and poultry products were staples. Above, a peasant milking sheep. Above right, gathering eggs. Right and below right, farmers in the field planting and plowing.

Below, peasants gathering grapes for wine.

Professions

As agricultural production improved and the population of Europe increased, new villages and towns sprang up. Craftsmen moved from the overpopulated manors into these trade centers. Merchants formed associations, or guilds, that gave them monopolies on trade by setting tolls and tariffs on goods brought into the cities from outside. Artisans, craftsmen, and other tradesmen, such as tailors, barbers, stonemasons, carpenters, shoemakers, and apothecaries, formed exclusive guilds. These guilds protected their own reputation and the public by insuring that only qualified craftsmen could provide goods and services. Young men entered the guild only after a long and thorough apprenticeship—usually seven years. Eventually, the guilds acquired so much power that the actual governing of the city fell into their hands. From the guilds, a new class—the bourgeoisie—would rise up to challenge the authority of the empire.

As a result of increased trade, money came back into circulation, bringing with it the need for bankers (below).

Left, a butcher slaughtering cattle. Below, a weaver works at a loom. In Flanders and Italy, the wool guilds became so prosperous that entire factories were set up to house all the stages of textile production—washing, dyeing, spinning, weaving—under one roof. Wholesale cloth merchants provided the capital and equipment.

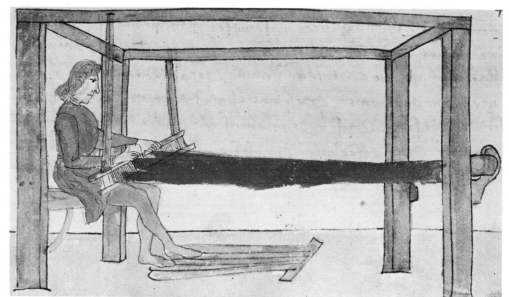

Above, craftsmen under the protection of Mercury, the Roman god of commerce: copyist, watchmaker, armorer, painter, sculptor, and organ maker. Top right, fishermen hauling in a catch. Center right, a mason laying bricks. Bottom right, artisans working with a burin, or engraving tool. Traveling merchants (below), who risked being robbed or killed on the roads, were a crucial trade link between cities.

had him deposed and replaced him with a friendlier pontiff.

Otto had won this particular contest, but the people of Rome resented being under the thumb of a German, and the rivalry between emperor and pope would continue for centuries. Otto's successor, Otto II, tried to annex southern Italy to the realm but died while still in his twenties. His son, Otto III, was crowned in 983 at the age of three and began to rule at sixteen. He too died young and without leaving an heir. A Bavarian cousin, Henry II, succeeded him; Henry also died childless and was the last of the Saxon line.

Conrad II, a descendant of Henry I's old opponent Conrad, became emperor in 1024 and began a new dynasty—the Salians. Under Conrad's son, Henry III, the empire reached what may have been the zenith of its power. An intensely devout and peace-loving ruler, Henry busied himself with purifying the monasteries by supporting the new, reform-minded Cluniac order of monks. He built a splendid imperial palace at Goslar, and he ordered the completion of the magnificent cathedrals of Mainz, Worms, and Spires. Henry detested simony—the selling of church offices—and he was probably the only medieval emperor who wasn't guilty of it. Most important, he strengthened the office of the pope during his reign by filling four papal vacancies with strong, independent prelates.

Henry IV, who succeeded him at the age of six, came to regret bitterly his father's preference in popes when he found himself locked in combat with perhaps the most controversial pope in the Church's history. Gregory VII, known as Gregory the Great, became pope in 1073 and immediately asserted his temporal authority: "If the pope is supreme judge in spiritual matters," he wrote to a friend, "why not also secular matters?" Since Charlemagne's time, bishops had been selected by kings and emperors—often for a price. Gregory found this practice of lay investiture inconsistent with the Church's dignity and issued decrees against it, and against simony and clerical marriage as well.

Henry, whose own vested interest rested on selecting bishops for himself, resisted the decree, and Gregory excommunicated five bishops who served as

The Salian dynasty, begun by Conrad II in 1024, ruled the empire for more than a century. Conrad and his son, Henry III, built the monumental castle of Nuremberg (above left) to serve as an imperial residence. Immediately above, interior of the cathedral of Worms, built under Henry III, where the Concordat of Worms was signed in 1122, putting an end to the struggle between the empire and the papacy over feudal investitures. Top, Henry IV and his court. Left, the courtyard of the fortress Runkel am Lahn, built in the thirteenth century to control the nearby town of Limburg.

Henry's counselors. Henry declared Gregory deposed, referring to him by his given name of "Hildebrand, not pope but false monk." Gregory responded by branding Henry anathema, excommunicating him and, in February 1076, declaring him deposed in turn. Although Henry had armies and weapons and Gregory had only moral persuasiveness to rely on, Henry's position proved the weaker in the face of outraged public opinion. Even the Saxons under Henry revolted, and the emperor found himself helpless. He decided to seek out Gregory in person and beg for absolution.

Finding Gregory was a problem, for Gregory had fled Rome and had found refuge in the Apennine village of Canossa, at the castle of his friend the beautiful Matilda, countess of Tuscany. At Canossa, one of the most dramatic events of the Middle Ages took place—a decisive confrontation between the pope and the emperor. Henry left his army behind and arrived at Canossa with a small retinue. Gregory himself described what took place next: "He presented himself at the gate of the castle, barefoot and clad only in wretched woollen garments, beseeching us with tears to grant him absolution and forgiveness." For three days, Henry knelt on the castle steps in the snow begging to be forgiven. Finally, Gregory relented and, in his words, "received him again into the bosom of Holy Mother Church."

The pope's treatment of Henry angered the Germans, and his victory proved to be more symbolic than substantial, for Henry soon returned to Germany, regained the support of his nobles, and in 1084 arrived in Rome with an army. Gregory excommunicated Henry again, but instead of garnering support for this act, Gregory was driven out of Rome. He found refuge in Salerno, but he had lost the will to fight and the desire to live. His spirit broken, Gregory announced, "I have loved righteousness and hated iniquity, wherefore I die in exile."

Had he been able to see into the future, he might have taken comfort, for although Henry had won this particular duel of nerves, the papacy would ultimately have the upper hand, a supremacy symbolized for all time by the fateful meeting at Canossa. Ironically, the impetuous Henry IV was also to die in exile, for his own family turned against him as a result of his support of Gregory's successor, Clement III. In 1105, Henry's son forced his father to abdicate. Henry died at Liège in 1106, unrepentant and still excommunicated, but the people of Liège, in defiance of Church authority, gave him a royal Christian burial anyway.

During the reign of his son, Henry V, the conflict between pope and emperor over lay investiture was

Above, a miniature from the manuscript De-cretum Gratiani, the Church's first systematic collection of canon laws, compiled by the monk Gratian (ca. 1140). It shows Christ conferring dual power upon the pope and the emperor. Below, an order by Andelasia, countess of Calabria and Sicily, giving instructions for the defense of a monastery against Saracen pirates. It is the oldest European document of its kind on paper.

Henry IV at Canossa

Perhaps the supreme dramatic encounter in the medieval conflict between Church and state occurred in 1077 between Pope Gregory VII and Emperor Henry IV at the village of Canossa near Parma, Italy. Gregory had issued a proclamation banning lay investiture, but Henry refused to comply. Gregory responded by excommunicating Henry. In the ensuing struggle, Gregory was able to turn Henry's own nobles in Germany against him, and Henry was forced to seek out the pope, who was staying at Canossa in the castle of Matilda of Tuscany. For three days, the emperor, barefoot and dressed in sackcloth, knelt outside the castle in the snow begging Gregory's forgiveness. At length, Gregory forgave him, and the emperor, promising to forego lay investiture, returned to Germany to deal with his rebellious nobles. Although Henry, who later gained public sympathy, eventually went back on his promise, the events at Canossa symbolized forever the subservience of state to Church.

Right, Matilda of Tuscany accepting her biography from her biographer, Doninzone. The countess was the most powerful landowner in central Italy in the eleventh century, but at her death her lands fell into the hands of Emperor Henry V.

M ATHILDIS LUCENS. PRECOR HOC CAPE CARA VOLUMEN

Left, the ruins of the tenth-century castle of Matilda of Tuscany, near the village of Canossa. The memory of the political impact of the meeting there between pope and emperor lasted for centuries. Eight hundred years later, when the German chancellor Otto von Bismarck came into conflict with the Catholic Church, he vowed he would "never go to Canossa."

Above, Matilda's seal. Facing page, bottom, two scenes from the struggle between Henry IV and Pope Gregory. The one on the left shows Henry and his antipope, "Clement III" (Guibert, archbishop of Ravenna), enthroned in Rome while Pope Gregory is being driven from the gates of the city. The scene on the right shows Gregory dying in exile at Salerno in 1084.

Before he became pope, Gregory VII (above) had gained renown as a reform-minded Benedictine monk. Gregory's papacy marked a turning point in Church history, for he paved the way for a later victory on the lay-investiture question in the Concordat of Worms.

Right, Pope Gregory's adversary, Emperor Henry IV, depicted on a silver shrine containing most of Charlemagne's remains. Henry's reign was undermined by the papacy and the German nobles. The nobles at first supported Henry in his fight to retain lay investiture, but when the pope excommunicated him, one group of nobles insisted that he beg for absolution. Henry died in exile—in 1106, after his own son, Henry V, forced him to abdicate.

Feudalism

After the deterioration of Charlemagne's empire, most of the political power passed into the hands of the nobles. The consequence was feudalism—a primitive system that varied greatly from region to region. The nobles, or lords, held fiefs, generally consisting of landed property, which could be as large as a kingdom or as small as a manorial estate. In some areas, a fief might consist merely of the right to collect taxes and duties. A feudal lord could be as powerful as a king or duke, or he might be a knight who ruled only a village or less. Under a rigid social hierarchy, the noble who granted the fief was the suzerain, or overlord, and the noble who received it was the vassal. To receive the fief, the vassal knelt before the suzerain and swore an oath of fealty which bound him to be loyal and to perform certain services. Often these services were military, but sometimes the vassal would have to give the lord money. The feudal contract benefited both parties: The suzerain gained armed warriors and the vassal gained the use of the land and the suzerain's protection in times of civil turmoil. By a process known as subinfeudation, the vassal himself could grant portions of his fief to lesser nobles and become a suzerain of sorts in his own right.

Falconry (above) was perhaps the chief leisure-time activity among nobles in the Middle Ages. In fact, this highly complicated sport became so fashionable that in some circles a noble wouldn't dream of appearing in public without a hawk on his wrist as a mark of dignity. Even bishops and abbots became enthusiasts. They would sometimes display their birds on the altar steps during mass.

The investiture of a youth into knighthood (below left) was the culmination of long years of apprenticeship in the arts of war and chivalry. Training began at the age of seven, when a page was chosen to serve a knight. At fourteen, the page became an esquire and received a sword, although he could not wear it girded at his side until the actual investiture ceremony. Below, a medieval banquet.

The ancient fortress of Carcassonne in southern France (left) was one of the architectural marvels of Europe. When it was completed, Carcassonne was widely considered impregnable. Typically, such castles were the feudal lord's residence and the administrative and judicial center of the territory.

Below, two knights jousting in a tournament. Tournaments provided sport and spectacle for the onlookers and fame for the participants, but they also functioned as war games, offering invaluable practice in the arts of combat. The rules were very formal and strict. The participants charged each other on their mounts; the lances were, in theory, to be aimed only at the opponent's shield, not his body. Once unhorsed, the knights dueled on foot until one of them formally surrendered on bended knee.

121

renewed with even more vigor. Henry V refused to cease his blatant wheeling and dealing in bishoprics. He went so far as to have himself crowned emperor by brute force, imprisoning the pope and the cardinals. Eventually, like his father, he was excommunicated for supporting an antipope, though he was finally reconciled with the Church in 1122, when he and Pope Calistus II settled the issue of investiture with the Concordat of Worms. Henry, the last of the Salian line, died without an heir.

The German nobles immediately took advantage of the succession dilemma and proposed that they elect the man who would wear the crown. They were divided into two opposing political factions, the Welfs (the papal party) and the Ghibellines (the imperial supporters). After intense debate among themselves, they elected Lothair, a Saxon duke, as the next emperor. Upon Lothair's death in 1137, the German nobles elected Conrad III, of the illustrious Hohenstaufen family, to the throne. Conrad went off on the

Second Crusade with Louis VII of France to recover the Holy Land and took part in the siege of Damascus. The siege failed, and Conrad returned home in ignominy.

Conrad's nephew and successor, Frederick, became king of the Germans when he was thirty and at once staked an outspoken claim to the empire. Frederick saw Germany and Italy as a sacred entity established on earth directly by God. He referred to the empire not merely as the Roman Empire but as the *Holy* Roman Empire. Frederick was physically unimposing—short, fair skinned, and yellow haired—but he did sport a ferocious red beard that led the Italians, who lived in fear of his invading armies, to call him Barbarossa.

Following a well-established tradition, Frederick Barbarossa got hold of the imperial crown by bargaining with the pope—or in this case two popes, Eugene III and his successor, Adrian IV. In 1153, Frederick agreed to help Pope Eugene suppress a rebellion of the revolutionary commune of Rome

Above, Frederick Barbarossa and the archbishop of Cologne in Rome for Frederick's coronation. The day after the ceremony, the independent-minded republicans of Rome, who were not enthusiastic about being ruled by a German, rioted in protest. Bitter fighting broke out in streets, and both the emperor and the pope were driven out of the city. Frederick invaded Italy six times in the hope of subduing the rebellious city-states. Right, Maria Laach. Dedicated in 1156, this Benedictine structure is an excellent example of a medieval German monastery.

led by Arnold of Brescia, an Italian monk and reformer and a champion of the Italian city-states. When Eugene died, Pope Adrian took up the cause that opposed the arrogant city-states, and he turned to Frederick Barbarossa for help. Frederick and his armies entered Italy in 1154, and by the following year the rebellious Arnold had been executed. Now, only one obstacle stood in the way of Frederick's ambition to be crowned emperor.

Frederick met Pope Adrian at Nepi, near Rome, where the pope rode up to him on horseback. According to traditional protocol, Frederick should have led the pope's mount by the bridle and held his stir-rup while he dismounted. This ceremony, called *strator,* was a symbolic recognition of the pope's superiority over a mere temporal king. In this instance, to the shock of onlookers, the pontiff sat waiting on horseback while the king made no move whatsoever to grab the stirrup. Finally, the offended pope had to get off the horse by himself. He refused Frederick the traditional "kiss of peace," as well as the imperial crown. For the next two days, Frederick and Adrian argued endlessly over this item of protocol until Frederick at length swallowed his pride and gave in. Then the pope went off some distance, got back on the horse, and rode in again. This time, Frederick

dutifully held the bridle and stirrup of the pope's horse as the pope dismounted. Frederick was then crowned emperor and was free to do as he pleased.

The Holy Roman emperor was also, in name, the king of Lombardy, although in fact no German ruler since Henry IV had even tried to control the Lombards. Frederick Barbarossa took his title seriously, and in 1158 he sent ultimatums to the towns of northern Italy asserting his royal prerogatives, which included the right to tax the Lombards to fill his German coffers. Unfortunately for Frederick, northern Italy was commune country, and Milan, Brescia, Cremona, and other city-states had been accruing

their own power since the tenth century. Although a few towns gave in to Frederick, others, Milan among them, preferred independence.

Frederick led his army to Milan and put the city under siege. The inhabitants within the walls resisted for two years. When Frederick finally captured the city in 1162, he burned it to the ground. This so infuriated the other cities of northern Italy—Bologna, Ferrara, Padua, and Cremona—that they banded together in 1167 to form the Lombard League. The pope, caught in the middle, decided to take his chances with the rebellious cities and excommunicated Frederick. In 1176, at the battle of Legnano, the

Daily life

The rhythm of daily life in a medieval city was governed by the light of the sun. No one cared what time it was—only how much daylight was left. Church bells rang at three-hour intervals beginning at dawn, when artisans and tradesmen would rise and set about their work and servants and housewives would line up for water at the town well. Horses and donkeys congested and befouled the narrow, unpaved streets, which became virtual mud troughs after a rain. Geese, pigs, pigeons, dogs, and cats ran loose as ever-present scavengers. All was not grim, however. Shops and buildings were brightly painted, and colorful signs advertised the occupant's trade—a unicorn for a goldsmith, a horse's head for a harness maker, a white arm with red stripes for a surgeon-barber. Shops were enclosed with shutters that opened horizontally into the street: The upper shutter served as a canopy, the lower shutter served as a counter for goods and foods, tantalizing passersby with their sights and smells. Peddlers hawking milk and cheese roamed the streets singing snatches of doggerel (forerunners of today's commercial jingles) about their wares. At sunset, people returned to their houses. All cooking was done over an open fire. Broths, stews, roasts, and fish were the main courses, augmented with fruits, pastries, and spiced wine. (Tomatoes, squash, corn, noodles, rice, chocolate, coffee, and tea were unknown, and only the wealthy could afford pepper.) With the onset of night, the gates of the city were locked shut, leaving only nightwatchmen and thieves to roam the unlit streets.

Scenes of urban life, as shown in medieval minia-
tures. Facing page, above, a busy market street in
Bologna. Below left, shoppers examining fish. In-
strumentalists and singers (below right) provided
background music while shoppers strolled. This
page, top, a wedding. Above, a buyer haggling
with a grain merchant.

Above and below, two domestic scenes. In the day-
time and evening, all activity centered on the
hearth. Members of the household prepared and
ate their meals and carried on tasks like sewing,
spinning, and weaving. The hearth also provided
needed illumination, for even on a bright day the
narrow windows covered with oiled parchment
admitted little light.

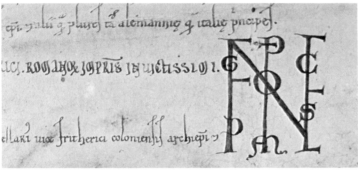

army of the Lombard League defeated Frederick's German troops. At the Treaty of Constance in 1183, Frederick agreed to the independence of the Lombard cities, while they in turn formally acknowledged Frederick as their supreme ruler, at least in theory. Under the treaty, all the Lombards were required to do was pay Frederick's expenses when he and his retinue happened to visit Italy.

Frederick had better luck at home in Germany, where he secured nearly full control over the German bishops. They were at times more loyal to him than to the pope. He defeated Henry of Saxony and destroyed the Welf power. He also established a new class of imperial civil servants to administer the German cities. Frederick staged elaborate festivals with lavish costumes and colorful pageantry that celebrated chivalry and knighthood—all of which won him the hearts of the pomp-loving Germans.

It was the love of chivalry that led Frederick to undertake, at the age of sixty-seven, the Third Crusade. The Moslem leader Saladin had captured Jerusalem two years before, in 1187, and Frederick felt it incumbent upon him in his holy office to recapture the Holy City for Christianity. Some historians think he may also have hoped to unite both the Eastern and Western empires in a new kingdom that would be as vast and powerful as the ancient Roman one. Frederick Barbarossa took off at the head of one hundred thousand men, but his army was attacked by guerrilla bands of Turks along the way. Many of his soldiers starved to death. The old emperor never reached Jerusalem; he drowned while crossing a river in Cilicia. It was hardly a glorious death for a chivalrous knight.

Frederick Barbarossa's son, Henry VI, journeyed to Rome to be crowned emperor by Pope Celestine III in St. Peter's in 1191. Like his father, Henry had glorious dreams of empire. He wanted to recover not only Italy but France and Spain besides. However, he

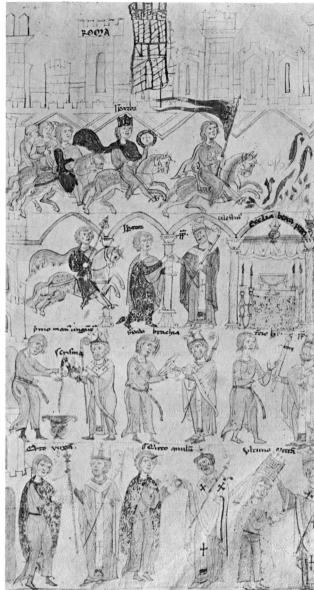

Frederick's son Henry VI (above left) added a new kingdom to the empire by marrying Constance, heir to the throne of Sicily. Above, the journey of Henry to Rome, where he was crowned emperor in 1191 by Pope Celestine III in St. Peter's. Henry is shown being anointed and receiving the symbols of his office—sword, scepter, ring, crown, and miter. When Henry died six years later, Constance (whose seal is seen at left) decided to raise their son, Frederick II, in Sicily.

died young, having gotten no farther than Sicily. His accomplishments there were impressive nonetheless. He managed to subdue the Normans, who had ruled Sicily and southern Italy for sixty years. To further strengthen his grip on the kingdom, he married Constance, the defeated Norman heiress to the Sicilian throne. The marriage made Henry king of Sicily as well as king of the Germans and emperor. At that moment, the empire united Poland, Bohemia, Austria, Holland, and Switzerland, as well as Germany and most of Italy (except for the Papal States, which remained in the pope's power).

Pope Innocent III (above) served as guardian of the four-year-old Frederick II, who became perhaps the best-educated ruler of the Middle Ages. Left, a page from Frederick's Tractatus de arte venandi cum avibus, a tract on hawking and on birds in general, considered the first work of modern ornithology. Facing page, a Sicilian mosaic of Frederick's coat of arms.

Constance, who had been secluded in nunneries in Palermo for much of her life, was thirty when she married the twenty-year-old Henry. For twelve years, she tried to bear him an heir and failed. When, at forty-two, she finally became pregnant, legend has it that she was so proud of the fact that she had a tent erected in the marketplace of a village near Ancona and gave birth to her baby in full view of the bewildered local villagers. (Nineteen cardinals and bishops also showed up for the occasion to make certain that the baby was really hers.) Presumably, the villagers and prelates were duly impressed. They had every right to be. The infant, Frederick II, would become one of the most extraordinary and enigmatic rulers of all time.

Henry died in 1197 when his son was three, and the provincial Constance, who wanted to keep her child with her in Sicily, renounced her son's claim to the German throne— a gesture that at once threw three generations of careful empire building into chaos. The following year, Constance herself died, after instructing in her will that her son be entrusted to the guardianship of the one man least likely to have any sympathy for a future emperor—Pope Innocent III. Innocent, naturally, was delighted by the choice. He had no intention of returning the child to his father's

kingdom in Germany and saw to it that Frederick remained out of the way in Palermo, where he grew up more or less on his own. Officially, he was a resident of the palace, but he was not closely supervised or cared for. Denied a systematic education, the child picked up much of his knowledge on the streets. It was an education unlike that of any other medieval ruler in Christendom.

Palermo had been held by the Moslems for two centuries before the Normans conquered it. The city was a melting pot that contained the best elements of three cultures—Jewish, Christian, and Islamic. The child learned Arabic, Latin, and Greek (he would eventually speak nine languages), and more important, he became an avid student of the city's Moslem culture. At the time, Islamic science and learning easily surpassed that of Europe. In an age when the confines of Christian dogma were absolute, Frederick received a far broader education than any royal tutor could have provided. He learned to evaluate and compare different religions and societies without prejudice.

The child may have been a pauper at times, but he was also the lawful king of Sicily, and he knew it. At the age of twelve, he abruptly dismissed the deputy regent who had been chosen by the pope to rule in his

name. The youth still lacked a power base, so three years later, when he was fifteen, he married Constance of Aragon, a much older woman whose appeal may have been her dowry—a troop of knights. With these knights, Frederick imposed his rule over Sicily. Luckily for Frederick, the current German king and emperor, Otto IV, had angered the pope and been excommunicated. Frederick was suddenly designated king of the Germans. The pope, in recommending Frederick to the German nobles, said that his ward was "as old in wisdom as he is young in years."

There was a catch, however. Frederick had to give his word to the pope that he wouldn't attempt to unite the kingdoms of Germany and Sicily because such a merger would leave the Papal States surrounded by a threatening power. Frederick also had to promise to undertake a Crusade to free Jerusalem from the Saracens.

Despite his German crown, Frederick's real love was Sicily, and once he had been anointed emperor at St. Peter's in 1220, he returned to the country of his childhood and ruled it and southern Italy as a separate dominion, legally severed from the empire. Under his hand, the governing apparatus was quickly transformed. Feudalism, which had favored the nobles, was abolished, and in its place Frederick established the first modern reign of divine-right despotism. He was, by and large, a benevolent despot. He introduced direct taxation, organized a professional army loyal to the king, and set rigid controls over commerce and industry by creating government monopolies for grain trade, textile manufacture, and slaughterhouses. He appointed jurists who codified laws into the Constitutions of Melfi. (The legal system had been in disarray since the time of Justinian in the sixth century.) Frederick's laws anticipated the rise of the centralized monarchies and nation-states

Pope Gregory IX (above right) excommunicated Frederick II after the emperor delayed his departure on a Crusade in 1227. Right, a tiara of Frederick's wife, Constance of Aragon. Facing page, top left, a coin issued by Frederick II. Frederick, in an effort to antagonize the pope, ordered the capture of a Genoese fleet of papal delegates (top right), but the imprisonment of these cardinals turned public opinion against him. In 1245, Pope Innocent IV also excommunicated Frederick, despite the protests of Frederick's minister, Thaddeus of Suessa, at the Council of Lyon (below).

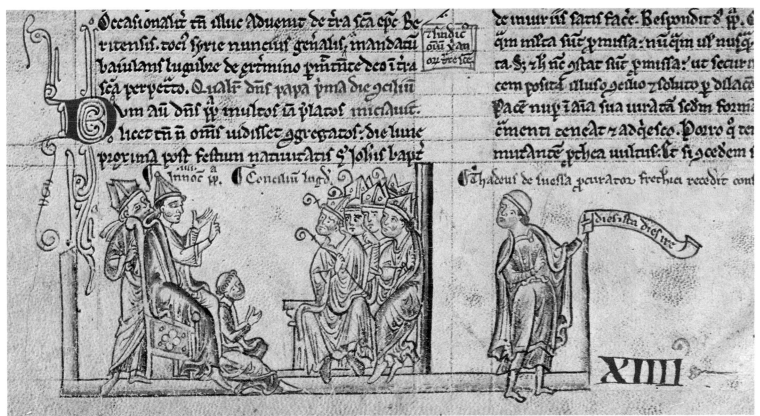

that would eventually supplant existing feudal baronies. He was, on the whole, a civilized man, who patronized science and was interested in mathematics, astronomy, and astrology. Frederick also wrote poetry and took an interest in art. In 1224, he founded the University of Naples, one of the few secular centers of learning in the Middle Ages.

The pope, meanwhile, kept urging Frederick to get on with the Crusade to the Holy Land that he had promised to undertake. In 1227, Frederick finally assembled a fleet and army at Brindisi and was about to embark when a plague struck, killing many of his soldiers. Frederick himself was desperately ill for sev-

eral months. The pope, on learning of the delay, uncharitably excommunicated him. When he recovered his strength, Frederick proceeded to the Holy Land anyway, assuming that the pope would rescind the excommunication. The pope, jealous of Frederick's growing reputation and power, chose instead to sabotage him. As Frederick led his armies to the outskirts of Jerusalem, envoys from the Vatican arrived to tell the assembled soldiers that all Christians were forbidden to serve under Frederick. Much as the pope wanted Jerusalem back, he sought the destruction of his rival even more.

Robbed of an army, Frederick was still able to

capture Jerusalem—not by force but by tact. He entered into discussions with the Moslem commander of the city, al-Kamil, and startled him with his thorough knowledge of Islamic literature, science, and philosophy. Al-Kamil was charmed by this literate foreign crusader who spoke so well in the Prophet's tongue. He graciously permitted Frederick to crown himself king of Jerusalem. Frederick's sacrilegious colloquy with the Saracen foe outraged his Christian followers, and when the emperor was boarding his ship at Acre for the voyage home, the Christian populace surrounded him and threw filth at him.

Christians back home were equally outraged, sus-

pecting that the emperor was more a friend to the Saracens than to the Christians. Frederick admittedly had fallen under a degree of Eastern influence. Like his Saracen friends, he maintained a harem at his palace. His troop of personal bodyguards was composed exclusively of Moslems, since Frederick reasoned that these troops could be counted on to be loyal in the face of papal interdictions.

Was this medieval ruler in fact an atheist? We simply don't know. We can only say for certain that he was, for his time, a uniquely knowledgeable student of comparative religion. But many of his contemporaries were convinced that he scorned all faiths. He

Accused by his enemies of being an infidel, Frederick did little to dispel the charge: He maintained a harem in his own palace and chose Saracens, who were free to ignore papal interdictions, to act as his personal bodyguards. Frederick quartered his loyal Saracen troops in the fortress of Lucera (immediately above). Top, the Romanesque-Gothic Castel del Monte in Apulia. This octagonal structure was built atop a thousand-foot hill because of the emperor's passion for falconry. It was Frederick's favorite residence. Above right, the throne room of the castle of Gioia del Colle.

was widely rumored to have once referred to Moses, Jesus, and Mohammed as "three conjurers" who had deceived their followers for their own selfish ends. Perhaps his deepest faith rested in the idea of the empire itself, which he saw as the universal instrument of God's order on earth. As for the Church, Frederick thought it should renounce all its wealth and political power and return to the poverty and saintliness of its early Christian beginnings.

The last twenty years of Frederick's rule were filled with strife. When Frederick tried to extend his Sicilian regime over northern Italy as well, the independent city-states naturally rebelled. Even Frederick's

Crusades

In 1095, after the Seljuk Turks swept across Asia Minor, threatening Byzantium and committing atrocities against Christian pilgrims to Jerusalem, Pope Urban II called on the warring nobles of Europe to unite under the Church's banner and set out on a holy war against Islam. "Undertake this journey for the remission of your sins, with the assurance of imperishable glory of the kingdom of Heaven," he told a group of Frankish aristocrats at Clermont-Ferrand. "God wills it!" the Frankish warriors were said to have replied, and within a year thousands of Europeans had embarked on the First Crusade. Three years later, the Crusaders captured Jerusalem itself, plundered the city, and murdered its inhabitants. However, Jerusalem proved easier to capture than to hold. The Moslems retook the city again and again, and over the next three hundred years, more than eight Crusades would be undertaken. The Crusades served many purposes: They strengthened the power and prestige of the Church, stimulated trade, exposed Europeans to the more sophisticated Arabic culture, encouraged chivalry, and provided ripe opportunities for plunder. Indeed, the crusading zeal may have brought out the three most resolute characteristics of medieval man: Christian idealism, the zest for battle, and economic greed.

A ship (above) takes on provisions before leaving for the East on a Crusade. The rising merchant class, particularly in the Italian seaports, thrived by supplying the expeditions to the Holy Land. The leader of the Sixth Crusade, the emperor Frederick II, spoke fluent Arabic. In 1229, he was able to recapture Jerusalem by negotiating directly with al-Kamil (right), the city's Moslem commander.

Left, a relief depicting Seljuk warriors, whose atrocities against Christian pilgrims provided the rationale for the First Crusade. The enormous Krak des Chevaliers (below) was built around 1200 to guard the Syrian coast near Tripoli.

The sack of Jerusalem (top), the climax of the First Crusade, was a large-scale, bloody undertaking. "If you had been there, you would have seen our feet colored to our ankles with the blood of the slain," one participant wrote afterward. The expedition was led by a group of nobles that included Godfrey of Bouillon (immediately above).

The ultimate aim of the First Crusade was the recapture of the church of the Holy Sepulcher (right), which stood in Jerusalem on the supposed site of Jesus' tomb. Later expeditions had baser goals. The Fourth Crusade, which some modern historians have dubbed "the businessmen's crusade," ignored the Moslem presence in Palestine and turned against the Byzantine Christians in Constantinople, reaping vast profits.

Pope Innocent IV, fearful of the invading armies of his imperial enemy, Frederick II, fled from Rome to address the Council of Lyon (left), which condemned, excommunicated, and deposed the emperor. A rival emperor was elected to replace Frederick, and the pope called on loyal Christians everywhere to mount a new Crusade that would rid the empire of the ungodly "antichrist."

Top, the last of the Hohenstaufen dynasty. It was widely rumored that Frederick II, who died suddenly in 1250 of dysentery, had been smothered to death by his less-than-dutiful son, Manfred (above). Right, Frederick's favorite (though illegitimate) son, King Enzio of Sardinia, imprisoned after losing a battle to the Bolognese. Above right, Conradin, Frederick's grandson and the last Hohenstaufen, being publicly beheaded in Naples by the troops of the victorious Charles of Anjou. Conradin was sixteen when he died.

son, Henry, was persuaded to join the coalition against the emperor. (Henry died as his father's prisoner in 1242.) The pope, siding with the independent cities, proclaimed an all-out holy war against the blasphemous antichrist. Welfs (who supported the pope) and Ghibellines (who supported the emperor) battled everywhere. No one was immune from the controversy. Lords and peasants, priests and laymen alike were forced to choose sides and take a stand. Even the mendicant orders of begging monks took up arms.

For a while, the war went Frederick's way. He invaded the Papal States and besieged Rome. He defeated a Genoese fleet that was carrying more than a hundred high-ranking Church officials to a papal council in Rome and imprisoned these cardinals and bishops in Apulia. Their capture hurt his cause, for it turned public opinion against him. In 1244, Pope Innocent IV, who seemed on the verge of capitulation fled Rome and convened a council in Lyon, which formally deposed Frederick. In 1249, Frederick suffered a greater loss: His favorite son, King Enzio of Sardinia, was captured at the battle of Fossalto by the Bolognese, who imprisoned him for the rest of his life.

A year later, while at the Castel Fiorentino in Apulia, Frederick died suddenly. (Rumor had it that his son Manfred had crept to his bedside and smothered him to death with a pillow.) The pope's elation over the demise of the antichrist was unbounded. "Let the heavens rejoice," he declared. "Let the earth be filled with gladness."

Frederick had failed to restore permanently the greatness and vastness of the empire. Unlike the Capetian monarchs in France, who had enlisted the support of the middle class against the barons, Frederick, because of his wars against the pope, had been compelled to rely increasingly on the support of the German nobles. To insure that support, he had been forced to grant them more and more power and independence that could only weaken the imperial power.

Although his son, Conrad IV, and grandson, Conradin, made feeble attempts to reclaim southern Italy and Sicily, their efforts failed. Conradin, the last legitimate heir of the Hohenstaufens, was never crowned emperor. He was defeated by the French king, Charles of Anjou, in 1268. Charles had him publicly beheaded in Naples and proceeded to rule Frederick's beloved southern kingdom in his own name. Sicily had passed into the hands of the French and was lost to the empire forever. Only Germany, which was little more than a feudal patchwork of petty tyrannies, remained a part of the empire. Henceforth, France, not Germany, would control the destiny of Europe.

Frederick II's court

Frederick II's lively and precocious intellect astounded his masters. He is said to have learned to read and write at four, and at fourteen he was steeped in philosophy, history, theology, and astronomy. He was profoundly learned in mathematics, the natural sciences, and music, and he knew seven languages. Frederick was exposed to many cultures and traditions. He grew up in Palermo, which was a thriving cosmopolitan center. Frederick chose to rule the empire from Sicily rather than Germany as his forefathers had done. He created a diversified, brilliant, and sophisticated court, with himself at the center. His cultural and intellectual reputation earned him the title of *stupor mundi,* "the wonder of the universe." Around him he assembled the best of the cultural world—Christian and Islamic. He invited the Provençal troubadours Folquet de Romans, Aimeric de Peguilhan, and Sordello da Goito. Many Sicilian poets also came to Frederick's court, among them Jacopo da Lentini and Guido delle Colonne. The Italian language made its first literary appearance under the emperor's aegis. Frederick himself was a good poet, an excellent conversationalist, and an expert in aristocratic arms. His treatise on falconry and birds, *Tractatus de arte venandi cum avibus,* was one of the most famous tracts of the Middle Ages, and it is viewed today as the first modern work of ornithology. The illustration (above) shows court musicians of the period.

Many historians have wondered why the empire wasn't allowed to expire quietly after Frederick. Its original function—the unification of Europe under a single Christian rule—was clearly out of the question. For all intents and purposes, the empire *had* died. No emperor was chosen to succeed Conrad IV, and for nearly twenty years, as various claimants failed to achieve the throne, Italy and Germany were thrown into chaos.

Eventually, however, Pope Gregory X, whose predecessors had done so much to weaken the empire, began to fear the growing power of the French king who ruled Sicily. Gregory decided to revive the empire so that it could serve as a geopolitical counterweight to the French. In 1272, he proposed that the fifty-five-year-old Count Rudolph of Hapsburg be named emperor. He was elected king in 1273 and crowned at Aachen that same year. Rudolph tried to reunite the fragmented German kingdom, but his path was blocked by the Bohemian king Ottocar II, who had taken advantage of the empire's comatose

When Rudolph I of Hapsburg attempted to reclaim some lost imperial territories, King Ottocar II of Bohemia stood in his way. Rudolph defeated him in the battle of Marchfeld in 1278. Above, Ottocar's tomb. The center of Ottocar's kingdom was the magnificent Hradčany Castle (left) in Prague, which eventually became an imperial capital. Below, Ottocar's seal.

condition to expand his own kingdom all the way to the Adriatic. The center of Ottocar's kingdom was the magnificent fortress of Hradčany in Prague. Rudolph and Ottocar went to war, and the outcome was decided in 1278 at the battle of Marchfeld in lower Austria. In the middle of the battle, Ottocar's own nobles deserted him. The Bohemian king, choosing not to retreat but to throw himself into the enemy's ranks, died in hand-to-hand combat.

Rudolph, as a result of his victory, acquired Austria and the other territories that came to be the central core of the great Hapsburg dominion. (The Hapsburgs would rule Austria from 1282 to 1918.) To help maintain his family's control over the conquered areas, Rudolph forced Ottocar's heir, Wenceslaus, to marry one of his daughters. Another daughter was dispatched to the elector of Saxony. Like centuries of Hapsburgs after him, Rudolph happily regarded his children as bargaining chips. He was less interested in the empire as a whole than in enlarging his own family's personal holdings.

Top, Rudolph of Hapsburg, from a stained-glass window of the cathedral of St. Stephen in Vienna. Rudolph, the first of the Hapsburg emperors, acquired Austria and other lands as a result of military victory, but it was his talent as a matchmaker for his daughters that really enlarged the empire. The Hapsburg family castle in Switzerland (immediately above), only a part of which still stands, was built around 1020 by one of the earliest recorded Hapsburg ancestors. Right, a document bearing the seal of Rudolph, in which the emperor bequeaths parts of Austria to his sons.

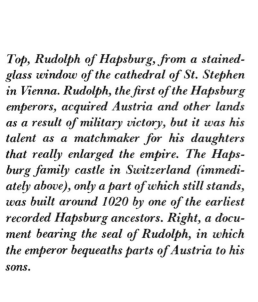

141

The pope may have given Rudolph the imperial crown, but the German nobles had the real power. Henceforth, most emperors would be chosen for their weaknesses rather than their strengths. Both the pope and the German barons and prelates who elected the emperor wanted a puppet, not a leader. Not surprisingly, Rudolph's successors accomplished little. Adolph of Nassau (1292–1298) was killed by the army of the Hapsburg Albert I, who took his victim's throne. Albert I was in turn assassinated in 1308 by a disgruntled nephew who felt that he had been cheated out of his share of a family inheritance.

Despite the desperate efforts of the Hapsburg clan, the crown passed next to a rival family, the Luxemburgs. Henry VII (1308–1313) even managed to muster an army and invade Italy. For a while, his prospects for the reconquest seemed glorious. The greatest poet of the age, Dante, came to Milan and threw himself at the German king's feet. "Time shall proclaim his vast munificence," Dante wrote in the *Divine Comedy*. Dante (a member of the Guelph party, the Italian counterpart of the Welfs) saw in Henry the last hope of overthrowing the tyranny of the pope, and he begged the citizens of his native Florence to open the city's gates to Henry. The people of Florence refused and sent Dante himself into exile for good measure. Henry was crowned emperor in 1312, but when he died suddenly of a fever not long afterward, the Italian campaign died with him. According to Dante, a special chair had been reserved for Henry in Paradise.

Although Henry's death was a blow to the empire, ironically, the papacy was also in disarray. In 1305, a French archbishop had become Pope Clement V. Four years later, he had uprooted the Holy See and moved it to Avignon. The popes remained in France for nearly seventy years, a period known as the Babylonian captivity, for the Avignon popes were regarded as puppets of the rising French monarchy. In 1378, Gregory XI brought the papacy back to Rome, but for the next forty years—a period known as the Great Schism—papal succession was clouded by total disorder. This was a period in which two or three rival popes would simultaneously claim to be the true pope.

Meanwhile, in Germany, a new ruler had to be chosen again. Traditionally, the all-powerful Diet of Electors, which consisted of seven dukes and archbishops, made the choice. The candidate they selected would receive the title "King of the Romans," and with title in hand, the designate would travel to the pope, who alone had the power to crown him Holy Roman emperor. The problem with this system was that there was often no general agreement as to

Rudolph's designs for expanding the empire didn't please the annexed Swiss cantons of Schwyz, Uri, and Unterwalden. On August 1, 1291, just seventeen days after Rudolph's death, the three cantons signed the Pact of Rutli (left), which founded the Eternal League and established Swiss independence.

who the seven electors should be.

When news of Henry VII's death reached Germany, two separate factions of electors chose rival kings—Frederick of Austria (a Hapsburg) and Ludwig IV of Bavaria (a Wittelsbach). Both appealed to Pope John XXII at Avignon. The pope agreed to recognize both of them, but only as kings, not as emperors. In the absence of a designated emperor, the pope suggested that perhaps the reins of the imperial government should be handed over to him. Ludwig and Frederick ignored his recommendation and went to war with each other. Ludwig won the war and took over the actual running of the empire, allowing Frederick to remain king, only to have the Avignon pope take away his German throne.

Ludwig next went to Italy, where he not only had himself crowned emperor by the people of Rome but also created a pope of his own, "Nicholas V." After returning to Germany, he convened a meeting of electors at Rense who decreed that henceforth the pope would have no say in approving future emperors-elect. Whoever the electors chose would automatically be proclaimed emperor, regardless of the pope's attitude.

The pope wasn't out of it yet, however. In Germany, a struggle broke out between Ludwig IV and the Luxemburg rulers of Bohemia over the posses-

sions of the Tyrol. The Avignon pope sided with the Luxemburg faction and persuaded the German electors that the fighting could be ended only by deposing Ludwig. They agreed and chose Charles IV of Luxemburg to replace him. Ludwig had no intention of giving up the crown and prepared to continue the civil war, but he died while hunting. The crown passed to Charles IV.

The new king, who was crowned in 1346 and ruled as emperor from 1355 to 1378, was realistic enough to see that the empire Charlemagne had founded could never be recovered, so he confined his excellent administrative abilities to maintaining peace. He fostered economic prosperity by introducing new agricultural methods. The king also moved the capital to Prague, where he founded a great university. When his advisers consulted him on problems of state, Charles would amuse himself by whittling on a willow branch, seemingly paying no attention, and then announce a decision said to be "full of wisdom."

However conscientious, Charles knew there was no hope of attaining a centralized rule over the haphazard federation of cities, duchies, margraves, archbishoprics, leagues, and principalities, whose rulers and boundaries changed with the seasons. The great families and dynasties warred with each other endlessly in

The castle of Rheinfels (above) was one of the strongholds in the Aragau canton in northern Switzerland. Below, the antipope "Nicholas V," a creation of Emperor Ludwig IV, who was opposed by the Avignon pope, John XXII. Right, the fortifications at Metz. In the twelfth century, Metz became a free imperial city, one of the richest and most populous in the empire.

the efforts to enlarge their personal fiefdoms. A new merchant class had arisen in the towns and was acquiring its own degree of political control. Each town thought only of its own interests and waged economic war on neighboring towns. Merchants who were foolhardy enough to venture beyond the city walls to trade with other cities risked being set upon by roving knights whose former chivalry had degenerated into cruel banditry.

Charles decided to concentrate mainly on enlarging his own kingdom of Bohemia and enriching its culture. He was so successful at this that his people called him the father of his country. As the historian

Barbara Tuchman has written, "He himself represented the nationalist tendencies that were making his imperial title obsolete."

In 1356, Charles abrogated his imperial power even further by promulgating a series of regulations known as the Golden Bull, so called because of the imperial golden seal affixed to the documents. The bull settled for good the question of who would sit on the Diet of Electors, and it handed over to the electors many prerogatives that had previously belonged to the emperor alone. The electors were to meet once a year to enact laws, and the emperor would merely carry out their decisions. Why did Charles surrender so much

Preceding pages, the fourteenth-century bridge of Charles IV in Prague. Charles, pictured with his wife above the door of St. Catherine's Oratory in Karlstein Castle (above left) and his son, Wenceslaus (below left), moved the imperial capital to Prague, which became an important cultural center. Charles also founded the University of Prague, the oldest in central Europe. Below, frescoes on the walls of the Chapel of Our Lady in Karlstein Castle depicting scenes from the life of Charles IV. Above, the elaborate jeweled crown of Charles IV, now in the treasury of the castle.

Charlemagne and the Holy Roman Empire

power? In fact, he didn't. He was simply acknowledging political realities that had existed for years. The days of imperial absolutism were long past.

In his old age Charles had to pay the electors enormous bribes in order to secure the succession of his son, Wenceslaus IV. Once paid, the electors kept their word, and in 1378, the eighteen-year-old Wenceslaus, a drunk, was duly elected. Like his father, he found the Germans and their affairs tiresome. He preferred to do his drinking in Bohemia. Although Wenceslaus had a particularly violent temper that flared up on occasion—almost always the wrong occasion—he was tolerant and good-natured for the most part. He was especially easygoing when it came to levying taxes, a trait that endeared him to to the people of Bohemia and infuriated the electors. In 1394, the electors had him arrested and thrown into prison. They released him only after he solemnly promised that he would take no action as head of state without first consulting them. In 1400, the electors deposed him for good (although he kept his title of king of Bohemia) and replaced him with the weakling Rupert II. Rupert reigned for ten years, but few people noticed.

The real force in the empire during these years was Wenceslaus' younger half brother, Sigismund of Luxemburg. At the age of nineteen, Sigismund had gone to Hungary and married the king's daughter, and soon he became king of Hungary. In 1396, he had led an army through the Balkans to Nicopolis to fight the Turks, who were threatening the empire from the east. In 1410, when the emperor Rupert died, there was, naturally, a dispute about who should succeed him. Sigismund claimed that the empire was rightfully his, but so did his cousin Jobst of Moravia. To add to the confusion, Wenceslaus claimed that he was still the lawful emperor.

An identical farce was at the same moment being played out in Italy and France with regard to the papacy, with "Benedict XIII" of Avignon, Gregory XII of Rome, and "John XXIII" of Naples all claiming to be pope. The survival of the empire and the papacy alike was in question.

The empire rallied first. Sigismund was confirmed emperor in 1411. He immediately set about putting the papacy back on its feet. The symbiotic dependency that had bound the two institutions during five hundred years of hatred, rivalry, and mutual need hadn't diminished. Sigismund convened an ecclesiastical conference—the Council of Constance (1414–1418)—to settle the matter of papal succession once and for all. The council rejected all three claimants and chose Martin V. Deciding to attend the council in person, Sigismund persuaded the Bohemian here-

In 1356, Charles IV set forth a series of documents known as the Golden Bull, named for the imperial golden seal (above). Seven copies exist today. The procedure for imperial succession was laid out once and for all: The bull fixed the number of electors at seven, and it also provided that the electors would meet once a year to enact laws that the emperor would be obliged to enforce.

tic John Huss to accompany him. Huss, who had publicly questioned the infallibility of immoral popes and had preached that the words of the Scriptures should take precedence over Church dogma, doubted the wisdom of his going, but Sigismund personally promised him safe conduct back to Bohemia even if the cardinals ruled against him. At Constance, though, Sigismund reneged on his promise and handed Huss, along with his friend Jerome of Prague, over to the Church officials. Huss was tried for heresy and burned at the stake. He became a national hero.

Sigismund continued to rule for more than twenty years after Huss' martyrdom, but he was never allowed to forget his betrayal. Huss' outraged followers,

149

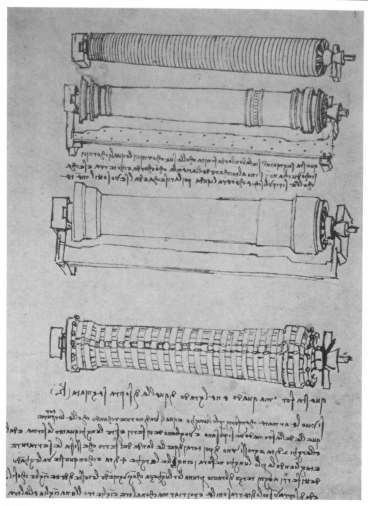

Firearms

"Important arts have been discovered against foes of the state, so that without a sword or any weapon requiring physical contact they could destroy all who offer resistance," wrote thirteenth-century Oxford scientist Roger Bacon. Bacon was referring to gunpowder, which had been used for centuries in China but was not imported to Europe until the early 1400s. Firearms eventually sounded the death knell of the feudal knight. Solid medieval castles were suddenly vulnerable to artillery. Battles were no longer decided by proud, richly attired nobles on horseback but by the common infantry. Above, drawings of firearms from the *Codex Atlanticus* of Leonardo da Vinci. Below, mortars at the battle of Grandson in 1476.

the Hussites, formed an army in Bohemia and Moravia and began a veritable holy war against Sigismund and the empire. Their cause was political as well as religious, for in his lifetime, Huss had encouraged intense nationalistic feelings in the Czechs of Bohemia. Nationalism was to be the empire's nemesis.

Sigismund's Hapsburg son-in-law, Albert II, succeeded him in 1438 and died the following year. His successor, also a Hapsburg, had better luck. Frederick III's reign lasted fifty-three years. The electors chose him because he seemed weak and easy to manipulate, and few historians have disputed their assessment. Frederick was indecisive and indolent. For him procrastination wasn't a vice but a policy. He was an immensely fat man and a heavy drinker, and crises made him lethargic. Therefore, he planned his imperial itinerary with the express purpose of avoiding crises. When revolts broke out in Austria and Hungary that urgently demanded his attention, he decided to visit Rome. There, in 1452, he married Eleanor, the daughter of the king of Portugal. Three days later he was formally anointed emperor by the pope. He was the last emperor to be crowned in Rome. "He was a useless emperor," one chronicler wrote shortly after his death, "and the nation during his long reign forgot that she had a king."

Frederick III did have his strong points. He was a generous patron of the arts when he had the funds. He was well read and was said to be an excellent late-night conversationalist. Alchemy and astrology interested him, but his main passion was the House of Hapsburg. Like most Hapsburgs, he believed that his family had a special authorization from God to rule, and he felt it only proper to put the interests of his family above those of the empire. He had all his documents and personal effects emblazoned with the initials *AEIOU,* which are generally thought to signify *Austriae est imperare orbi universo* ("it is Austria's destiny to rule the whole world"). It also meant that the office of Roman emperor belonged to the ruling house of Austria.

Frederick's only significant act as a statesman was to marry off his son Maximilian to Mary of Burgundy, the daughter of Charles the Bold. Burgundy at that time had the richest trade, industry, and agriculture in western Europe. As a center of the arts, the gallant court of Burgundy was second to none. The territory of Burgundy included most of present-day Belgium and the Netherlands as well as substantial portions of France. The cities of Ghent, Bruges, Antwerp, and Brussels now belonged to the empire. Thus, in a single stroke, the Hapsburgs became the preeminent family of Europe.

As an emperor and leader, Maximilian I, who

ruled from 1493 to 1519, was an obvious improvement over his self-absorbed father. Even Machiavelli had high praise for him: "A wise, prudent, God-fearing prince, a just ruler, a great general, brave in peril, bearing fatigue like the most hardened soldier." He was also chivalrous, charming, handsome, and well educated.

Maximilian hoped to regain Italy for the empire, but his many campaigns there ended in failure, largely because the stingy electors refused to provide him with the necessary funds. (At times, the emperor was so poor that he couldn't pay for his dinner.) Despite his great abilities, Maximilian's hands were tied. The power of the emperor had been so reduced over the centuries that there was little he could accomplish. His only recourse was to emulate his father and resort to diplomatic marriages, which he did brilliantly. His son Philip was betrothed to Juana, the

Top, the emperor Wenceslaus IV arriving at Reims in 1398. Wenceslaus, a drunken, irresponsible son of Charles IV, was deposed by the imperial electors in 1400; eleven years later, his half brother Sigismund (left) was named emperor. Above, Frederick III of Hapsburg, who ruled for fifty-three years, and his wife, Eleanor.

Council of Constance

In 1414, the emperor Sigismund convened the ecumenical Council of Constance to rescue the papacy from impending dissolution. The trouble had begun in 1309, when Pope Clement V, a Frenchman who was reviled by the people of Rome, had moved the Holy See to the town of Avignon in southern France. The Curia remained in Avignon—under the thumb of the French king—for the next sixty-nine years, a period known as the Babylonian captivity. In 1378, Gregory XI brought the Curia back to Rome, but he died soon afterward, and two rival popes succeeded him. One of them ruled from Rome, the other from Avignon. During this period, known as the Great Schism, each pope claimed to be the only true vicar of Christ, and neither pope would step down. In fact, by 1414 there were *three* papal claimants—"Benedict XIII" of Avignon, Gregory XII of Rome, and "John XXIII" of Naples, an antipope who so sullied papal dignity that no true pope would adopt the name John

until 1958. The Council of Constance declared all three claimants deposed and designated a new pope, Martin V. The council attended to other business as well. The Bohemian heretic John Huss, in spite of imperial promises of safe conduct, was tried and burned at the stake along with his friend Jerome of Prague.

Facing page, above far left, the arrival of German nobles at the Council of Constance. The council attracted thirty-three cardinals, nine hundred bishops, and more than a thousand theologians. Among the council's accomplishments was the deposition of the antipope "John XXIII" (facing page, top right), whose scandalous personal life made him the least fit of the three papal claimants. Facing page, center right, the arrival of the emperor Sigismund at Constance on Christmas Eve, 1414. The trial (facing page, below far left) and execution (this page, below) of the heretic and Bohemian nationalist John Huss and his friend Jerome of Prague (this page, below right) eventu-

ally brought on the Hussite Wars. The historic council drew enormous crowds. There was much pageantry in the city, with many processions (above left) and many vendors who set up shop in the streets to sell their wares, such as snails (facing page, below right). Above right, Sigismund, and above center, Pope Martin V, who was elected by the council to replace the three existing rival popes.

153

daughter of Ferdinand and Isabella of Spain. While it wasn't a match that every father might wish for his son—Juana was insane—by Hapsburg criteria it was ideal. It brought Spain, Naples, Sicily, and the rich Spanish colonies of the New World into the family. Although Philip lived to be only twenty-eight, he gave the family two sons—Charles V and Ferdinand I.

Charles, who was only six when his father died in 1506, was raised in Burgundy. French, not German, was his first language. He became king of the Netherlands at fifteen, and at sixteen, when his Spanish grandfather died, he went to Spain and was proclaimed sovereign there. When his other grandfather,

the emperor Maximilian, died in 1519, Charles went to Germany and bribed the electors to choose him as emperor. He had to pay a high price because both Francis I of France and Henry VIII of England had put in bids too.

Almost at once the young emperor was forced into a conflict, the outcome of which would ultimately spell the empire's doom. A German monk named Martin Luther had publicly denied both the spiritual and temporal authority of the Church and had exalted the dignity of the German nation and proclaimed its right to have its own religion and its own church. The princes and nobles of Germany lost no

154

Charles V (far left) was elected emperor over his rivals, Francis I of France and Henry VIII of England. In addition to the usual imperial conflicts with popes and wars with other countries, Charles was forced to deal with the Protestant Reformation, spearheaded by a German monk named Martin Luther (top left, in a Lucas Cranach painting). Above left, Charles' signature, and above, an engraving of German cavalry.

time in rushing to his support, for they stood to gain all the Church properties in their domains. The pope excommunicated Luther and ordered the emperor to punish him.

By promising him safe conduct, Charles persuaded Luther to appear before the imperial diet at Worms in 1521, and the two argued with each other face to face. Luther's nationalism infuriated Charles. "The empire of old had not many masters but one," he told the monk, "and it is our intention to be that one." Because Luther had the support of many members of the diet, Charles was powerless to prevent the monk's escape to the castle of the elector of Saxony. Charles

155

Preceding page, a hunt in honor of Charles V, organized by John Frederick, the powerful elector of Saxony (painted in 1545 by Lucas Cranach, the elector's court painter). Above, the great hall of Albrechtsburg, the palatial residence of the electors of Lower Saxony. Left, the burg of Dankwarderode in Brunswick (formerly known as lower Saxony).

Emperor Maximilian I (right, in a painting by Albrecht Dürer), who was praised by Machiavelli as "a wise, prudent, God-fearing prince, a just ruler," had little power, but he was a shrewd Hapsburg matchmaker. He married his son Philip to the Spanish infanta. Maximilian II (below right), who came to power some thirty years after Maximilian I, was openly sympathetic toward the Protestants.

did manage to push through the Edict of Worms, which made outlaws of Luther and his followers, after many of the electors had returned home.

Charles could have pursued Luther even further, but he was involved in a war with Francis I of France that took up most of his attention. Charles did well in Italy, where he captured Genoa and Milan, but elsewhere the French, who had made treaties with the German Lutheran princes, had the better of it. Pope Clement VII also refused to support him, weakening him considerably. By 1555, Charles, faced with the necessity of compromising with the Protestants, was forced to agree to the Peace of Augsburg, which formally granted the German princes the right to recognize the Lutheran religion. He delegated the sad task of signing the document to his brother, Ferdinand. Charles then retired to an almost monkish life in Spain, abdicating the imperial throne in favor of Ferdinand and leaving the Hapsburg lands divided between Austria and Spain. He died in 1558.

The emperors who followed Ferdinand—Maximilian II (1564–1576) and Rudolph II (1576–1612)—only had authority over the diminishing anti-Protestant factions there. Maximilian was openly conciliatory toward the Lutherans. Rudolph, who was politically incompetent, had fits of insanity and otherwise devoted himself entirely to alchemy, astrology, and art collecting. His brother Matthias (1612–1619), who deposed him, tried to appease the leaders of a Protestant rebellion that had broken out in Bohemia. Matthias' staunchly Catholic cousin, Ferdinand II, who followed him to the throne in 1619, had grand schemes. He wanted to restore the empire to all of its old glory. The Bohemians showed what they thought of the empire by hurling two imperial envoys out a window. The event came to be called the Defenestration of Prague, and it led to the Thirty Years' War. At first, Ferdinand gained the upper hand by winning a victory against the Protestants at the Battle

Rudolph II and astronomy

Rudolph II of Hapsburg, who became emperor in 1576, suffered from long bouts of profound depression that left him unable to rule. He moved to Prague and locked himself away in his castle there to devote himself to magic, astrology, and astronomy. The greatest astronomers of the day were welcomed into Prague, where they received imperial protection from Church authorities. Nightly, the emperor studied the stars with his friends and masters, such as Tycho Brahe and Johannes Kepler. Eventually, the old emperor, whose depressions worsened and who based many of his acts of state on astrological calculations, was declared mentally unfit and removed from power in 1607.

Rudolph II (above left) was obsessed with astronomy. In 1599, he summoned the Danish astronomer Tycho Brahe (above right) to his court in Prague, where Rudolph received the astronomer standing up and bareheaded. Below left, instruments used by Copernicus, which can still be seen at the University of Cracow. Below right, an astronomical table of the period.

When Johannes Kepler (top) became Rudolph II's court astronomer, he attempted to carry on his predecessor's mission of refuting the theories of Copernicus (immediately above). After much study, however, Kepler became convinced that Copernicus had been correct.

Above, Tycho Brahe's celestial globe, which was constructed at Antwerp in 1601. Right, the palace observatory at Uranienborg, where Brahe worked with his assistant, Johannes Kepler. Brahe's main achievements were improving astronomical instruments and making exact determinations of the position of the stars and planets. When Brahe left the court at Prague, his pupil Kepler was chosen by Rudolph II to succeed him.

The Thirty Years' War

The twin specters of Protestantism and nationalism had been gathering force for more than a century when, in 1617, the arch-Catholic Ferdinand II of Hapsburg was named king of Bohemia. The following year, a group of Protestant Czech nobles, horrified by Ferdinand's plans to restore Catholic orthodoxy and imperial authority, gathered in a rump assembly at Hradčany Castle in Prague. Here, they tossed two of Ferdinand's hapless royal governors out a castle window to the ground seventy feet below. (Luckily, they landed on a manure pile and escaped unhurt.) The rebels then formally deposed Ferdinand as king of Bohemia and replaced him with Frederick V, a rigorous Calvinist. The religious, dynastic, and territorial war that ensued continued for three decades, involving all the major countries of Europe. Because of its shifting alliances and participants, the war is usually divided by historians into distinct stages.

The Bohemian period, 1618–1625

Ferdinand, who was crowned emperor in 1619, immediately looked to his European Catholic allies for assistance in quelling the Protestant revolt. He found plenty of sup-

The Danish-Swedish period, 1625–1635

Defeated and humiliated, the rebellious Protestants eventually found a new ally—Denmark's King Christian IV. With the support of a few thousand troops from

From left to right, Cardinal Richelieu of France, Chancellor Axel Oxenstierna of Sweden and General Matthias Gallas.

England, Christian marched on Germany. Against him Ferdinand employed one of the empire's greatest generals, the controversial Albrecht of Wallenstein. Wallenstein's army not only drove King Christian out of Germany but even overran the Danish peninsula. Having achieved another stunning military success, Ferdinand

followed it with a stunning act of political plunder. The Edict of Restitution, which he promulgated in 1629, demanded that Catholic ecclesiastical holdings that had been confiscated by Protestant princes during the past seventy-five years now be handed over to him. This measure would have made the Hapsburgs the richest monarchs in Europe. France and Sweden now grew anxious. Sweden's King Gustavus II, a far abler military tactician than King Christian, declared a "holy war" and led a Swedish army into Germany, defeating Baron Tilly at Breitenfeld. Other victories followed, until at length the emperor sent Wallenstein himself to try to stop the Swedes at Lutzen in Saxony in 1632. Gustavus also won that battle, but unfortunately he was one of its casualties, and

The Swedish-French period, 1635–1648

Catholic France under Cardinal Richelieu felt that peace with the Hapsburg empire would threaten the French state. A war that had begun as a religious conflict was becoming a struggle for European hegemony. The armies of Ferdinand's ally, Philip IV of Spain, defeated the French and threatened Paris; Austrian forces moved into Burgundy. Paris was in a panic, but Richelieu fought back partly by calling in the Swedes and the Dutch. The Swedish general Johan Banér soundly defeated the emperor's armies at Wittstock in 1636. A disastrous series of campaigns followed, led by the incompetent and

Above, Philip IV of Spain. Right, General Johan Banér at the battle of Wittestock.

Left, door with imperial seal in Hradčany Castle in Prague, where the emissaries of Ferdinand II (right) were defenestrated.

port—from the pope, from Spanish troops, and from Maximilian of Bavaria. Ferdinand also benefited from a good deal of factionalism in his enemies' ranks, for traditional Lutherans abhorred the growing number of radical Calvinists as much as they abhorred the pope himself. Lutheran

Saxony, for instance, refused to support the Czech rebels and instead took advantage of the civil turmoil to seize parts of Bohemia for itself. In November of 1620, outside Prague, the Protestant armies met the forces of Ferdinand's Catholic League, commanded by the brilliant "monk in arms," Baron Tilly. The result, known as the Battle of the White Mountain, ended after two hours of fighting in a total rout of the Bohemian rebels. Frederick fled to Holland, his brief reign over Bohemia permanently ended. (He would be known to history as frederick the Winter King.) Ferdinand then began recatholicizing the Czechs. It was a period of ruthless repression. Ferdinand confiscated the landed estates of approximately half the Bohemian nobles and redistributed them to the

Church and among prominent Catholic aristocrats. Military leaders and intellectuals alike were executed, as were many Protestant clergymen. For the moment, the power of the Hapsburgs and the empire seemed greater than it had since the days of Charles V a century before.

Right, Albrecht of Wallenstein, a mercenary imperial general who may have wished to become a monarch in his own right.

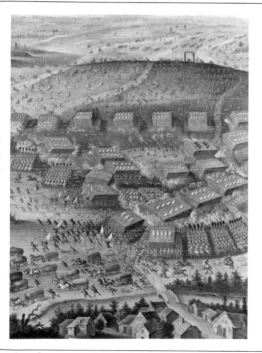

Left, the battle of Breitenfeld (1631), where Swedish troops under King Gustavus II (right) defeated the imperial forces.

Sweden's political leadership passed into the hands of the country's cautious chancellor, Axel Oxenstierna. The Swedes, defeated the following year, entered into talks with Wallenstein, who had begun acting independently of Ferdinand to negotiate in secret with both the Swedes and the French. Wallenstein's role has puzzled historians. Some think he may have wanted to become a monarch in his own right—the ruler of a new, unified Germany—rather than remain the emperor's mercenary. Ferdinand probably thought so too: Wallenstein was killed in 1634 by assassins who were afterward rewarded by the emperor. (Wallenstein has been regarded by Germans as a national hero ever since.) In 1635, the Swedes signed a treaty directly with the emperor at Prague.

drunken general Matthias Gallas, who came to be known as the "destroyer of armies"—his own. Civilians, too, suffered terribly, as the French crossed the Rhine and devastated the German countryside. Ferdinand II died in 1637 and was succeeded by Ferdinand III, who fared even worse against the French armies, in part because of two French generals, Turenne and Enghien. In 1648, Turenne clinched victory in Bavaria and Enghien routed the Spanish at Lens. This forced the emperor to sign the Peace of Westphalia, which ended the war, gave local sovereignty to German Protestant princes, recognized the independence of Holland and guaranteed that France would thereafter play the dominant role in the European balance of power.

Left, Ferdinand III. Right, the town hall of Münster, where one of the treaties of the Peace of Westphalia was signed.

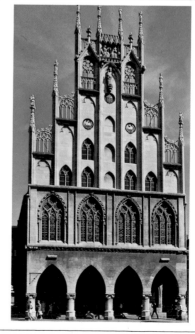

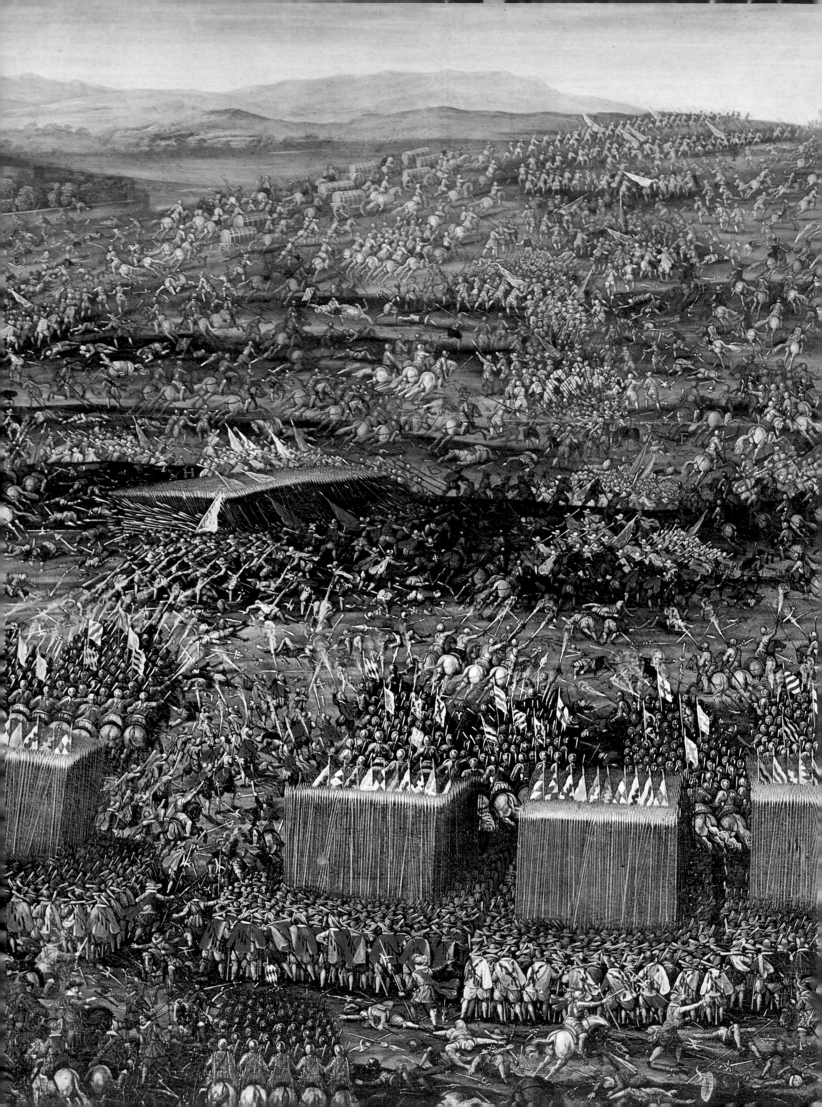

of the White Mountain, fought near Prague in 1620. But the war spread through all of Europe as Protestants everywhere joined the struggle against the now hated empire. The entrance of Sweden and France on the Protestant side decided the issue.

After Ferdinand's death in 1637, his son, Ferdinand III, had no choice but to face the fact that there was no hope of ever again reuniting the Catholic world. With the humiliating Treaty of Westphalia in 1648, in which the emperor formally recognized the individual sovereignty of all the territorial princes within the empire (there were more than 340 of them), the Holy Roman Empire was effectively dismantled.

The empire continued to exist in name, but it was nothing more than a loose federation of the various German princes who happened to support the Hapsburg rule of Austria. Although the Hapsburgs exercised real authority only in Austria, they continued to go through the solemn medieval charade of crowning emperor after emperor. A so-called Diet of Deputation would meet regularly to debate questions of precedence and title: Should certain envoys be seated in chairs upholstered in red cloth or green cloth? Should imperial dinners be served on gold plates or silver plates? The members of the diet were the laughing-

Preceding pages, the Battle of the White Mountain, fought near Prague on November 8, 1620. Here the Catholic troops of Ferdinand of Hapsburg defeated the Protestant nationalist armies of the king of Bohemia. Above, a meeting at Munster of the delegates of the powers engaged in the Thirty Years' War. The war ended in 1648 with the Peace of Westphalia. Facing page, signatures on the Treaty of Westphalia.

stock of Europe. The eighteenth-century Prussian leader Frederick the Great compared them to dogs in a yard baying at the moon.

In 1806, Napoleon, who thought of himself as the new Charlemagne, decided to depose the last emperor, Francis II, and incorporate the Holy Roman Empire into the "new order" he was attempting to establish throughout Europe. Even when Francis II was defeated by Napoleon at Austerlitz, he refused to hand over the by now meaningless title. Instead, he formally dissolved the empire before Napoleon could get his hands on it. It was only a gesture, but it was long overdue.

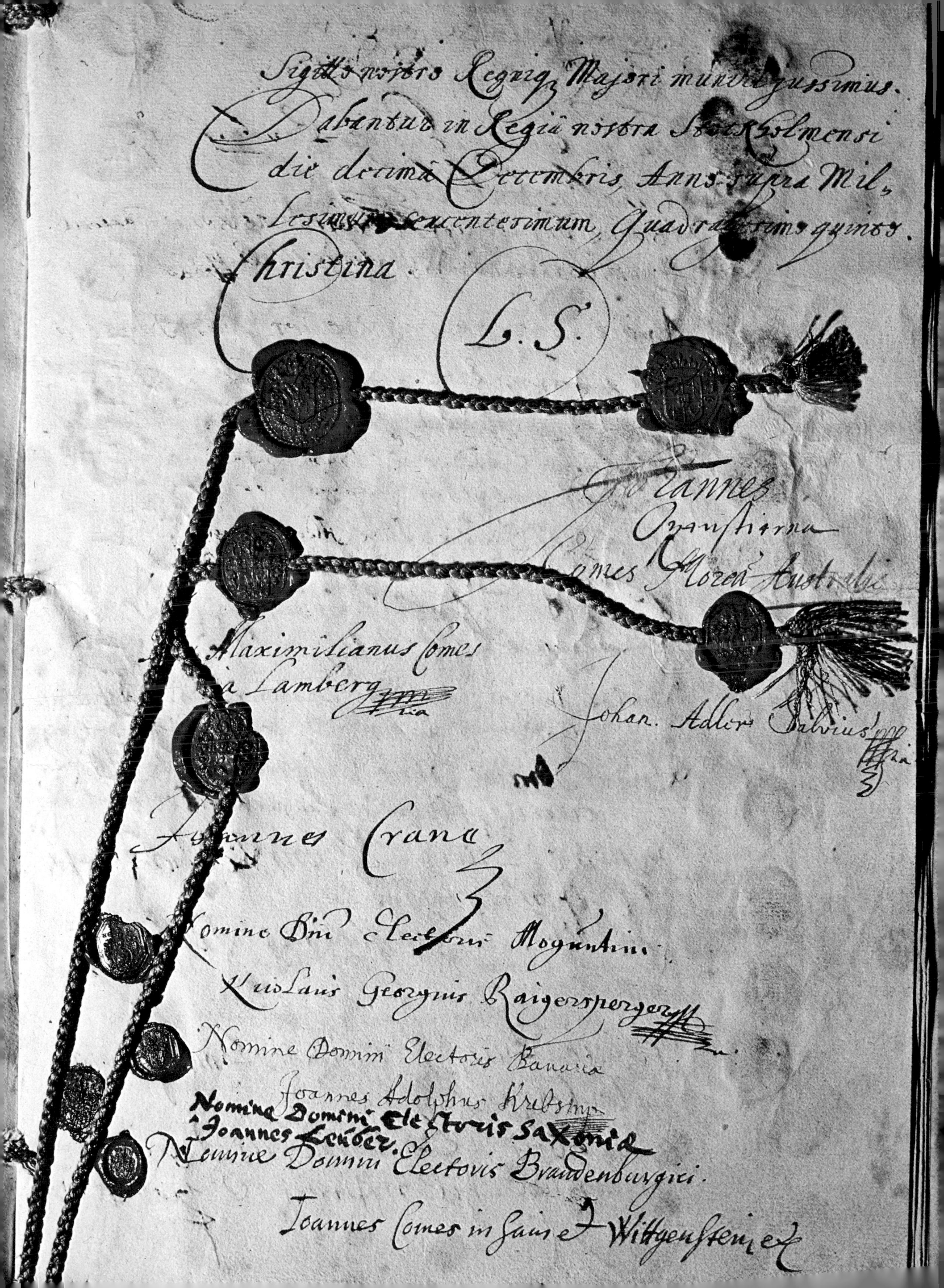

Sigillo nostro Regiæ Majori muniri jussimus.
Dabantur in Regia nostra Stockholmensi
die decima Decembris, Anno supra Mil=
lesium sexcentesimum Quadragesimo quinto.

Christina

L. S.

Johannes
Oxenstierna
Comes Moræ Australis

Maximilianus Comes
a Lamberg

Johan. Adler Salvius

Joannes Crane

Nomine Dñi Electoris Moguntini.

Nicolaus Georgius Raigersperger

Nomine Domini Electoris Bavariæ

Joannes Adolphus Krebstein

Nomine Domini Electoris Saxoniæ
Joannes Leuber
Nomine Domini Electoris Brandenburgici.

Joannes Comes in Hansa & Wittgenstein

Photography Credits

Arborio-Mella: p. 93 bottom, p. 100 top right and bottom right, p. 103 bottom, p. 110 bottom, p. 131, p. 133 top left and bottom, p. 136 center right, p. 138 top left and bottom, p. 154 top right, p. 160 top right, p. 161 center right / *Bavaria-M. Jeiter:* p. 99 bottom left, p. 107 top, p. 116 center right, p. 125 / *Bibliothèque Nationale:* p. 100 top left / *Cauchetier:* p. 71 top and bottom left / *Costa:* p. 10 bottom, p. 18 top left, p. 25 bottom right, p. 29 top right, p. 30 top left, p. 34 bottom, p. 36 top, p. 39 top, p. 49 bottom, p. 51 center left and bottom, p. 54 top right, p. 55 top right and bottom right, p. 61 center right, p. 82 bottom right, p. 87, p. 91 top right, p. 97 top left, p. 108 top right, p. 111 center, p. 122 bottom, p. 128 center, p. 143, p. 155, p. 160 bottom right, p. 161 top right, pp. 164–165 / *Dilia-Neubert:* p. 140 bottom left / *Dulevant:* p. 91 bottom, p. 93 top, p. 123 / *A. Ferrari:* p. 59 top / *M. Ferrari:* p. 21 bottom left / *Fiore:* p. 20 bottom, p. 37 top right and bottom right, p. 39 bottom, p. 41 center right, p. 63 top right, p. 70 center, p. 72 bottom right / *Frezzato:* p. 128 top / *Giraudon:* p. 90 left / *Hassmann:* p. 89, p. 99 right / *Magnum-Hopker:* pp. 112–113 / *Magnum-Lessing:* p. 59 bottom, p. 97 top right and bottom, p. 114 top, p. 115, p. 116 top left and bottom, p. 137 bottom right, p. 141 top and bottom right, p. 144 top, p. 148 top left, p. 154 left, p. 158 top, p. 160 bottom left, p. 162 center third picture from left, p. 163 bottom left and right / *Mandel:* p. 105 bottom left / *Meyer:* p. 9, p. 96 bottom left, p. 149, p. 160 top left / *Östereichische Nationalbibliothek:* p. 142 top, p. 148 bottom left, p. 151 bottom right / *Pedicini:* p. 130 left, p. 138 center right, p. 139 / *Pedone:* p. 15 bottom, p. 20 top left, p. 31, p. 40 bottom right, p. 54 top left, p. 134 bottom right, p. 135 bottom / *Perogalli:* p. 15 top / *Pubbliaerfoto:* p. 53 top, p. 135 top / *Pucciarelli:* p. 12 top, p. 19 top and bottom, p. 23 top, center left, and bottom left, pp. 32–33, p. 42 top and bottom, p. 44, p. 51 top and center right, p. 54 bottom, p. 55 top left, pp. 60–61 top, p. 61 bottom right, p. 63 bottom, p. 66 top right, p. 67, p. 74, p. 75 top left, p. 79 center left, p. 79 bottom right, p. 81, p. 82 top and bottom left, p. 83 top right, p. 86 right, p. 109 top left, right, and bottom, p. 111 top right and bottom left, p. 116 top right, p. 117 top, p. 118 bottom right, p. 119 top left, p. 120 top, p. 122 top, p. 126 bottom left and right, p. 128 bottom, p. 130 right, p. 132 bottom, p. 133 top right, p. 138 center left, p. 140 top, p. 148 top right and bottom right, p. 152 top left, center right, and bottom left and right, p. 153 top left, top right, and bottom left and right, p. 161 bottom right / *Radici:* p. 162 top right / *Radnicky:* pp. 146–147 / *Ricciarini-Bevilacqua:* p. 25 bottom left, p. 27 bottom right, p. 66 bottom right, p. 71 bottom right / *Ricciarini-Simion:* p. 29 bottom right, p. 40 left, p. 75 center right and bottom right, p. 83 top left / *Ricciarini-Tomsich:* p. 10 top, p. 22 top left and right, p. 25 center, p. 36 bottom left and right, p. 37 top left and bottom left, p. 50, p. 55 bottom left, p. 60 left, p. 77 top right, p. 91 top left, p. 109 center / *Rizzoli:* p. 11, p. 12 bottom, p. 13, p. 14, p. 17, p. 20 top right, p. 23 bottom right, p. 24, p. 26 top left and bottom, p. 27 bottom left, p. 29 bottom left, p. 30 top right and bottom, p. 34 top left and right, p. 35, p. 38 right, p. 40 top right, p. 41 top right and bottom left and right, p. 43, p. 45 bottom left, p. 46, p. 47, p. 48 right, p. 52, p. 53 bottom, p. 56, p. 57, p. 58 left, p. 60 bottom right, p. 61 left, p. 62, p. 66 bottom left, p. 68 bottom, p. 70 bottom, p. 72 top, p. 75 top right and bottom left, p. 76, p. 77 top left, p. 78, p. 79 top, p. 80 top left and right, p. 83 bottom, p. 84 bottom, p. 85, p. 86 left, p. 96 top

right and bottom right, p. 100 bottom left, p. 101 left and top right, p. 102, p. 103 top right and left, p. 104, p. 105 right, p. 108 bottom, p. 110 center, p. 111 bottom right, p. 119 bottom left and right, p. 120 bottom right and left, p. 121 top, p. 127 center, p. 129 top right and bottom, p. 134 top right, p. 136 top, center left, and bottom, p. 137 bottom left, p. 140 bottom right, p. 142 bottom, p. 144 bottom, p. 145, p. 150, p. 151 top, p. 152 top right, p. 153 top center, p. 154 bottom right, p. 159, p. 161 left, p. 162 center second picture from left and bottom left and right, p. 163 top right, center left, and right, p. 166 / *Lores Riva:* p. 105 top left, p. 114 bottom, p. 124 left / *Scala:* p. 45 right, p. 68 top, p. 69, p. 118 top, p. 119 top right, p. 132 top, p. 134 left, p. 137 top / *SEF:* p. 27 top, p. 48 left, p. 58 right, p. 77 bottom, p. 79 bottom left, p. 90 right, p. 118 bottom left, p. 121 bottom / *Spielmann:* p. 98, p. 99 center left, p. 106, p. 107 bottom left and right / *Titus:* p. 16, p. 18 top right and center right, p. 21 top and bottom right, p. 22 bottom, p. 23 center right, p. 25 top, p. 38 left, p. 41 bottom center, p. 49 top, p. 72 bottom left, p. 73 right, p. 79 center right, p. 80 bottom, p. 84 top, p. 92 top and bottom, p. 99 left, p. 101 bottom right, p. 108 top left, p. 110 top, p. 111 top left, p. 117 bottom, p. 126 top and bottom right, p. 127 top left, right, and bottom, p. 129 top left, p. 151 bottom left, pp. 156–157, p. 158 bottom, p. 162 center first picture from left, p. 163 top left, p. 167 / *Titus-Beaujard:* p. 28, p. 66 top left, *Titusedi:* p. 29 top left, p. 70 top / *Ufficio Nazionale Svizzero del Turismo-Giegel:* p. 141 bottom left / *Unedi:* pp. 64–65

Index

GONE A-WHALING

*The Lure of the Sea and
the Hunt for the Great Whale*

GONE A-WHALING

The Lure of the Sea and the Hunt for the Great Whale

by

JIM MURPHY

CLARION BOOKS

New York

CLARION BOOKS
a Houghton Mifflin Company imprint
215 Park Avenue South, New York, NY 10003

Text copyright © 1998 by Jim Murphy

Printed in the USA.
Text is 12 point New Baskerville.
Book design by Sylvia Frezzolini Severance.

Library of Congress Cataloging-in-Publication Data

Murphy, Jim, 1947–
Gone a-whaling : the lure of the sea and the hunt for the great whale /
by Jim Murphy.
p.   cm.
Includes bibliographical references (p. 193) and index.
Summary: Surveys the history of the whaling industry from its earliest days to the
present, focusing on the young boys who managed to sign on for whaling voyages.
ISBN 0-395-69847-2
1. Whaling—History—Juvenile literature. [1. Whaling—History.]
I. Title.
SH383.M87   1998
306.3'64—dc21   97-13051
                            CIP
                            AC

CRW 10 9 8 7 6 5 4 3 2 1

FRONTISPIECE: Dead whales were a common sight in whaling towns.
Here two Nantucket youngsters play on the carcasses of some
long-finned pilot whales in the late 1890s.

For Alison—
  my inspiration, my pal,
  my at-home editor,
  my research advisor
  and helper,
  my calm in the middle
  of all storms,
  and, most of all,
  my one and only love

CONTENTS

*For millions of years whales swam the world's oceans in peace. Here humpback
whales have surfaced, mouths wide open to gather in food, while
hungry birds circle, hoping for leftovers.*

CHAPTER ONE
Enticed by the Riches

In the year 1690 some persons were on a high hill observing the whales spouting and sporting with each other, when one observed; "there"—pointing to the sea—"is a green pasture where our children's grand-children will go for bread."

Obed Macy,
History of Nantucket

THE WATER IN THE BAY was calm. Mewing gulls soared and dipped feverishly, searching for fish, before gliding off toward the rocky shore. For a few seconds, all was quiet and serene.

Suddenly, the water erupted as a forty-ton right whale broke the surface, its tail flukes driving its massive body nearly clear of the water. A shower of spray flew from its flippers as the whale did a half turn, paused a second at the height of its jump, then came down, landing on its back with a thunderous, watery clap.

On the other side of the bay a second right whale seemed to answer with its own playful leap. Other whales surfaced, and soon the bay was filled with the huge black creatures. The immature whales and adult males cruised the deeper water spouting lazily, while close to shore, the pregnant females were about to give birth. The long journey from the summer feeding grounds had come to an end and a new generation of whales was about to appear.

Ever since whales in their present form began appearing about 30 million years ago, scenes like this one were common around the world. Whales of all kinds swam the oceans, mated and gave birth, fed and played. They were able to thrive in part because the seas were rich with food; another reason for their success was that they had few natural enemies. It's impossible to know precisely how many whales lived in the world's seas thousands of years ago. Marine biologists estimate that there were as many as 4.5 million of the largest whales, plus millions more of the smaller whales, which includes their close relatives, the dolphins and porpoises.

This peaceful existence was disrupted by the arrival of humans. At first, humans were confined to watching the whales from the shore—awed and frightened by their size, and amazed by their grace and powerful leaping ability. Actual contact with the mighty creatures was limited to the instances when a dead whale washed ashore or when one accidentally beached itself.

Such encounters were rare, but Neolithic humans quickly discovered the incredible value of a whale carcass. A single large whale contained tons of meat, which could be dried to feed a village for months. Oil squeezed from the blubber created a very bright light when burned. The long bones, especially the ribs, were used for building homes and other structures, while the springy baleen (which is also referred to as bone) that came from the mouths of some whales was carved into combs, ornaments, and a variety of other useful items. Even the vertebrae made very nice basins and pots.

The hardships of day-to-day survival forced these people to be extremely careful and creative with each whale that came their way. "The skins covering the livers [were] made into drum heads," whaling historian Ivan T. Sanderson speculates; "the guts [were] shredded and used as twine for sewing skins. . . . Sinews from the tail flukes were doubtless used . . . to bind stone and bone weapons and tools to shafts. In fact, whales must have been taken apart completely and every bit of them used."

It's not surprising that as human populations around the world increased, so did the demand for whale products. Why wait for the occasional whale to float up on shore? people reasoned. Why not go out and get

A twelfth-century drawing showing a beached whale being hacked apart for blubber, meat, and bones. Notice that the artist gave the whale long, sharp teeth and an angry, nasty disposition, both products of his imagination.

A dead whale had many uses. In areas where wood was scarce, the long, curved bones from the rib cage could become the framework for a house or meeting hall.

Northern, Pacific, and Southern Right Whales

OTHER COMMON NAMES: black right whale, right whale, true whale (all species); Biscayan right whale, Atlantic right whale (northern right only); ice baleen white (southern right only)

FAMILY: *Balaenidae*

SPECIES: *Eubalaena glacialis* (northern); *Eubalaena australis* (southern); *Eubalaena japonica* (Pacific)

The right whale was the first whale commercial hunters went after. It was the "right" whale to hunt because it was a slow, lumbering swimmer that stayed close to shore; it was placid and amiable, which made approaching it in a boat easy; it floated when dead; and it provided large quantities of valuable oil, meat, and baleen.

After killing off the right whales that frequented European waters, whalers followed their migratory trail from Europe to the Americas (both North and South), up to the Pacific

one? So humans entered the whale's domain intent on killing. Archaeological evidence, such as whale bones found in ancient garbage pits, suggests that wherever whales swam near the shoreline, boats went out to get them.

At first, the whales were used strictly for the community that killed them. How did this affect whale populations? "Any primitive whaling community which managed to kill two or three whales a year was doing rather well for itself," answers historian Samuel Eliot Morison. "There was no need to kill northwest, and into the Sea of Japan. Cetologists have divided right whales into three separate species, the northern right whale (which lives in waters north of the equator in the Atlantic Ocean), southern right whale (which lives south of the equator), and the Pacific right whale. Aside from some minor cranial differences, the right whales look remarkably alike, having dark, rotund bodies with irregular white patches on the belly.

An adult right can reach a length of 60 feet and weigh 80 tons. Its blubber ranges in thickness from 16 inches to 28 inches and represents 30 to 45 percent of the animal's total weight. Despite its ponderous bulk, a playful right can heave its body high above the ocean's surface in a graceful breach, and it is smart enough to use its tail to catch a breeze and "sail" for miles with little effort.

To feed, a right whale swims along at a leisurely pace, mouth wide open to gather in copepods and other crustaceans that float on the water's surface. After closing its mouth, it uses its tongue to press out the water through an interwoven screen of approximately 540 baleen plates.

These species have been protected from hunters since 1937, but only the southern right whale seems to be increasing in population. There are between 3,000 and 5,000 southern right whales left, while the northern and Pacific right populations hover around 300 to 600, a number that might be too small to survive.

BIRTH SIZE AND WEIGHT: 15 to 20 feet, 2,000 pounds
ADULT SIZE AND WEIGHT: 36 to 60 feet, 60,000 to 160,000 pounds
SWIMMING SPEEDS: 3 to 6½ mph when cruising or migrating, 7 to 11 mph fleeing
GROUP SIZE: 2 to 3, with some groups as large as 12; many more congregate at
    feeding grounds

more anyway. . . . Consequently, early man posed no real threat to the continuing prosperity of the whale nation."

Unfortunately for the whales, inland communities began asking for oil and baleen products—enough so that by A.D. 1000 some hunters began to take extra whales. These first commercial whalers were the Basques, a fiercely independent people who lived in scattered enclaves along the shores of northern Spain's Bay of Biscay. Business was so good for the Basques that

Scene at a typical shore station shows a lookout (top left) scanning the ocean for whales, while fellow workers cut up and carry blubber ashore. The cooking process to extract oil is done in the brick tryworks to the right.

other people in Europe and in other areas of the world soon began sending out their own ships.

America entered the whaling business almost as soon as the first European settlers began arriving from the Continent. One book, *Brief Relation of the Discovery and Plantation of New England*, published in the early 1600s, tried to entice prospective colonists with this observation: "Whales of the best kind for oil and bone are said to abound near Cape Cod which for that reason is spoken of as likely to be a place of good fishing."

In fact, great numbers of whales haunted the New England coast three hundred years ago, especially in the winter. When the Pilgrims entered Plymouth Bay in 1620, there were so many whales "playing hard by the

Mayflower, [that] many of [the colonists] were eager to undertake their pursuit especially as there were among the ship's company a number of men skilled in whaling." The author of these words, a man identified only as Mount, went on to say that the ship's captain "professed we might make three or four thousand pounds worth of oil." Incidentally, it appears that before the *Mayflower* made its historic journey, it had been used as a whaler. And after safely depositing the Pilgrims in the New World, the ship headed straight for Greenland, where it was engaged in whaling for a number of years.

Despite the obvious dangers, whaling was never an exclusively adult male activity. Before commercial whaling began, the entire community often became involved. Everyone, including little children, was taught to recognize distant whale spouts and raise the alarm. And every able-bodied person was ready to grab a rope to haul the huge body up onto shore, where it could be butchered.

Even after whaling became an established business and ships had to sail hundreds and hundreds of miles to find whales, boys nineteen years old and younger could always be found on them. Every ship had one or two cabin boys to help with various small chores. It was not unusual for cabin boys to be as young as ten or eleven years old. In addition, many boys accompanied their fathers, who had gone to sea with their fathers before them, and so on back in time.

Whaling companies rarely bothered to write down the names and ages of their crews. The few instances where they were recorded show that whaling was a young person's job. When the *Elizabeth* sailed from Salem in 1836, twenty of the twenty-six common seamen were under the age of twenty-four. Of these, nine were nineteen years old or younger. When you consider that the American whaling fleet once numbered 750 ships, it becomes obvious that over the years thousands and thousands of boys joined in this dangerous and deadly work.

Some of these boys kept journals or wrote home about their day-to-day experiences aboard whaling ships. Their writing is rich in detail and emotion,

Family Tree

Whales are mammals. Like all mammals, whales breathe air through nostrils, they give birth to live young that nurse from their mothers, and they are warm-blooded. Paleobiologists believe that *Ambulocetus natans*, an animal that lived 55 million years ago and could walk on land and swim in water, was the common ancestor to all ancient and modern whales. From *Ambulocetus* evolved ancient whales, and from them modern whales. Scientists call whales cetaceans and have divided them into three distinct groups or suborders. The *Archaeoceti* are the ancient whales and are all extinct. Living whales are either *Mysticeti* (whales with baleen) or *Odontoceti* (whales with teeth). There are 13 separate families of cetaceans, and they contain 76 or more different kinds of whales and dolphins. The chart below shows suborder and family relationships.

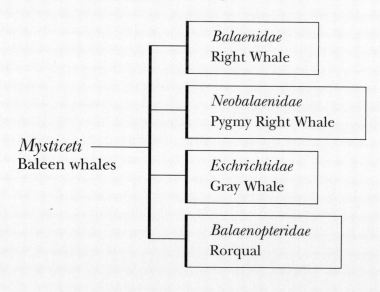

Mysticeti
Baleen whales

Balaenidae
Right Whale

Neobalaenidae
Pygmy Right Whale

Eschrichtidae
Gray Whale

Balaenopteridae
Rorqual

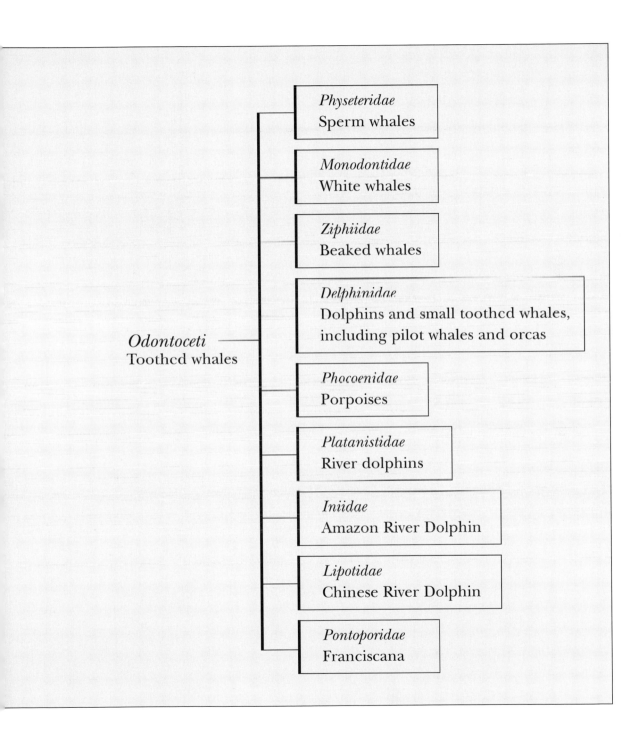

and they seem to have been, on the whole, curious about almost everything around them—the ships' officers and crew members, the food served, the working of the ships, and the hunting of the whales.

Few of these boys spent much time thinking about the pain suffered by the whales or the consequences of massive commercial hunting. As far as these boys (and for that matter most adults before the twentieth century)

An extraordinarily rare photograph of a British whaling crew. Boy in front row (left) is wearing a pair of wooden cleat shoes, used for walking on a whale carcass when it is floating alongside the ship.

were concerned, whales were things to be killed, chopped up, and made into a variety of usable items.

There were a few people—a very few—who realized that whales were unique, intelligent creatures capable of feeling pain, and that the aggressive hunting might have grave consequences. Such individuals were in the minority until fairly recently. One such person was the French naturalist the comte de Lacépède.

Lacépède wrote a natural history of whales in 1804 in which he expressed these concerns. "Enticed by the riches that would come from vanquishing the whales," Lacépède said about those who hunted whales, "man disturbed the peace of their vast wilderness, violated their haven, wiped out all those unable to steal away."

Lacépède's condemnation of the whaling industry was passionate, but even he knew that his voice was only one against many. The Basques killed so many Biscayan right whales that by 1500 it was no longer economically feasible to hunt them (that is, not enough whales could be found to pay for the ship, gear, and various supplies); after several unprofitable voyages they and other European whalers went after another kind of right whale, the bowhead. Meanwhile, Americans went after right whales along their coast and reduced their numbers dramatically. They then turned their sights and harpoons on a very common deep-water whale, the sperm whale.

By the time Lacépède was writing, this hunting pattern was firmly established. "Since man shall never change," he concluded sadly, "only when [the whales] cease to exist shall these enormous species cease to be the victims of his self-interest. They flee before [man], but it is no use; man's resourcefulness transports him to the ends of the earth. Death is their only refuge now."

This charcoal drawing of an unidentified boy destined to go to sea was done in the 1850s and entitled "Eager for Adventure." Boys thought of going on a whaling voyage as a grand and glorious romp, a little like attending summer camp for modern youths.

CHAPTER TWO

So We Were All Soon Aboard

There are several whalemen now fitting in our port. . . . Active
young men from the country and others would now have a good
opportunity of obtaining situations on board those vessels,
where the wages . . . are equal and in most cases
superior to those in merchant ships.

New Bedford Mercury, *October 22, 1822*

HARISON BODFISH GREW UP IN the tiny village of West Tisbury on Martha's Vineyard, an island off the coast of Massachusetts. Harty spent most of his days near water, playing along the rocky coast, fishing, setting out eel pots, and following the comings and goings of the ships. Even a trip to the store reinforced the notion that the sea was the center of life.

West Tisbury had two general stores, both, as Harty recalled, "carrying everything under the sun that man or beast required." It was here that a number of captains and officers from whaling ships would gather, especially in winter. "Grouped around the stove, they would talk about whaling, fishing, and all manner of things pertaining to their work. . . . When they congregated in Nathan Mayhew's, or Rotch's store, the atmosphere became pretty salty in a short time."

These men talked about the hardships of being at sea for long periods and the brutal nature of their work. Some of the men walked with limps or carried livid scars as proof. But these weren't the stories that Harty remembered best—or what fueled his imagination. No, he remembered their tales of riding out terrible storms, their descriptions of exotic, faraway islands, and, most of all, the way they battled and killed the giant whales. For Harty, a whaleship was filled with heroes, and life at sea was full of adventure.

Harty wasn't alone in his view of whaling. Thousands of children living along the coasts of the United States felt the same way. Clifford Ashley fondly recalled his childhood days in the whaling port of New Bedford: "The unpoliced ships and grass-grown wharves made marvelous playgrounds. We learned to swim from the bob-stays of the old hulks. . . . We swarmed over

The whaleship Sunbeam *is being readied for a voyage from New Bedford in 1904. Such a scene was often a boy's first introduction to the glamorous world of whaling.*

the rigging and slid down the backstays, spun the wheels, and on rainy days gathered in the cabins and played games and pretended one thing or another; and always it was something that smacked of the sea."

Many of these children were related to whaleship captains, officers, or seamen, or to people who built the ships or provided casks to hold the oil, harpoons, sails, and other supplies and gear. Harty Bodfish's father was a blacksmith and drew most of his income from whaling-related work; Clifford Ashley's uncle was an officer on a whaler. While it was natural for these youngsters to turn to whaling as a livelihood, the lure of the sea and whaling stretched far inland as well.

School texts and books on natural history routinely discussed whales, though rarely as remarkable animals that were intelligent, cared for their young, or could suffer pain. Whales were seen chiefly as valuable commodities. One book, *Gately's Universal Educator*, says only this about the sperm whale: "The *Cachalot*, or sperm whale, has the nasal, frontal, and maxillary

A drawing from Gately's Universal Educator *shows marine plants and fish off the coast of Newfoundland. A "natural" part of the scene has a bow-head whale moments away from being harpooned.*

bones filled with a fatty matter called *spermaceti*, used in the manufacture of cosmetics and ointments. Some whales yield six thousand pounds of this substance." An equally brief entry about the Greenland whale (bowhead) ends with "This whale furnishes the most oil, which is taken from the fat enveloping the body."

Whales were also viewed as dangerous and destructive creatures. One author, the Reverend J. G. Wood, felt whales were a threat to people because

Bowhead Whale

OTHER COMMON NAMES: great polar whale, arctic whale, arctic right whale, Greenland right whale, Greenland whale, the Whale

FAMILY: *Balaenidae*
SPECIES: *Balaena mysticetus*

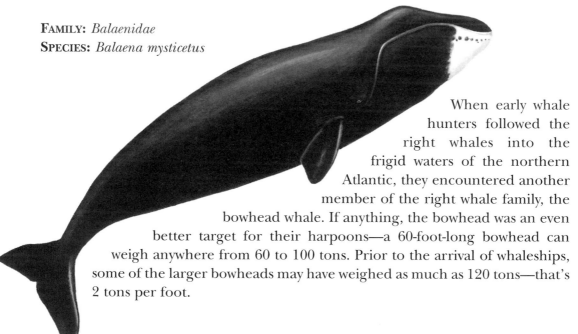

When early whale hunters followed the right whales into the frigid waters of the northern Atlantic, they encountered another member of the right whale family, the bowhead whale. If anything, the bowhead was an even better target for their harpoons—a 60-foot-long bowhead can weigh anywhere from 60 to 100 tons. Prior to the arrival of whaleships, some of the larger bowheads may have weighed as much as 120 tons—that's 2 tons per foot.

some varieties ate fish, thus reducing the supply for humans. The sperm whale, he insisted, is "destructive among lesser fishes . . . and can at one gulp swallow a shoal of fishes down its enormous gullet." Reverend Wood closed his discussion with a ringing endorsement of whaling: "With . . . few and simple weapons, the fishers contrive to secure the monster of the waters—a beautiful instance of the superiority of reason over brute strength. The whale-fisher . . . achieves a task which may be compared to a mouse attack-

Bowheads were hunted chiefly for their baleen. Their huge, bow-shaped mouths hold between 460 and 720 plates, some of which can be 14 feet long. After killing one of them, whalers would cut the baleen out of its mouth and discard the blubber and meat.

Like its right whale cousins, the bowhead is a slow, leisurely swimmer, easy to approach in a boat, and it floats when dead. In addition, the mother-calf bond is extremely strong and contributed to this whale's near extinction. Whalers would harpoon a calf and then wait for the mother to come to its rescue. A certain eighteenth-century whaleman reported that one mother was struck with six harpoons and still remained at the side of her injured calf.

Information about the bowheads is still extremely scarce. We know, for instance, that as the ice thickens in the fall, they head south. But we have no idea where they go. One reason for this lack of information is that there are very few bowheads to study. Scientists estimate that there are only 6,000 to 12,000 of them left, and that these are scattered over vast areas of the northern waters in small groups.

BIRTH SIZE AND WEIGHT: 13 to 15 feet, birth weight unknown
ADULT SIZE AND WEIGHT: 46 to 60 feet, 120,000 to 200,000 pounds
SWIMMING SPEEDS: 3 to 3½ mph cruising or migrating, 10 to 12 mph fleeing
GROUP SIZE: 1 to 6, though as many as 14 have been spotted traveling together

ing and killing a wolf with a reel of thread and a crochet needle." The message was clear: We were better off without whales, and those who killed them were heroes.

As if this were not enough, fresh bodies were also drawn into whaling through effective advertisements. The following is a typical ad published throughout eastern-seaboard states during the 1850s:

WANTED LANDSMEN: 1,000 stout young men, Americans, wanted for the fleet of whaleships now fitting out. . . . None but industrious young men with good recommendations taken. Such will have superior chances for advancement. Outfits to the amount of $75.00 furnished to each individual before proceeding to sea.

Persons desirous to avail themselves of the present splendid opportunity to see the world and at the same time acquire a profitable business will do well to make early application.

Farm boys from the interior read these ads and flocked to the whaling ports to sign on. Today we might call these boys foolish or gullible, but the truth is that they had few other real opportunities available to them. In the seventeenth, eighteenth, and nineteenth centuries the majority of Americans lived on farms or in small rural communities. They faced a lifetime of hard physical labor at very low wages. Even the cities offered little in the line of exciting work for unskilled and uneducated kids. They might get a tedious job in a factory, or spend their days on a loading platform. No wonder an ad such as the one above caught their attention and sparked a desire to travel.

When a boy finally made it to the docks, he had his first shock of reality. This was a crowded, chaotic place, nothing at all like the quiet, friendly hometown he had left behind. No face was familiar, and the air was filled with shouted orders and commands and the hurried clatter of horse-drawn wagons. Some ships swarmed with sailors making ready to depart, while

Captain James W. Buddington (seated and not at all interested in looking at the camera) and the crew of the whaling ship Margarett *in 1908.*

other ships were having their precious oil and baleen unloaded. Out of all of this came one individual with a friendly smile and a helping hand—the ship's agent.

The agent's job was to recruit crew members for a ship and have them sign articles of agreement. The "articles" was a contract that legally bound the individual to the whaleship for the duration of its voyage. When potential crew members were in short supply, an agent would say almost anything to get an individual to sign on. George A. Dodge recalled his experience in 1831. "It was the custom to have an agent in Boston to ship green hands from the country. They told fine stories about whaling profits and what a pleasant voyage it was and held out every inducement."

Or take the case of a young boy from London named Frank T. Bullen. He went to sea for the first time when he was twelve years old, sailing aboard a sleek two-masted schooner. For six years Frank crisscrossed the ocean aboard various merchant ships, where he had little contact with whalers. Then, one day, he wound up in America, alone and without any cash.

"I found myself roaming the streets of New Bedford, Massachusetts," he remembered, "and mighty anxious to get away. . . . My money was all gone, [so] I was hungry for a ship; and when a long, keen-looking man with a goat-like beard, and a mouth stained with dry tobacco-juice, hailed me one afternoon at the street corner, I answered very promptly, scenting a berth."

It turned out that the man represented a local shipowner and was, indeed, looking for seamen. The two then went to a nearby building, where Frank was given articles of agreement to sign. Frank did not bother to read the paper. "Sailors are naturally and usually careless about the nature of the 'articles' they sign, their chief anxiety being to get to sea, and under somebody's charge. . . . I signed and passed on, engaged to go I knew not where, in some ship I did not know even the name of."

Accompanied by several large, glowering men, Frank and some others who had also signed on were led to the wharf where their ship was docked. It was only when he saw the vessel that Frank realized what he had done. "I was booked for the sailor's horror—a cruise in a whaler. Badly as I wanted to get to sea, I had not bargained for this."

It was a horror to Frank because a whaleship's voyage could last anywhere from one to three years, and sometimes longer. One ship, the *Nile*, left New London, Connecticut, in May 1858 and did not return until April 1869—a voyage of eleven years! A ship's agent would probably not go out of his way to tell a prospective hand the planned length of the voyage, and if the boy did not (or could not) read the articles, he wouldn't know this detail until it was too late. Frank was used to much shorter trips, from one to three months, so the prospect of being aboard a ship for over a year seemed like a prison term to him. "[I] would have run some risks to get ashore again," he added ruefully, "but they took no chances, so we were all soon aboard."

Most kids did not have to be tricked the way Frank Bullen was. They volunteered eagerly for any position offered. The only problem they faced was getting their parents to approve. By the mid-nineteenth century, any boy under the age of seventeen had to have the written permission of his parents in order to legally work on a whaling ship.

Generally, boys living in a whaling community had an easier time getting this consent. Parents were aware of what would be expected of their son on such a voyage and whether he could handle the work. Often, they knew the captain or officers of the ship and could assume they would look out for their son's welfare.

Younger boys usually began their careers as cabin boys. Every ship signed on at least one cabin boy; larger vessels might have two or even three. Cabin boys did a variety of jobs—serving meals to the captain and officers, lighting lamps at dusk, helping clean the deck of the blood and unwanted pieces of whale, to name just a few. They were also there to learn the ways of a ship and the sea, and especially the job of a whaleman. At any moment, a sailor might be injured or killed, or desert the ship. At these times, the cabin boy might be called on to literally step into an older man's shoes and perform his job.

By far, the largest number of boys signed on as regular hands. Charles Erskine was just fifteen when he told his mother he wanted to go to sea, but she refused to sign a letter of release. "I knew it would almost break her poor heart; but I kept coaxing and teasing, teasing and coaxing, until I had almost bothered the life out of her. At last I gained her consent, and was made one of the happiest boys in all Boston."

Evidently, Harty Bodfish met less resistance. Harty was sixteen when a neighbor, Captain Cyrus Manter, brought a brand-new whaling ship into port. "Bright with fresh paint and varnish, her sails snow-white and covered with flags, the *Belvedere* was a beautiful and impressive sight. I felt a longing to go to sea, and on that ship."

A young boy stands between the massive jaws of a sperm whale.

Harty drove the captain home that day and peppered the man with questions about the *Belvedere* and how it handled in the water. At some point during the ride, Captain Manter turned to his young driver. "'Harty,' he said, 'we're sailing in two weeks, you'd better come along.' And I agreed to go."

With the good captain there to support him (and to reassure his parents), Harty received the needed permission without much fuss. The very next thing he says is "Three of us boys from the Vineyard shipped to sail on that voyage and five Dartmouth boys. We sailed from New Bedford on the 17th of August, 1880, for a voyage 'not to exceed two years,' according to the articles. Our destination was the Arctic Ocean."

Not even the actual sailing seemed to cause much of a stir for Harty or his family. "Sailing for a whaling voyage was far too common . . . to attract more than passing attention. There was the usual bustle around the wharf, the last minute details to be attended to, relatives to say good-bye, and that's about all. We were clear, under way, and out of sight of land in a few hours."

Of course, parental support was not always so easy to come by, as fourteen year-old George Fred Tilton was to learn. On two occasions George Fred had attempted to sign on whaling ships using a forged letter of permission. Both times he'd been caught before the ships sailed.

"When I say that I felt blue, I mean just that. . . . But I said to myself, 'I'll get away yet!'" So George Fred studied the shipping news every day waiting for a ship to appear.

One day, he saw that the whaleship *Union* would be leaving New Bedford in a week for a fifteen-month cruise. "I made up my mind that when the *Union* sailed, George Fred would be among those present, but I kept right on working and being the best behaved boy you ever saw."

The day before the *Union* was to leave, George Fred left home and begged a ride to New Bedford. Once there, he went directly to the wharf where the ship was tied up. "There were boys playing around on the wharf and on the vessel, and a number of men standing around talking."

Watching for his chance, George Fred joined the crowd of noisy boys and

George Fred Tilton posed for this photograph when he was fourteen years old, several months before he ran away from home to sail on the Union.

then slipped aboard the *Union*. When no one was looking, "I dropped down into the hatchway, then into the lower hold, and worked my way clear up into the 'eye' of the vessel, just as forward as I could get. There I made myself as comfortable as I could, and settled down for the night. I didn't have a very pleasant night's rest, but if I was afraid, it was mostly of being caught."

The next day, a tug towed the *Union* out to sea. George Fred could hear the officers barking out orders, sailors scurrying about, and sails being set. Soon, the ship was plowing through the choppy water.

"It sounded like the devil and it seemed as if the water would burst right through the planking. There was an awful smell down there, too, mostly of oil casks and bilge water, but I was too scared to be sick. I stayed right there until the second morning."

George Fred knew they were probably far out to sea, too far, he hoped, for the captain to turn back. He crawled over some casks and made his way to the hatchway. With a feeling of triumph, he "caught hold of the coamings and hauled myself on deck. There was no land in sight. My first voyage had really begun."

Most boys who stepped aboard a whaler had no idea what the weeks and months ahead would be like. They set sail with the same enthusiasm and spirit of adventure as George Fred. A few did pause long enough to wonder if they had made the wisest decision. Eighteen-year-old Enoch Carter Cloud had a chance meeting just before signing on the *Henry Kneeland* that set him to thinking.

"I met a stranger today on one of the wharves," Enoch recalled. "[He] accosted me in a friendly manner and inquired 'If I was bound a Whaling.' I replied in the affirmative. 'Take my advice young man,' said he, 'and don't go!' He then turned and left me. I may possibly have cause to think of this when it is too late! Time will show!"

Captain Obed Starbuck came from a long line of whaling captains;
he became a mate when he was eighteen and captain a few years
later. Don't let his impish smile fool you. He was a tough, no-non-
sense captain who completed three successful whaling voyages to the
Pacific in the space of four years—an amazing accomplishment—
and retired a very wealthy man before he was forty.

CHAPTER THREE
Work Like Horses and Live Like Pigs

We have got the poorest set of green hands that a ship had—
dull, O dear, how dull it appears that they will
never learn anything.

Log entry by Captain Charles Starbuck
of the ship Peru, *1851*

THE *UNION* WAS UNDER FULL SAIL, slowly plowing through a choppy sea. The ship pitched and swayed, responding to the movement of the water and the way the wind caught the great sheets of canvas sail. An officer of the ship spotted George Fred standing alone on deck and asked him what he was doing there. When George Fred told him how he'd snuck on board, the officer immediately ordered him to report to the captain.

"All the tales of tough skippers that I had ever heard came back to me and I dreaded the reception waiting for me on the poop. I wished that the deck was a mile long."

All too soon, George Fred was standing before the captain, feeling very much like a little boy. George Fred probably considered making up some far-fetched story about playing on the ship and accidentally falling asleep belowdecks. If he did, the sight of the captain's stern expression put this out of his mind; George Fred confessed to stowing away. The young boy recalled the brief conversation that followed.

"'What in the world did you stow away for?' [the captain] asked. 'Because my people wouldn't give me permission to ship,' I answered. 'Do you know where you are going,' inquired the captain. 'Why whaling, I suppose,' I replied. 'Yes, you are,' said the captain, half to himself; 'I can't put back now.'"

Not only couldn't he turn his ship around, the captain had no ship-to-shore communications to let George Fred's parents know where he was. If he encountered a ship heading toward New Bedford, he could send a note back with it. Otherwise, he had to wait until they stopped at their next port to post a letter to them, which might take weeks or even months to arrive.

Instead of bawling out George Fred, the captain proved to be quite lenient. He informed the boy that everyone works on a whaling ship. Next he issued George Fred clothing and assigned him a bunk in the forecastle with the other sailors.

It was at this point that George Fred learned his first, painful lesson about an open-sea voyage. "Almost from the minute that I found out that I wasn't going to be killed, I commenced to get seasick. And good Lord, wasn't I sick."

George Fred had been on boats all of his life, but these were usually small vessels on calm water. Now there was no land to fix his eyes on and steady himself. The only things in sight were the ocean and the ship, and these were both in perpetual and often contrary motion. The deck went up and down, at the same time rolling from one side to the other, while the ocean moved in a hundred different ways all at once. Sunlight bounced off the water in a blinding, dizzying way.

Just about every green hand went through the same physical initiation. One of the more vivid pictures of such suffering was given by young Moses Morrell, who sailed in 1822. His ship, the *Hero*, left Nantucket in January and hit rough, wintry seas the first day out. "Most all our hands being unaccustomed to the motion of the ship, those countenances that before had been expressions of pleasure and health, in a moment became dejected, pale and terrific—such a scene is difficult to describe. Literally, it was a floating hospital. Some would lay prostrate on the deck, as regardless of the spray as it was of them. Others were laying on their chests, sighing to be home where some friendly hand would administer to their wants."

Robert Weir became ill almost as soon as the whaling bark *Clara Bell* left port. Five days later he was still seasick. "And oh! how dreadfully sick I was. Saw two sharks, one about 12 ft. long and the other 5 or 6 ft. I felt very much tempted to throw myself to them for food."

Veteran sailors were particularly hard on the new men and boys. After describing the wretched condition of the new hands, Moses Morrell ended with this observation: "Their shipmates, more accustomed to the boisterous elements, stood and laughed at their calamity." Not only did the experienced hands make fun of the seasick greenies, they often played practical jokes on them.

In addition to keeping a journal, Robert Weir also did quick drawings of shipboard activities. A daily routine on his ship was to scrub it clean every evening as the sun set.

Fourteen-year-old William Fish Williams recalled one bit of "medical" advice an older sailor offered him. He was told to swallow a piece of raw salt pork tied to a string and then pull it back up to induce vomiting. After that, of course, William passed along this bit of advice to all new hands who came after him. They needed "a thorough house cleaning," William explained, "and the sooner it was accomplished the sooner they got well."

Lesson number two of shipboard life was that, sick or not, there was work to be done. Hard work. The ship had to be scrubbed clean, and all the brass polished with brick dust and brine. Thousands of feet of whale line needed to be stretched out and then coiled neatly in tubs. Enoch Cloud remembered being "up at 4 and hard at work; grinding harpoons, lances & spades; making foxes, etc., a general preparation for taking Whales."

A few boys loved the assignments given to them. "My special job," Harty Bodfish recalled with pride, "was scraping and oiling the royal-masts and gilding the trucks which ornamented the extreme tip of each mast. Some of the men were too short to reach, and some that were tall enough couldn't stand the height."

Harty's delight in going aloft made him an exception. Most boys were scared to death of climbing high above the deck and dangling amid the ropes and canvas while the ship pitched and rolled wildly. "To be ordered aloft to help furl a sail," William Fish Williams recalled, "especially at night, must have been torture to the poor devils too sick to stand up on deck much less go into the rigging."

But go they did. At home they might complain about having to do a simple chore, but on board back talk of any kind usually earned them a loud verbal rebuke or worse. "We had a bucko mate of the type you read about, who would strike first and explain afterward," Harty Bodfish said of his first trip out. "We green hands were allowed two weeks to learn the rigging and box the compass, and after that we were supposed to be able to find our way around and to take our regular trick at the wheel."

Of course, Harty was lucky. He was on a ship captained by a friend of the

High above the rolling deck of the Sunbeam, *a man stands masthead watch, while another is snugly positioned between the sails. Harty Bodfish enjoyed climbing above the topmost lookout position to paint the very tip of the mast.*

A young boy and an older hand wrestle with a tangled sail during a gale.

family, so this mate never hit him or any of the other boys on the *Belvedere*. Still, the mate's quick temper "put the fear of God into us without question."

Strict discipline was necessary on any oceangoing sailing vessel. A sudden change in weather might send gale-force winds and surging waves to pound the ship. At times like these a missed or delayed order could cause a ship to capsize or send it crashing onto a rocky coast. But while order and discipline were vital, many officers went to extremes.

Frank Bullen was able to avoid verbal and physical abuse because he already knew the workings of a sailing ship. When a surly fourth mate ordered Bullen to "skip aloft 'n' loose dat foretaupsle," the young man was

Discipline aboard a whaleship was often harsh, as shown in this drawing from Browne's Whaling Voyage. *Crew members were required to watch the punishment being inflicted, an event the young boy (foreground left) will probably never forget.*

able to climb up and loosen the fore-topsail without hesitation. The other green hands on Bullen's ship had no idea what the officers were telling them to do, which resulted in ruthless bullying.

Perched safely above, Bullen watched as "the farmers, and bakers, and draymen were being driven about mercilessly amid a perfect hurricane of profanity and blows. . . . Such brutality I never witnessed before. I knew how desperately ill all those poor wretches were, how helpless and awkward they would be [even] if quite hale and hearty; but the officers seemed to be incapable of any feelings of compassion whatever."

Once the ship was on its way, the captain would call all hands together on deck to give a little speech. These talks were fairly uniform from captain to captain. He advised the crew of general rules on board ship, such as obeying orders and not wasting food, or fighting. He also gave them some details about where they were headed. The captain on Robert Weir's ship "gave us a short harangue of which I noticed these few words—he'd give us plenty to eat and plenty to do—if we acted like men he'd treat us like men—no swearing etc. etc. etc."

A few captains used this moment to scare new hands into obedience. After the *Theresa* had cleared San Francisco Bay in 1907, Captain Higgins made this brief announcement: "Just remember, I'm boss on this ship. When you get an order, jump. If I catch any one of you wasting grub, I'll put him on bread and water for a month and dock the rations of the whole watch. You greenies have got just a week to box the compass and learn the ropes. . . . Let every man work for the ship. . . . [If] any dirty work goes on, I'll break the rascal who does it."

Immediately after such a talk, the crew was divided into two watches and each hand assigned to a specific whaleboat. The average whaler carried three or four whaleboats, and each one required six men to operate it. Unless a boy was unusually big, he was generally assigned to the stroke oar. When George Fred learned he would be at this position, he pointed out that "this oar is nearest the stern and the lightest in the boat."

Boat practice was a common feature early in a voyage. In this picture, the whaleboat has been lowered and the men are undoing the lines and getting ready to push away from the ship.

Boys were not given this oar out of sympathy for their small size. If they did not realize it by this time, they would very soon: A whaling ship was a commercial endeavor. Their mission, their reason for existing, was to kill as many whales as possible and bring back the oil and baleen. Boys were given the stroke oar because, as Frank Bullen realized, "Whenever one of them [made a mistake rowing], which was about every other stroke, his failure made little difference to the boat's progress."

As with every other activity, each crew had to practice handling their whaleboat. Such drills included lowering the thirty-foot-long, six-hundred-pound boat along with its one thousand pounds of gear as quickly as possible, scrambling into proper position, and pushing clear of the whaler. Getting to a whale required both sailing and rowing skills, so these were practiced for hours in calm and choppy seas. Robert Weir's first boat drill was called when he was high up in the masthead. The sea was calm, he remembered, and there were few clouds in the sky. Suddenly, he heard the urgent command of the mate: "Man the boats."

"Down I had to scramble to be at my post for the Larboard boat. All four boats were lowered, and after maneuvering about for practice within a mile of the vessel—going through all the motions of harpooning and avoiding a struck whale, we raced to the ship and *our* boat beat [all the others]."

The boat crew of the John R. Manta *paused just long enough to have this picture snapped.*

Sperm Whale

OTHER COMMON NAMES: great sperm whale, cachalot

FAMILY: *Physeteridae*
SPECIES: *Physeter catodon*

In 1712, Captain Christopher Hussey of Nantucket and his crew of eleven got lost in a howling storm. All night, they struggled to keep their thirty-foot-long sloop from flipping over, while being driven farther and farther out to sea. As the sun began to rise, they were in a soupy fog when a giant black mass surfaced just twenty feet away. It was a whale of some sort, Captain Hussey guessed, but one with a huge, squarish head he had never seen before. Hussey wasn't interested in whale biology; he was a hunter. He grabbed a nearby harpoon and slammed it into the side of the strange creature. His aim was true, and in a remarkably short time, the whale was dead, and Captain Hussey became the first commercial whaler to kill a sperm whale.

Hussey's accident changed the course of whaling. The sperm whale turned out to have an extraordinarily large supply of high-quality oil, and ships by the hundreds set out to get sperms. And because they can be found anywhere where the

This was grueling exercise even for the biggest and strongest boys and could last anywhere from thirty minutes to several hours. When they stepped back on board the ship, their clothes were soaked through with sweat and sea spray, and their hands burned with blisters from the constant friction on the oar handle. If the captain didn't like what he had just seen, he might order the entire drill done over.

water is deeper than 650 feet, whalers soon found themselves circling the globe in their pursuit.

Few whalemen understood what a truly unique animal the sperm whale is. Here is the undisputed diving champion of the mammalian world, capable of descending to depths of two miles and staying underwater for over two hours. These dives allow the sperm whale to gather in the ton of food it needs to survive every day. Its favorite food is squid, but it will also feast on schools of cod, barracuda, ray, or albacore, along with some seals and sharks measuring up to 10 feet. To capture fleeing prey, it has an impressive array of 36 to 50 teeth in its lower jaw.

An adult male can measure 60 feet in length and weigh 50 tons. Despite its bulk, it loves to breach and lobtail (slap the surface of the water with its tail), and can swim at great speeds if alarmed. While older males tend to travel alone, sperm whales frequently travel in groups of 20 to 50, and in several exceptional sightings, hundreds and even thousands have been spotted together.

Sperm whales were extensively exploited by whalers for almost 250 years, and while they are now a common sight in some locations, we have no real idea how many of them exist.

BIRTH SIZE AND WEIGHT: 11½ to 15 feet, 2,000 pounds
ADULT SIZE AND WEIGHT: 36 to 60 feet, 40,000 to 100,000 pounds
SWIMMING SPEEDS: 3 to 9 mph cruising or migrating, 21 to 27 mph fleeing
GROUP SIZE: 1 to 50, though there have been some sightings of hundreds of them traveling together

The first weeks of any voyage saw many such practice sessions. But, as Frank Bullen observed, "[We] learned very fast under the terrible imprecations and storm of blows from the iron-fisted and iron-hearted officers, so that . . . the skipper was satisfied of our ability to deal with a 'fish' should he be lucky enough to 'raise' one."

They were suffering these hardships in order to hunt whales. But where were they? "It was the habit of the whales up to about 1748 to set in along-shore," says marine historian Frances Diane Robotti. "The whaling was done in the immediate vicinity of the coast and seldom beyond sight of the land. . . . By 1761 the North Atlantic was practically devoid of Right Whales . . . and soon the Greenland Right Whale [the bowhead] was all but exterminated in his habitat."

At the time, few people believed the idea that any animal could be completely wiped out of existence through overhunting. Most felt that the whales had simply become terrified by the hunters and fled to different and distant parts of the seas. We know now that this isn't true. We also know that hunting has always had a particularly severe impact on whales. "Whales have local populations called stocks," says writer Robert McNally, "each with its own range. The stocks intermingle little."

If, say, a stock of right whales that frequented a particular bay off the Massachusetts coast is killed off, it is not likely that other right whales will enter the emptied area and colonize it. "When a stock is exterminated," McNally concludes grimly, "it is gone for good."

With large whales close to shore either gone or in limited supply, bigger ships were built to search for whales farther out at sea. The next whale hunted was the sperm whale. By the mid-nineteenth century, ships leaving a New England port had to sail all the way to the Pacific Ocean in order to find enough sperm whales to make a trip profitable.

Smaller whales remained a common sight everywhere. Because of their size, dolphins and porpoises did not yield enough oil to be hunted commercially, so large schools still existed. Clifford Ashley was on deck one night when "I was startled . . . by an unusual commotion forward. We had driven into a school of porpoises, breaching and gamboling all about us."

Such sightings often gave boys their first taste of what a hunt might be like. Ashley had no time to admire either the beauty or the leaping ability of the porpoises near his ship. Instead, he was swept along in the excitement that followed. "There was a scramble for harpoons, and in a moment the boat-steerers were out on the back ropes in a race to get [a porpoise]. There were two misses before Smalley drove his iron into one, for a porpoise's movements are erratic as a rabbit's. Flopping and bleeding like a stuck pig, the animal was hauled to deck. That night we had the first fresh meat in weeks, and for two days we feasted on porpoise steaks and liver."

Enoch Carter Cloud was lucky enough to see some large whales on his third day out. "Proved to be a school of 'fin-backs.' Truly novel & strange! Look where you would, these mighty leviathans were seen, surging, rolling & spouting, throwing the high spray high in the air, and 'sounding,' for another general surge and spouting."

There was no rush to the whaleboats, however. While an eighty-five-foot-

A young sailor aboard the Sunbeam *hacks meat from a recently harpooned porpoise.*

long fin whale can yield a great deal of oil, it can also swim along at over twenty miles per hour, much faster than any sailing ship could go. "This species are not easily taken," Enoch concluded his entry, "and Whalemen give them a wide birth." They gave them wide berth, that is, until steam-powered engines were used in whalers.

Unlike Enoch, most greenies were not yet in the mood to be fascinated by the new world they had entered. For the majority, these first days tended to blend together in a blur of seasickness, hard work, and harsh treatment—and the realization that there was no escape. "We have to work like horses and live like pigs," a weary Robert Weir sighed after several days. "Eyes beginning to open—rather dearly bought independence."

The only escape came when it was time to go below into the tiny forecastle to grab a quick meal or turn in for the night. "The room itself was terribly cramped," says Robert McNally, "twelve to sixteen feet square with the butt of the foremast occupying the center of the floor. The bunks, sixteen or eighteen of them, were built into the sides. Light entered only from the hatch, which was also the way in or out, not only for the men, but also for [any water] the whaler shipped." Space was so precious that there wasn't even room for benches. Sailors sat on their sea chests, which lined the floor next to their bunks.

If a boy was lucky, he had a mattress of straw or corn husks, known as a donkey's breakfast, to cushion the hard wooden slats of his bunk. There he would curl up in a tight ball, think about home, and hope that sleep came quickly.

Enoch Cloud's opinion of the forecastle was anything but positive. "Well, what is it, and what is it not?" he asked. "It is not home!! It is a hole in the foreward between deck of the ship . . . about 9 feet by 16 in which 21 men are to live for 30 or 36 months. A thick dark cloud of tobacco smoke pervades this 'castle' and an occasional 'growl' indicates another party's presence."

Frank Bullen found it difficult to relax during the opening days of his cruise. He would lie in his bunk for hours, staring at the slats of the one

Jamie McKenzie made his first whaling voyage in 1853, when he was fourteen. He had this photograph taken three years later and presented it to his cousin, Mary E. Smith.

above him. The stench of gurry filled his nostrils, while cockroaches scurried about searching for food. All around him the greenies "were groaning in misery from the stifling atmosphere which made their sickness so much worse." With so many bodies crammed into such a tiny, windowless space, the air grew warm and fetid. "There was a rainbow-coloured halo round the flame of the lamp, showing how very bad the air was."

Eventually, the groans blended with the creaking of the ship and the sound of someone above pacing on the deck. Frank closed his eyes, and "in a very few minutes oblivion came, making me as happy as any man can be in *this* world."

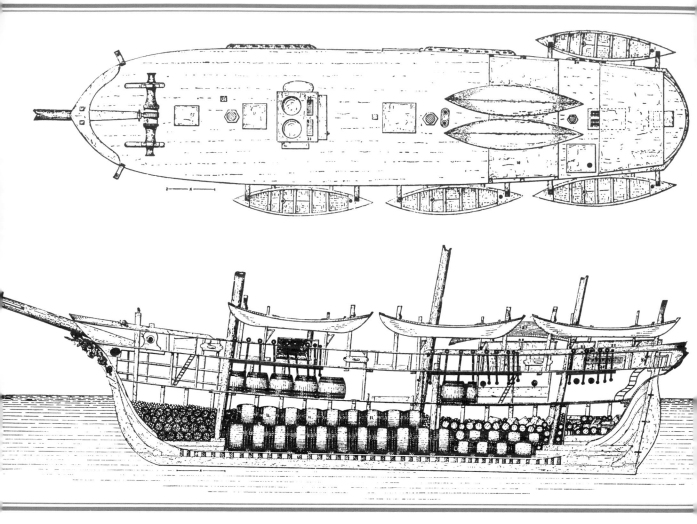

Above-deck and cutaway views of the Alice Knowles, *built in 1883. The above-deck view shows the position of the four whaleboats and two spare whaleboats when not in use. Cutting in the whale was done on the starboard side of the ship; boiling or trying out took place in the two round kettles to the right of the forward whaleboat. The belowdecks storage area for various-sized casks is shown in the cutaway. The forecastle (just above the small casks in the forward section) has bunks drawn in.*

CHAPTER FOUR
It All Seems So Strange

At 9 A.M. all hands came on board and made all sail and went
to sea with 32 men and wone Lady all told.

Journal entry by
Captain Valentine Lewis, 1866

EVENTUALLY, A BOY WOULD BEGIN to find his sea legs. Walking along the deck of the rolling ship became easier, and the queasy, upset stomach settled down some. Robert Weir began his diary entry for his eighth day of sailing with a chipper "Commenced the day at the masthead feeling quite well."

These boys were also growing accustomed to the new kinds of jobs they were expected to perform. Two weeks after leaving port, Weir was equally happy to report that "I am getting quite used to the work now—and my hands can testify to that quite plainly—for they are as hard as horn inside— pulling & Hauling on hard ropes—and the outside have a most beautiful . . . brown color."

A change took place aboard ship at this time, too. The greenies were not skilled seamen yet, but they jumped to a task when an order was given and made fewer mistakes. Most important, the whaleboat crews were acquiring a sense of teamwork, their oars slicing through the water effortlessly and with real power. Seeing this, the captain and officers could ease up a bit in the way they treated the crew. "It was interesting to note the rapid transforma-

51

tion of the greenhorns into sailors," William Fish Williams observed during the second week of a voyage. "There was a general mellowing effect in the growing understanding of the various members of the crew, both forward and aft."

Frank Bullen's description of this transformation was much more earthy. "Our landsmen got so thoroughly drilled, that within a week of leaving port

Gray Whale

OTHER COMMON NAMES: California gray whale, grayback whale, Pacific gray whale, devilfish, hardhead, mussel digger, scrag whale

FAMILY: *Eschrichtidae*
SPECIES: *Eschrichtius robustus*

The gray whale presented a handsome target to early whalers. It was fairly large (between 40 and 46 feet and weighing up to 35 tons), and it stayed in shallow water in order to feed. In addition, grays often attempted to help injured companions. In one documented incident, a wounded female gray whale was sinking and about to die, when two males lifted her from the water and held her aloft until she recovered enough to swim off. Of course, hunters used this habit to great advantage: The North Atlantic population was extinct by the early eighteenth century, the Korean grays were wiped out soon after, while those that frequented the California coast were reduced to just a few hundred by 1900.

Fortunately, grays are hardy creatures and reproduce fairly quickly (a gray whale can give birth every year and a half to two years, while a right gives birth only they hardly knew themselves for the clumsy clodhoppers they at first appeared to be."

Now that the new men and boys were settling in, they began to look more closely at the world they had chosen to inhabit. Naturally, the people closest to them—their companions in the forecastle—were given very careful scrutiny.

Enoch Carter Cloud took a rather dim view of his fellow crewmen. Enoch

every three to four years). Females are fiercely protective of their young and will attack anything that threatens them (a trait that earned them the nickname of "devilfish"). As a result, most of the young survive to grow up and eventually breed. Today the gray whale population stands at between 15,000 and 25,000.

One of the most amazing things about gray whales is their migratory journey. In the summer they travel north to the Arctic feeding grounds, where they plow along the bottom taking in mouthfuls of shrimplike amphipods and straining the water through short baleen plates. When winter approaches, the grays set off down the coast for the southern breeding lagoons in the Gulf of California. Their 12,000-mile round trip is the longest migration of any mammal.

It is during this southern journey that grays display an incredible energy reserve. For not only do they have to swim for weeks on end, but this is a time of frequent breaching, lobtailing, and surf riding. And when they reach the breeding grounds off Mexico, they are greeted by crowds of enthusiastic whale watchers, where, despite their nickname of "devilfish," they prove to be remarkably friendly and approachable.

BIRTH SIZE AND WEIGHT: 15 to 16½ feet, 1,000 pounds
ADULT SIZE AND WEIGHT: 40 to 46 feet, 30,000 to 70,000 pounds
SWIMMING SPEEDS: 2½ to 6 mph cruising or migrating, 10 to 11 mph fleeing
GROUP SIZE: 1 to 3, with as many as 18 traveling together; larger congregations are sometimes seen in breeding grounds

considered himself a good Christian, so he was offended to see them gambling on Sundays. "This holy day is spent by the majority of the crew in raffling with coppers, for tobacco! I have made a careful calculation, concerning the characters of Whalemen; and I find that out of every 100 men in the service, 75 are run-away-apprentices; of the remaining 25, 20 are fugitives from justice—leaving a remainder of 5 honest men!"

Many boys shared Enoch's view of whaling crews. William Fish Williams felt that "some very poor specimens of humanity went to sea" and that "the majority [of the crew] spent their spare time telling lewd stories or describing their various love affairs in much detail." Frank Bullen looked around the forecastle and could only say, "A motley crowd they were."

None of these broad characterizations should be taken as absolute fact. It's true that whaling attracted men and boys who considered themselves tough and adventuresome individuals. And because a whaling ship could operate fairly efficiently as long as it set out with a few skilled whalemen, many of the common sailors were indeed uneducated and unskilled. Few of them were out-and-out criminals, troublemakers, or no-accounts, however. No captain would tolerate such a person for long. So why did a number of boys have such a low opinion of their fellow crew members?

These boys all came on board with some deeply ingrained prejudices. In addition to feeling that he was the only true Christian on his ship, Enoch Cloud was also displeased with the national composition of the crew. When he signed on, he was assured by the agent that he would sail only with Americans. Yet he found himself living with "English, Irish, French, Dutch, Portuguese & Spaniards!" Referring to the animals brought along as pets or a food supply, he went on to add, "We might add to the above list, goats, fowls, hogs & dogs, but . . . beg the pardon of the 'lower race,' for associating their names with a portion of the crew!"

William Fish Williams' view was clouded by the fact that his father was a whaling captain. William had been on ships from birth and had by the age of ten a veteran sailor's grasp of the sea, the ship, and whaling. As such he

Pages from the log of the John P. West, *1885. Drawings of whales indicate that a whale had been killed; numbers above the head record the amount of oil gotten. Whenever another ship was encountered, a drawing of it was also entered.*

had little patience or liking for the inexperienced hands. Frank Bullen was another story altogether. Most of his sailing time had been aboard sleek and majestic clipper ships. He found everything about whaling—from the crew to the officers to the ship itself—inferior to his past experiences and, thus, beneath him.

None of these boys were mean-spirited or bad. They simply reflected the attitudes and prejudices of their parents and of their communities at large. For them, race, ancestry, religion, and wealth counted heavily for a person's social position and as an indicator of character. What is more, when they stepped aboard a whaler, they entered a place of clear and rigid class distinctions.

Take the living arrangements: The captain had a number of small, private rooms at the very back of the ship. Just ahead of him came the mates or officers, each having a single private room. The captain and officers ate in the main cabin with meals served by a cabin boy, who also bunked in the stern area.

Forward of the officers, at midship, was the steerage section where the boatsteerers, blacksmith, cooper, carpenter, cook, and another cabin boy slept and ate. At the very front of the ship was the forecastle, home of the common sailors. Even within these areas, a certain caste system reigned. In general, the closer an individual's bunk or room was to the captain's, the higher his status on the ship. Boys usually ended up sleeping at the very front of the forecastle, where the space narrowed to a point and the bunks were made smaller to fit the awkward shape.

"The rules regarding quarters were strict and might seem unfair," George Fred Tilton observed. "The officers had the run of the ship on deck and could go anywhere below if necessary. . . . The seamen had to stay forward; . . . the boatsteerers were obliged to keep to the waist; and if a man left his section of the ship without good reason he was generally punished."

There is another reason why the boys whose letters and journals come down to us viewed shipmates with a cold eye. Remember, as greenies they were often picked on and ridiculed by the older, more experienced sailors. Most boys did not fight back, either verbally or with their fists. Instead, they let their pens extract a measure of revenge on their oppressors.

Despite such a rigid and traditional life, there were at least two ways in which a whaling ship sometimes proved to be unusually liberal and well ahead of the time. First, many blacks were employed aboard whaling ships, and not just as common seamen either. When William Fish Williams sailed aboard the *Florence* in 1873, both the fourth mate and one of the boatsteerers were black. A few blacks were even able to take the money from their various whaling voyages and become shipowners.

As always, a lack of clear, detailed records makes it difficult to know precisely how many blacks shipped aboard whalers or how many of them were under the age of nineteen. Historian Martha S. Putney combed the crew lists at the National Archives and at the Old Dartmouth Historical Society and discovered that on whalers leaving from New Bedford, "at least 3,189

A wood engraving of Captain Paul Cuffee. Cuffee was a highly esteemed resident of New Bedford as well as a successful shipbuilder, shipmaster and owner, exporter-importer, and navigation instructor. When he captained the Traveller *in 1815, he had an all-black crew that included his sixteen-year-old son, William (who later became a captain too).*

identifiable blacks held 4,064 positions on the ships from 1803 to 1860." Of the one hundred whaling voyages that left from Newport, Rhode Island, over 10 percent of the crews were blacks.

The same holds true for the other major whaling centers, Nantucket and Salem, as well as the many smaller ones that dotted the eastern seacoast. Thousands of blacks were able to find work aboard whalers, and many even advanced in rank and stature.

Initially, blacks found acceptance because most shipowners from Nantucket and Salem were members of the Society of Friends, also known as

Captain Absalom F. Boston probably heard stories about whaling from his grandfather, Prince Boston. Absalom Boston sailed for many years out of Nantucket before being given command of the ship Industry, *which left from Nantucket in 1822 with an all-black crew.*

Quakers. Because of their religious beliefs, Quakers had had their own property seized and been shunned socially in England, where their society had been founded. Many had fled to the American colonies, hoping to escape such prejudice, only to be persecuted again, most notably by the Puritans. Here, then, were people who had firsthand experience with prejudice and who believed that all humans should be treated with fairness and dignity. Quakers were also among the first in America to actively take an antislavery stance and to work for its abolition. So when Quaker shipowners staffed their ships, they literally practiced what they preached.

The tolerance of the Nantucket and Salem owners was so widely known that runaway slaves from the south often went into whaling to maintain their freedom. One unidentified runaway was on board a whaler in the Pacific when he wrote a letter to the American and Foreign Anti-Slavery Society that appeared in their 1853 annual report. In it, he detailed his escape from a southern slaveholder and flight to the north. At first, he stayed in Brooklyn, he told them, but "I fled from Brooklyn because I could not sleep, as I was so near the slaveholding country I thought I could not be safe until I had gone to the other side of the globe."

But whaleship owners were also hardnosed (some would say ruthless) businessmen. No one stayed employed on a whaleship unless he could handle the jobs assigned him. When Joseph Miller, Philip Bailey, Henry Tucker, and other blacks were made boatsteerers, they earned those promotions because they had the skill to lead men and kill whales, and not because of the color of their skin. Even more impressive was the fact that these and other blacks made numerous voyages for the same owners, a sure sign that they were highly skilled at their jobs.

As the American fleet grew during the eighteenth and early nineteenth centuries, the demand for sailors who were experienced whale hunters also grew. Non-Quaker owners, desperate for reliable help, relaxed their discriminatory hiring practices and began taking on blacks as well. Most ships carried at least one or two blacks, though even the incomplete records indicate that the average was probably higher. In 1843, for instance, 26 of 89 ships that sailed from New Bedford had five or more blacks on board. And in May 1822, the whaling ship *Industry* left Nantucket manned entirely by a black crew and officers, including Captain Absalom F. Boston.

Despite the fact that thousands of blacks found employment in whaling, they did not escape prejudice entirely. The number of blacks who became mates was small in relation to the number of experienced blacks available. Owners were very hesitant to put a black in charge of a predominantly white crew, fearing rebellion and reduced profits. In addition, blacks had to work harder and longer for those promotions. Frederick A. Lawton shipped aboard the whaler *Charles* in 1830 when he was fourteen and stayed with the ship as a common seaman for eleven years. Any white sailor who worked on a ship that long would have been made a boatsteerer or mate somewhere along the line. Finally, after thirty-two years of whaling, Lawton was promoted to first mate, a rank he deserved decades earlier.

Another indication of the obstacles faced by black sailors was that very few were ever made captains. So far, it would seem that only nine—Absalom F. Boston, Pardon Cook, Paul Cuffee, William Cuffee, Samuel Harris, Amos Haskins, Alvin Phelps, Edward J. Pompey, and Petter Green—have been identified as having command of a whaler.

To add to their burdens, black sailors also faced prejudice from white crew members. One young white sailor, Roger Wilit, wrote an angry letter home in which he complained, "We are forced to sleep with the coloreds and breath the same air as them. . . . Unless things change I will leeve the ship at the first chance."

Even Harty Bodfish's boyish good cheer could not hide an ugly streak of racial prejudice. "We had a mixed crew," he said of the sailors on his first ship, "and it was well mixed too. There were niggers, Portugees, and several other nationalities." Harty then went on to note that he and a young man named McDermott were the only whites in the forecastle.

So while many blacks found employment aboard whalers and even

Captain Amos Haskins as he appeared in 1850, when he took command of the Massasoit. *Haskins was thirty-four and had twenty-two men under him, twelve of whom were black.*

respect and advancement, their lot was certainly more difficult than that of the white sailors. "The reason why they are not there as seamen often," said Captain Edmund Gardner in 1863, "and very rarely there as officers is the same that must be given for their exclusion from every other position of authority and fellowship." For those who did not understand him, Captain Gardner added, "It is, without doubt, almost wholly owing to the prejudice of the whites."

Getting used to living and working with black sailors was one situation boys had to deal with. Another was that many captains brought along their wives and families.

The first captain to do this was Laban Russell. When he left Nantucket in 1817, he was accompanied by his wife, Mary, and their twelve-year-old son,

William, who was signed on as a cabin boy. The voyage must have gone well, because the entire family—which had grown to include another son named Charles—went out again in 1823.

Ten years after the Russells' historic voyage, whaling wives and children were fairly common. By the middle of the 1860s, hundreds of women were sailing to faraway ports on whaling ships. The appearance of a captain's wife on board was so common that these ships were referred to as "lady ships."

Most of these women accompanied their husbands in order to keep their families together. In addition, they wanted to be of real value to their husbands. Mary Brewster stepped aboard her husband's ship in May 1849 filled with confidence: "I am going and in the end hope I may be a useful companion, a soother of woes, a calmer of troubles and a friend in need."

Susan A. Stimson stepped off her husband's ship in 1850 just long enough to have her photograph taken. She would eventually go on three extended whaling voyages.

Almost without exception, the women proved to be extremely useful not just to their husbands but to everyone on board. For a captain, having his wife by his side meant bringing his home—and many of its comforts and distractions—with him. A conversation with his wife about her day or the children provided a welcome relief from the usual talk aboard an all-male ship, talk that revolved around whales, the weather, and crude jokes. The captain could watch his children at play, listen to (and make recommendations about) their lessons, and, especially if one of the children was a boy, give instruction in navigation and the whaling business. In every way possible, a captain's voyage was made more bearable by having his wife and family with him.

For a woman, the story was very different. Often she had traded a spacious home on land for a small, dark, damp space that never stopped moving. Seasickness, homesickness, and boredom affected her as much as any of the crew, and she had to get used to the idea of being the only woman on the ship. Eliza Williams (William Fish Williams' mother) sounded a bit lost when she spoke about her first day at sea: "Now I am in the place that is to be my home, posibly for 3 or 4 years; but I can not make it appear to me so yet it all seems so strange, so many Men and not one Woman beside myself; the little Cabin that is to be all my own is quite pretty; as well as I can wish, or expect on board a ship. I have a rose geranium to pet . . . and I see there is a kitten on board." After this assessment, Eliza added a somber afterthought: "I think it will not all be as pleasant as it is today."

The greatest part of a woman's day was spent doing domestic chores—washing, ironing, mending clothes, supervising meals, embroidering quilts, cleaning her family's living quarters, or giving school and music lessons to her children. A surprising number brought aboard upright pianos, melodeons, and parlor organs. A fifteen-year-old sailor, William Wright, remembered "the happy sound of music coming from below as we stewed a large whale."

As if caring for a husband, children, and living space were not enough, the women also interacted with the crew. It was not at all unusual for them

After her husband, who was captain of the Cicero, *left Mary Crocker Stickney in New Bedford for a whaling voyage in the Pacific, she grew bored and lonely. Instead of mooning around at home for three years, she boarded another whaling ship and sailed by herself to the South Atlantic island of St. Helena in order to join up with him.*

to hold Bible reading classes, tend to sick and injured sailors, teach crew members (especially the younger ones) how to read and do simple math, help the cook vary the preparation of meals, or organize activities to keep the crew occupied. Jane Worth was enterprising enough to assemble an orchestra, which may have been more comical than musical, if we believe the mate's comment: "Two violins, tambourine, and a coal chisel. Made more noise than music, I guess, but answers for a pastime."

These women were determined and energetic individuals—they had to be to step aboard a whaler—and a number of them actively participated in the running of the ship. It's known that a few took regular turns at the helm and stood watches. Honor Earle passed all the required tests and was officially rated as navigator on the *Charles W. Morgan* from 1890 to 1906.

Many men felt there was no place for a woman on board a ship or that, if she had to be there, she should stay belowdecks with "her children and sewing," as one disgruntled sailor remarked. An all-too-typical reaction came from the American writer Mark Twain when he met a captain's wife who knew a great deal about sailing and whaling (probably more than Twain did) and was not shy about sharing her opinions either. "I have just met an estimable lady, Mrs. Captain Jollopson, whose husband (with her assistance)

Back in New Bedford after lengthy cruises, this group of whaling wives put on their best bonnets and had their picture taken. Despite their frilly appearance, whaling wives were tough and determined, and they knew the sea as well as most sailors.

commands the whaling bark *Lucretia Wilkerson.*" Those who disapproved of having a woman on a whaling ship put aside the term "lady ship" and referred to the vessel as a "hen frigate."

The vast majority of men who actually sailed on a lady ship came to respect and admire these women. George Fred Tilton was certainly one of those. One day young George Fred got into a heated argument with his captain and even raised his fist to hit the older man. "The captain then told the mate to go and get the irons, but Mrs. Smith interfered. She came on deck and spoke to her husband. I don't know what she said, but he answered her by saying, 'Go below, Lucy. Mutiny on my ship!'"

There followed several moments of tense silence because Lucy Smith would not leave the deck, an act of defiance that none of the crew would dare commit. Instead, she began speaking in a voice so soft, her husband had to calm down to hear her words. A much-relieved George Fred was happy to report, "I didn't have any irons put on me, but I have always felt that if it hadn't been for her . . . I would have been ironed and like enough worse things would have happened to me."

Another telling incident was reported by William Fish Williams. His mother, Eliza, was a rather quiet and shy person, and he had always assumed that she was timid as well. Then one day a fight broke out between two men. One of them was slashed across the abdomen so badly that, as William recalled, "his bowels were in his shirt."

After the bleeding man was carried to a shady spot on deck, it was Eliza Williams who nestled the dying man's head in her lap, wiped his forehead with a cool, wet cloth, and gave him water to ease his suffering. "I often marvelled at my mother's courage and control of her nerves under real danger or trying conditions," William said proudly. "Here was an awful situation . . . but she was as cool as any man on the ship."

Or take the case of Caroline Mayhew, who sailed with her husband, William, on the *Powhatan.* She was the daughter of a doctor, so she had a practical knowledge of medicine. She was also an accomplished navigator.

Then in 1846 smallpox swept the ship, striking most of the crew and officers, including her husband. At this point, Caroline Mayhew did what any good sailor would do—she took command of the ship, becoming chief medical officer, navigator, and captain until the disease ran its course and the men were able to return to duty.

Make no mistake about it: The whaling business was dominated by white males, and thus neither blacks nor women were truly able to demonstrate their skills or leadership abilities to the fullest. Still, both had more freedom than their counterparts on land, and many took advantage of every opportunity that came their way. With few exceptions they would probably agree with the sentiments expressed by Mary Lawrence when she considered what those on land must think of her: "I imagine that I was looked upon by them as an object of pity. But I do not believe that I would exchange situations with any one of them."

Sailing to the Pacific meant traveling around treacherous Cape Horn,
where strong currents, high winds, and fierce storms sent many ships
and their crews to a watery grave. This ship has been so battered by a
typhoon's winds and waves that the crew has given up trying to control
it and climbed into the rigging to avoid being swept away.

CHAPTER FIVE
Nothing So Electrifying

The Skipper's on the quarter-deck
a-squinting at the sails,
When up aloft the lookout sights
a school of whales
Now clear away the boats, my boys,
and after him we'll travel,
But if you get too near his fluke,
he'll kick you to the devil!

J. C. Colcord, Roll and Go

ROBERT WEIR CAME UP ONTO the rolling deck of the *Clara Bell* and paused to look around. "The sea was in glorious commotion," he observed a bit shakily. "We would see an enormous wave come rolling toward us—with every prospect of being overwhelmed—but no—God is there—our vessel would glide gently over it—through a brilliant dash of spray and foam."

To Weir, the sea was wild, ready to swallow up the ship in one frothy gulp. To the experienced hands, it was just "a bit of weather," and nothing to break the normal running of the ship. And since a whale had to be spotted before it could be killed, this meant standing watch high up in the masts.

Normally, four crew members stood watch at a time, two in the foremast, two in the aftermast. If they were lucky, the ship might have a tiny platform to stand on with hoops to keep them from tumbling to the deck below. Many ships (especially those built before 1860) did not have this luxury; instead, the men had to sit or stand on the highest yardarms without railings to catch them should they slip. Owners hoped this dangerous position would keep lookouts extra alert during their watch. Extra protection was provided only when hunting in bitter cold areas, such as the Arctic. Here, a platform with railings was assembled with a canvas wrapping to keep out the wind and snow. This enclosed shelter came to be called a crow's nest.

Weir scrambled up the ropes until he was nearly at the top of the hundred-foot mast. Any confidence the young man had gained during his first days of sailing probably deserted him at this time. The deck had been rolling and pitching in the choppy seas, but up here was a hundred times worse. The mast whipped back and forth with stomach-churning regularity, and Weir often found himself suspended over the boiling sea. "The ship was almost on her beam ends by the wind, and the spray dashing nearly to the fore-top [sail]," he said. "Often a big lurch of the ship will knock half the ideas out of ones head."

From this swaying perch Weir and the other lookouts strained with eyes and spyglasses, hoping to be the first to spot a whale. A greenhorn was usually paired with an experienced hand who might, if he was generous, teach the new man what to look for in the endless expanse of water. William Fish Williams was proud to report that "having good eyes and knowing fairly well a sperm whale's spout from that of a finback [fin whale] or sulphur-bottom [blue] whale, I frequently stood a trick at the masthead."

Of course, overhunting had so reduced the numbers of right and sperm whales in the Atlantic that days and weeks might slide by without anyone's seeing any. Sailors on lookout would become bored and distracted, chat with their lookout companion, and often lapse into daydreaming.

To keep the lookouts alert, captains often offered a prize of ten pounds of tobacco to the first seaman to spot the particular whale they happened to be hunting. The tobacco might be used by the winner or traded for other items, such as food or alcohol, at the islands where they stopped during the long voyage. Still, prize or no prize, whales along overhunted routes could be scarce.

This doesn't mean the oceans were empty. Far from it. Greenies were

The bow whaleboat of the Sunbeam *being lowered into the gently rolling water.*

surprised and delighted by the abundance of life they encountered. Robert Weir seemed almost breathless in his reporting of fish and birds. "Saw a school of cowfish and they appeared somewhat like the bodies of cows tumbling about in the water—saw plenty of flying fish—never imagined there were half so many in the sea—saw some land swallows one or two of which lit in the rigging—they did not remain long—rested an hour or more and then went *home*—happy creatures."

Such a casual reference to home—even that of a bird—could bring out other, more melancholy thoughts. Weir's mind often drifted while he was on lookout. Near the end of one particularly boring stint, "while looking for whales or rather *nothing*," he found himself thinking of his father and sister. "I had pleasant thoughts of those I left so unkindly and abruptly but I console myself that it will be some relief to dear father, for me to be off his hands. I also amused myself by singing all the psalms and hymns, chants, etc., that dear Emma [his sister] and myself used to sing in our little Church."

Eventually, despite all the distractions, the hours of watching would pay off. A lookout would see something unusual—a dark shape, a vapor spout—two or three miles away from the ship. Quickly, he leaned forward, every muscle tensed, eyes squinting, trying to determine whether or not he had spotted a whale. The moment he was sure, he cried out, "There blows! There blows!"

Robert Weir wasn't lucky enough to win the tobacco on his ship. He was in his bunk, half asleep, when the first whales were located. "A little before 6 o'clock this morning heard the cheering cry from mast head 'there blows' 'there blows'—'there goes flukes.'"

"There is nothing so electrifying as that cry from the masthead," said William Fish Williams, and most boys aboard whaling ships would agree with him. They had sought out a whaleship in order to experience adventure, and now that moment had come. There were a few—a very few—who did not relish the call. Frank Bullen hadn't been happy to come aboard a whaler in the first place, so when he heard the alert, he described it as "a long mournful sound." Two minutes later, he was on deck. "At last," he sighed, "the long dreaded moment had arrived."

Happy or not, the cry "There blows" had an instantaneous effect. Every hand on deck stopped what he was doing and turned to search for the whales. Those below tumbled from their bunks and scurried to join the others up top. Even the captain, who was usually the picture of calm, deliberate movement, leaped into action.

"The Captain was on deck in a moment," Weir went on, "and after

The whaleboat moves away from the ship.

singing out Where away & how far off—jumped into the rigging with his glass—presently the lookout cries again there blows half a dozen times—all is now excitement; a general rush is made to get a sight."

Tense seconds passed. Not a sound was made. The crew waited, poised for action, while the captain sighted the animals in his spyglass. Sometimes the sighting was a false alarm and everyone went back to what he was doing.

But many times there were whales, and they were the kind the whalers intended to hunt. When this happened, as Weir recounts, the captain "sings out get the boats ready—then there is a confusion; each boat crew rushes to their respective boats, and assist the Boat steerers in preparing the boats for dropping."

Every boy's heart was pounding furiously by this time. They had had

Humpback Whale

OTHER COMMON NAMES: humpbacked whale, hump whale, hunchback whale

FAMILY: *Balaenopteridae*
SPECIES: *Megaptera novaeangliae*

The humpback whale doesn't really have a hump. It received its name because it arches its back and dorsal fin sharply when it dives, creating a high and very visible triangle. A much more accurate description can be found in its Latin genus name, for the Greek word *Megaptera* means "big wing." This refers to the humpback's exceptionally long flippers, which can measure nearly 17 feet in length.

orders barked at them before, but now there was a heightened urgency to the voices, a sense that everything was at stake and that time was running out. Before had been play; this was for real.

"I was the most excited and anxious boy in the world," George Fred Tilton recalled about his first whale. "I wanted to lower and get him and I don't suppose that anyone ever moved any faster than I did when we got the order to lower."

The humpback is probably the most energetic of all whales, and is well known for spectacular breaching, lobtailing, and flipper slapping. This, plus a rather peaceful and friendly personality, make it a favorite among whale watchers. Imagine how surprised some of these people would be to learn that this 30-ton creature is capable of using its flippers to smash in the skulls of attacking killer whales.

Humpbacks also sing, creating an intricate medley of moans, groans, bellows, wheezes, whines, and gurgles. No one knows how they make these sounds, or whether they constitute some kind of speech, but cetologists believe they are associated with mating, since they are sung exclusively in the whale's breeding grounds. These songs so intrigue humans that they have been made into two best selling recordings and even incorporated into popular and classical music.

Sadly, humpbacks were just as popular with whale hunters. Their relatively slow swimming speed, their habit of staying close to shore, and their natural curiosity made them easy targets. Whalers managed to kill over 100,000 of these giants, so that only 6,000 to 12,000 of them survive today.

BIRTH SIZE AND WEIGHT: 13¼ to 16½ feet, 2,000 to 4,000 pounds
ADULT SIZE AND WEIGHT: 40 to 50 feet, 50,000 to 60,000 pounds
SWIMMING SPEEDS: 3 to 9 mph cruising or migrating, 21 to 27 mph fleeing
GROUP SIZE: 1 to 3, with some groups of 15; larger groups can often be found in good feeding and breeding areas

The mate and harpooneer leaped into the whaleboat and it was lowered, with the crew scrambling down the lines after it. The harpooneer (also known as the boatsteerer) rowed the forward oar, while the five crew members took their assigned positions. The whaleboat was commanded, or "headed," by the mate, called the boatheader. He stood at the back of the boat to steer it, and was the only one who saw the whale as they approached it.

"A stroke or two of the oars were given to get clear of the ship," Bullen recalled, "then the oars were shipped and up went the sails. . . . The beautiful craft started off like some big bird. . . . The other boats were coming flying along behind us, spreading wider apart as they came."

"Off we go after the Captain's directions," an excited Weir recalled. "The whale is down now and we are about half a mile from the ship—presently we see a flag floating from the mainmast. The whales are up. We see them from the boat—off we put—again on them fast—get about three ship's length when they lift their flukes and sound again."

Every time the whales appeared, the boat's course was altered to head them off. Again and again this happened as the chase went on. If the whales were close by when initially sighted or if they were at rest, the chase might be over in the space of a half hour or so. Most chases took from one to three hours, with some lasting much longer.

Robert Weir's first real chase lasted "three, four, or more hours." And more often than not, all of the crew's work went for nothing. The whales would hear or see the approaching whaleboats and outmaneuver their hunters. After his long pursuit, Weir's boat had to give up: "We turn about and go on board disheartened—tired & disgusted—such is the sad history of the first whale we saw, chased & didn't get."

But many whaleboat crews—thousands of them every year—managed to get within striking distance of a whale. When they were close to the whale, the harpooneer would ship his oar and stand, his eleven-foot-long weapon raised to strike. All was still in the boat; no one moved or spoke.

Only the harpooneer and boatheader were facing the whale during these tense moments. The rest of the crew sat with backs to their prey, oars at the ready. Frank Bullen couldn't control his curiosity and stole a peek over his shoulder—and probably wished he hadn't. "His great black head, like the broad bow of a dumb barge, driving waves before it, loomed high and menacing to me."

Evidently, this whale had not heard or seen Bullen's whaleboat, because

A lot is going on at one time as the whaleboats from four ships pursue a shoal of sperm whales in 1833. Closest to the viewer, a harpooneer is about to drive a second harpoon into his whale; to his left, a mortally injured whale is being lanced; behind this whale, a whaleboat is being taken for a Nantucket sleighride; while at the right in the distance, two whaleboat crews strain to haul a dead whale back to their ship.

it did not sound. Then suddenly, when the mate thought they were as close as they could safely get, he yelled, "Give't to him, Louey, give't to him!" and the harpooneer struck.

"To see Louis raise his harpoon high above his head, and with a hoarse grunt of satisfaction plunge it into the black, shining mass beside him up to the hitches, was indeed a sight to be remembered. Quick as thought he snatched up a second harpoon, and as the whale rolled from us it flew from his hands, burying itself like the former one, but lower down the body."

When the boatheader was certain they were securely fastened on to the whale, he ordered the rowers to back the boat away from the creature. A whale in pain might roll and thrash around wildly, trying to dislodge the harpoons. Or it might slap its tail while sounding and accidentally crush a whaleboat and its crew. What happened depended on the type of whale struck and its temperament.

One boy, Bryce Anders, was surprised at how easy it was to kill a humpback whale. "We found [these] whales, so tame that we couldn't help getting them, and got four in the first three days that we cruised."

Other species, such as the sperm whale, were regarded with awe and respect because of their fighting ability. After putting the two harpoons into their sperm whale, Frank Bullen's boat backed away to a safe distance. "[The whale] made a fearful to-do over it, rolling completely over several times backward and forward, at the same time smiting the sea with its mighty tail, making an almost deafening noise and pother."

While the whale struggled to free itself, one of the stranger customs of the hunt took place. The harpooneer would leave his spot at the bow and make his way over legs, oars, and equipment to the stern to take charge of the tiller. Meanwhile the mate worked his way to the front to take up the lance. The harpoon's sole purpose was to wound the whale and allow the crew to attach a rope to it. The lance was a long, thin shaft of metal with a razor-edged head meant to be thrust into a vital organ of the whale to kill it. Because the boatheader outranked the harpooneer, he was usually given the honor of inflicting the fatal wound.

After five or ten minutes of furious thrashing, most whales sounded, hoping to escape their attackers. Bullen's whale dove, pulling the harpoon line after it. When the first tub of line was nearly gone, the line was tied to one in the second tub. Still, the whale kept diving, pulling out more and more line. Two other whaleboats came alongside Bullen's, and their lines were attached, along with drogues, square pieces of plank meant to slow the creature down. But still it kept diving. "So our friend was getting along somewhere below with 7,200 feet of 1½-inch rope."

Whalemen were clever hunters. Knowing that whales were very protective parents, they often harpooned a calf first and then waited for the mother to return to help her injured baby.

Eventually, the whale surfaced and the whaleboats moved closer. All but 600 feet of the line was cut off, and this short piece was tied to Bullen's boat. This was hardly done when "the whale started off to windward at tremendous rate," towing Bullen's boat behind it. Whalemen referred to this as a "Nantucket sleighride," though there was nothing fun about it, as Bullen made clear. "The speed at which he went made it appear as if a gale of wind was blowing, and we flew along the sea surface, leaping from crest to crest of the waves with an incessant succession of cracks like pistol-shots. The flying spray drenched us and prevented us from seeing him."

One crew member bailed water from the boat, while the others pulled on the rope, hoping to get closer to the whale. "Inch by inch we gained on him, encouraged by the hoarse objurgations of the mate, whose excitement was intense."

At this point, the whale could have sounded again and pulled the whaleboat with it. Enoch Cloud did witness such a moment. He was watching another whaleboat being towed by a struck whale when "suddenly—as quick as thought—boat, crew & whale vanished! A sickening feeling of horror oppressed me as I saw that the whale had taken the boat down with him (a frequent occurrence) and my heart almost sank as I thought of 6 brave messmates being so quickly hurried into eternity!"

Luckily for Bullen, his whale kept to the surface. "After what seemed a terribly long chase, we found his speed slackening, and we redoubled our efforts."

Soon they were next to the exhausted creature. Again the whaleboat edged close to the massive animal and the mate raised the lance high. "Now the mate hurls his quivering lance with such hearty good-will that every inch of its slender shaft disappears within the huge body."

The whale thrashed some more, spinning around to face its attackers, but the animal was tired and disoriented. The lance had done its job. Blood was now filling the animal's lungs and choking it. "As I looked he spouted, and the vapour was red with his blood." This was followed by the "flurry," the dying agony, of the great animal.

"Turning upon his side, he began to move in a circular direction, slowly at first, then faster and faster, until he was rushing round at tremendous speed, his great head raised quite out of the water at times, clashing his enormous jaws. Torrents of blood poured from his spout-hole, accompanied by hoarse bellowings . . . caused by the laboring breath trying to pass through the clogged air passages. . . . In a few minutes he subsided slowly in death, his mighty body reclined on one side, the fin uppermost waving limply as he rolled to the swell, while small waves broke gently over the carcass in a low, monotonous surf, intensifying the profound silence that had succeeded the tumult of our conflict with the late monarch of the deep."

The average person witnessing the harpooning and death of a whale would have been shocked and revolted by the blood and gore as well as the obvious suffering of the animal. There was nothing romantic about the event. Curiously, boys who wrote about the killing of a whale managed to distance themselves from the more unpleasant aspects by being coldly rational. The world needed the oil and baleen, they explained, and their job was to harvest it. When pressed about the issue, they would probably agree with Harty Bodfish's answer: "I felt no other emotion in lowering than the hunting instinct which I regard as a prominent part of the make-up of all normal men."

If these arguments failed to convince the listener, a whale hunter would fall back on various quotations from the Bible. A favorite scripture line came from Genesis 1:26: "And God said, 'Let us make man in our image, after our likeness: and let them have dominion over the fish of the sea, and over the fowl of the air, and over the cattle, and over all the earth, and over every creeping thing that creepeth upon the earth.'" Even in the face of a whale's great suffering, few westerners in the nineteenth century dared question that the word "dominion" gave humans the right to hunt any animal.

Not everyone on a whaler could maintain an unemotional stance after witnessing the death of a whale. Eliza Williams rarely saw a whale killed, because it usually happened far away from her husband's ship. Then one day a whale was harpooned only a hundred yards from where she stood on the deck. "I was astonished . . . to see how thick he threw the blood out of his spout holes. . . . The whale went down and stopped some minutes, and when he came up it seemed as if he threw the blood thicker than before. He came up near the boats and threw blood all in the boats and all over some of the men."

Eliza was so upset by the animal's suffering that her stomach began to grow queasy. "I did not like to look at the poor whale in his misery any longer and so came down below to write a few words about it."

Eliza could flee the sight, but the greenies could not. Many were so upset and nauseated by their first taste of blood that they resolved to abandon whaling just as soon as their voyage was over. After Enoch Cloud took part in the killing of a whale, he said, "It was the most terrible sight I ever witnessed. We pulled up to her—Capt. Vinall darted his lance—and 3 hearty cheers burst from the 4 boats as a stream of blood shot from her spout holes, full 30 feet in the air! I never knew before what it is to sail through a sea of blood! My feelings were now most peculiar! It is painful to witness the death of the smallest of God's created beings, much more, one in which life is so vigorously maintained as the Whale!"

There was no escape for Enoch or any of the others who might find the slaughter of whales upsetting. The great battle was over, but there was no time to rest. The crew rowed to the whale, hacked a hole in its tail, and secured a tow rope. Next, the oars were unshipped and the crew began the long, hard chore of towing their prize to the ship. When Frank Bullen's whale died, the whaleship was between three and four miles away.

Almost immediately, his whaleboat bumped into some "great masses of white, semi-transparent-looking substances . . . of huge size and irregular shape." Bullen took a boat hook and hauled in a chunk "as thick as a stout man's body" for inspection. When he asked the mate what it was, he was told that a dying whale always "ejected the contents of his stomach." They were floating in a rather large area of whale vomit!

Eventually, the whale was pulled next to the ship on the starboard side, flukes forward. A fluke chain was passed around the small section of the body, just forward of the tail, and secured; then the whaleboats were hoisted and made fast.

Everyone on deck, including the captain, would lean over the railing to view the dead whale. Using the 110-foot-long ship as a gauge, Bullen estimated the length of their whale as seventy feet. The experienced hands knew this whale would yield well over one hundred barrels of oil. No wonder, then, that the ship's captain, a man who had been as sullen and as cold as a rain cloud, appeared to cheer up. Bullen recalled that "the skipper's grim face actually looked almost pleased as he contemplated the colossal proportions of the latest additions to our stock."

The captain was so happy that he actually called a halt to work and sent the entire crew off to have dinner "with an intimation to look sharp over it." Though the tough task of killing the whale was over, even harder work had to be done before anyone could really rest.

Elton Cowen wanted to show how dangerous the sperm whale could be. Here a whaleboat has been overturned and the crew sent flying by the jaw snap of a harpooned sperm.

This line-drawing print makes the cutting-in process look extremely neat and tidy.

CHAPTER SIX
A Foot of Oil on Deck

The scrubbed decks and tidied ship becomes a floating charnel house. . . . [A] whale has tons of red flesh which oozes the scarlet fluid when dissected. The crew is not only oil-soaked but blood spattered. The men wade in blood.

Frances Diane Robotti, Whaling and Old Salem

THE MEAL WAS BOLTED DOWN and the weary crew assembled on deck for the next phase of work. Experienced hands had probably told the greenies about the "cutting in" and "trying out" processes, but a simple description, no matter how detailed, couldn't prepare anyone for what would take place. The ship they had scrubbed and polished so carefully would become an oily, bloody shambles; every man and boy would be a butcher.

First, the cutting stage was lowered. The cutting stage was nothing more than three long planks and a railing attached to wooden arms. The men leaned against the railing for balance and leverage while wielding their long cutting spades. Cutting in was considered such an important job that only the mates and sometimes even the captain did it.

Using their long spades, the cutters made a hole in the body just above one of the fins. A man jumped down onto the whale to insert the huge hook that would help tear off the blubber. Because the carcass was spattered with slippery blood and oil, this task was dangerous even on a calm sea. In rough seas, with the ship and whale bobbing about, the likelihood that this man would take an unwanted bath increased. Such a fall was more than simply embarrassing; it could prove fatal, since, as William Fish Williams observed, "Sharks . . . have a remarkably keen scent for blood as shown by the speed with which they will collect around a ship when cutting in a whale."

The hook chain was passed through a giant block and tackle attached to the masthead, and the crew was ordered to "heave away." Every muscle strained as the chain grew taut against the giant carcass that might weigh thirty, forty, or more tons. In Herman Melville's novel *Moby-Dick*, the narrator described what happened to the ship. "When instantly, the entire ship careens over on her side; every bolt in her starts like the nailheads of an old house in frosty weather; she trembles, quivers, and nods her frightened mastheads to the sky. More and more she leans over to the whale."

As the crew pulled on the chains, the cutters went to work, slicing through the skin and blubber behind the head. The whale would begin to roll over as the chain pulled at the flap of blubber. As a diagonal cut was made around the body, the whale continued to roll and the blubber continued to peel off in a long strip. Because blubber is wrapped around a whale body like a blanket, this sheet of skin and fat is called the blanket piece. When the blanket piece stretched up some twenty feet, another hole was made in the blubber still attached to the whale's body and a second hook inserted. Then a slice was made across the blubber above the second hook, freeing the first blanket piece. The long slab of blubber was lowered to the deck, where crewmen cut it into smaller and smaller pieces for boiling. Meanwhile, the cutters had already begun to tear off another blanket piece.

Drawings of the cutting-in process show the work as clean and orderly. In reality, the blanket piece dripped enough oil and blood to soak a man's clothes through. And the swaying mass of blubber weighed hundreds of pounds and could knock senseless anyone who inadvertently got in its way.

While the blubber was being cut off and prepared, the hatch to the try-works was removed to reveal two or three enormous metal try-pots. The

The truth is revealed in this photograph. The blanket piece is not so much sliced off the whale as ripped from its body.

tryworks were approximately ten feet by eight feet square and five feet high and made of brick and mortar. Between the fire and the deck, a basin called the goose pen was kept filled with water to prevent the intense heat from igniting the ship itself.

The thin slices of blubber, known as books or bibles, were tossed into a pot until it was filled to the top; then a wood fire was lit. As the pot heated, the blubber at the bottom sizzled and popped like bacon in a pan, shriveling up and forcing out its oil. The level of oil rose and continued boiling out oil in the pieces above.

After the blanket has been landed on deck, the men go to work cutting it into smaller and smaller pieces.

The deck of the Daisy is littered with bits and pieces of blubber, meat, and intestines. Blubber is being dumped belowdecks to be stored until it can be cooked.

A half hour or so later, most of the oil had been boiled out of the blubber, and cooked bible pieces began floating to the top of the pot. These pieces, called scraps, were golden brown and very crisp, and crew members often nibbled on small chunks as a snack. The rest of the scraps were saved and would eventually get tossed into the fire. Enough oil remained in them to produce a clear, fierce flame. The whale had been killed and butchered, and now it even provided the fuel to boil itself down.

The three try-pots of this ship are cooking away, black smoke rising into the air as a sign of a successful hunt.

Besides the blubber, other parts of the whale were commercially valuable. Three items were routinely harvested from the twenty-five-foot-long head of a sperm whale. The upper part of the head contains the case, a large cavity that holds up to 500 gallons of spermaceti. Spermaceti is an extremely high quality oil, and thus fetched a higher price than regular whale oil at market.

After describing how the head was severed from the body and hoisted clear of the water, William Fish Williams related how this precious oil was retrieved. "At first, [a] bucket was filled by pressing it into the case with a

The case of a small sperm whale has been cut from the jawbone and is being hauled up onto the deck.

A cut is made in the top of the case, and then a chain and tackle pull the oily flap back to open it.

pole but, finally, a man got into the case and filled the bucket as it was lowered to him from the deck."

On Frank Bullen's ship, the procedure was exactly the same, though a gusting wind complicated the work. Every time a full bucket was handed up, "the grease blew about, drenching most of us engaged in an altogether unpleasant fashion."

Robert Weir was so intrigued by the way oil was taken from a whale's case that he made this sketch of the scene. This case was large enough for two men to climb inside to bail the oil. To the right of center, a man has slipped and gotten an oily bath from his own bucket.

Below the case is an oil-rich substance called the junk. "Layer after layer, eight to ten inches thick, was sliced off, cut into suitable pieces, and passed into the tanks," Frank Bullen recalled. "So full was [the junk] of spermaceti that one could take a piece as large as one's head . . . and squeeze it like a sponge, expressing the spermaceti in showers, until nothing remained but a tiny ball of fibre."

Finally, the sperm whale's jaw was hacked off and lashed to a rail away from where the men were working. A typical jawbone may be twenty to twenty-five feet long and contains thirty-six teeth. Later, the teeth would be pulled out and stored for leisure time when the men would carve intricate designs on them called scrimshaw.

Right, bowhead, and humpback whales do not have a case or teeth in their heads. Their heads were valuable only because they contain baleen, which is often referred to as whalebone or simply bone. Baleen is a springy, elastic substance that had hundreds of uses before the steel spring and plastic were invented. Everything from horse whips to corset stays to the springs for sofas and carriages was fashioned out of it.

The lower jaw of a sperm whale has been parked on the deck of the whaler Costa Rica Packet *for later use.*

Sei Whale

OTHER COMMON NAMES: pollack whale,
coalfish whale, sardine whale,
Japan finner, Rudolph's rorqual

FAMILY: *Balaenopteridae*
SPECIES: *Balaenoptera borealis*

The sei (pronounced say) whale has a long, sleek body capable of reaching a speed of 40 miles per hour when alarmed. Because of its great speed, early whalers rarely bothered to hunt this species, and the population grew to over 200,000.

Sei whales can be found worldwide in deep, temperate waters, where they skim the surface for krill, copepods, small squid, sardines, cod, and herring, then strain water through a sieve of 300 to 410 fine baleen plates. They do not dive very deeply,

Harty Bodfish was so impressed by the quantity of baleen in a bowhead that he made a detailed report in his journal. "There are 780 slabs of bone in each mouth, secured to the skull by muscle two or three inches thick. . . . The size of these slabs is from six inches in length to twelve and a half feet, the longest slab being midway of the jaw, growing shorter both ways, so that the very shortest are next to the throat and at the tip-end, or chin."

Harty went on to describe how the head was chopped from the body and hauled on deck, where "the men go around it clearing away the blubber and cutting the muscle that holds the bone. Continuous strain on the tackles lifts rarely below a few feet, so that they can be followed by "fluke prints," swirls left by the beat of a tail just below the surface.

There are two distinct groups of seis, one in the northern hemisphere, the other in the southern hemisphere. Northern seis grow to a maximum of around 59 feet and weigh over 20 tons, while their southern cousins can reach 70 feet and weigh 30 tons or more.

Seis are the only whales that exhibit an often irregular migratory pattern. They do follow the normal pattern of going to colder water in summer, warmer water in winter, but from time to time large schools will suddenly appear in unexpected locations. Unfortunately, they were regular enough in their visits to Antarctica to offer a prime target to whalers after the steam chaser was developed. Today their population is estimated to be between 40,000 and 60,000.

BIRTH SIZE AND WEIGHT: 14½ to 15¼ feet, 1,600 pounds
ADULT SIZE AND WEIGHT: 59 to 70 feet, 40,000 to 60,000 pounds
SWIMMING SPEEDS: 3 to 22 mph cruising or migrating, 36 to 40 mph fleeing
GROUP SIZE: 2 to 5; groups of up to 50 can be found at good feeding grounds

the head, and when the [baleen] is clear, it will fall to the deck spread out flat. . . . After this is done, the skull is hove overboard and the men knock the 'oysters' or muscles and gum fragments from the slabs of bone with heads of axes. Then it is bundled up, four or five slabs in a bundle, and stowed below or on deck wherever it is convenient. Later it must be washed and scraped to remove all the gum."

As an historical sidelight, Harty added that "the bark *Northern Light* took one [bowhead] that produced 3181 pounds of bone after it was washed and dried." Around when Harty first sailed, the price of bone was at $1.96 per pound, which meant the baleen alone brought in over $6,200.

The final product from a whale—and the most valuable—was ambergris. Sperm whales are the only whales to produce ambergris, which was used in perfumes to intensify and preserve for long periods of time any odor that was combined with it. This waxy, nearly odorless substance was so rare that the price per pound often reached several hundred dollars, depending on the supply. One whaler, the *Splendid*, took 983 pounds of it from a single whale and then disposed of it for $125,000.

A perfume user might know that an exotic-sounding substance called ambergris was in the perfume, but few knew what it really was or where in the whale it was produced. "It is of a scabious nature," Clifford Ashley explained, "and results from a squid's beak having punctured the wall of the intestine. Nature forms a cicatrix about this beak in an effort to throw it off. Eventually this either passes naturally out of the whale's system, or it clogs up the passage and the whale dies."

A sperm whale carrying ambergris usually excreted it while struggling to break free of a harpoon. The crew of the whaleboat would then scoop up the floating chunks while waiting for their ship to arrive. If a dead whale was found floating in the water, or if a whale appeared sick, the cutters would slice along the length of the intestines in search of this valuable substance.

The cutting in and trying out of a big whale took about three days, with work going on around the clock in six-hour shifts. Half the ship's crew worked while the other half rested or ate. All the while, a sullen, dark smoke curled from the tryworks, staining the sails and blackening the masts and decks with a coat of dark grease. The stench of cooking blubber stuck in the men's nostrils and permeated food, bedding, and water.

At night, the light from the blazing ovens glowed a lurid yellow-orange, visible for miles to passing ships. The cutting, chopping, mincing, and boiling of blubber never stopped for a moment.

The mates constantly monitored the work of the less-experienced hands, barking out orders for them to look lively or to be careful of spilling the precious oil. Still, the thoughts of a bone-weary greenie often wandered. Some thought of the warm, cozy homes they had left behind or simply longed to be clean and asleep. George Fred Tilton spent most of these hours recalling how scared he had been when he'd gotten close to his live whale. "Well, we got our whale, cut him in, tried him out, and stowed the oil below, but I hadn't got over my scare enough to learn just how it was done."

There were even some moments of humor. Frank Bullen was amazed at how much oil dripped from the blanket pieces or was spilled. "There was nearly a foot of oil on deck in the waist, and uproarious was the laughter when some hapless individual . . . slid across the deck and sat down with a loud splash in the deepest accumulation."

Eventually, the work would be completed. The days when every bit of a whale had a use were long gone. Only the oil, baleen or teeth, and ambergris were harvested. A few hundred pounds of whale meat might be sent to the cook for food, but most of the whale was considered useless.

The head and any stray chunks of meat or bone were tossed overboard. The order would be given to "Haul in the chains! Let the carcass go astern!"

The peeled white body of the headless whale slowly floated away from the ship. The water all around it bubbled angrily as the sharks rushed in to tear and rip their way into the cavity, and a slick of blood and oil stained the ocean. Screeching sea vultures circled the great mass, then dove to pick at the flesh and bones that bobbed above water. The scene of the burial was visible for a very long time—hours if the sea was calm.

No one on board had time to watch the whale being devoured. More important work had to be done. Lookouts went aloft again to search the sea for more whales. The ship had to be scrubbed clean and made ready for the next whale, and the men had to clean themselves and their clothes.

If he was lucky, a boy would get several days to rest and regain his strength. If he was really lucky, another whale would be spotted instantly, taken, and the entire messy procedure of trying out would be done again. For by this time he realized how many whales it would take to fill the ship's

Trying out a whale did not stop until the last drop of oil went into a cask. The fires of this ship's tryworks cast a smoky glow as the crew worked in shifts throughout the night to cut up and boil its latest victim.

belly full of oil and baleen—and the ship would not head home until that had been accomplished.

As for the whale, or what was left of it, the sharks' feeding frenzy went on until bones and internal organs were devoured or sank into the dark waters. Three days before, the whale had been a powerful, thinking creature swimming to its feeding grounds. Now its pieces were food for the scavengers that inhabit the ooze on the ocean's floor.

Whenever whales were hard to find, whalers found something else to hunt and sell, such as seals or elephant seals. One shore gang from the Neptune managed to kill 33,340 seals during a five-month stay on one island.

CHAPTER SEVEN
A Strange Uneven Sort of Life

*Home sweet home, and those we have left behind us are con-
stantly in our minds. Little do those on shore know a sailor's
feelings, separated from all that they hold dear on earth, with
almost a certainty of being apart for three or four long years—
enough to make a man's hair grow grey at the thought of it.*

Log entry by Captain Charles Starbuck
of the ship Peru, *1851*

THE STORY OF WHALE HUNTING was one of constant searching and exploration. When ships sailed, they followed very precise routes that brought them to established whale grounds. The voyage Enoch Cloud took was fairly typical.

His ship left New Bedford in the middle of August 1851 and headed toward the Azores, islands off the coast of Portugal. They lowered to chase a few whales along the way but had no luck. But the voyage was young, and as they sailed along the coast of Africa in September, Enoch could still be excited by "the thrilling cry of 'there-re-re, she blows!'" These chases resulted in sore muscles, but no whales, so Enoch's ship sailed to Brazil, then headed south down the South American coast and around Cape Horn.

Once in the Pacific, they managed to kill their first whale on December 5. Despite taking a large sperm whale in early February 1852, the prospects of filling the hold were slim and a new course was set. "Capt. Vinall has determined to proceed to the Japan Sea," Enoch said matter-of-factly on February 13; "if we do not fall in with whales there we will proceed to the Okhotsk; & if unsuccessful there, we will go on to the Arctic."

Such trips covered thousands and thousands of miles, and often meant that ships entered unfamiliar waters. Along the way, captains and officers were careful to enter in the ship's log book the exact location of every island, barrier reef, or sandbar they came across. When the whaleship *Maria* spotted land one night, Captain George Gardner made this log entry:

Sunday, December 19, 1824. At 4:30 P.M., saw low land to the SE [southeast] 3 leagues; tacked ship to the ENE [east northeast] at midnight stood to SSW; at 8 A.M. saw land again. It appears to be a small island. . . . Very low. Lat. 21—45 South, Long. 155—10 west.

These very precise entries meant a ship could revisit an island in the future to get water or provisions; it also meant it could avoid a dangerous coast during a stormy night. American whaleships mapped the remotest areas of the world's oceans so thoroughly and accurately that American aviators used these charts during World War II.

This wide-ranging quest for the elusive whales had another consequence as well. Many weeks, even months, slid by when no whales were sighted. Some sailors probably began to wonder if whales had disappeared for good (and in some cases this was, sadly, true). Up in the yardarms, the lookouts scanned an endless expanse of glittering water and tried not to nod off.

Frank Bullen's ship had gone only four weeks without spotting a whale, and he was already weary with boredom. Then the wind died and his ship sat for several days, bobbing up and down listlessly. "Except to a few whose minds to them are kingdoms, and others who can hardly be said to have any minds at all, the long monotony of unsuccessful seeking for whales is very wearying. . . . Some of the crew must become idiotic, or, in sheer rage at want of interest in their lives, commit mutiny."

The officers did their best to keep their crews alert and sane. Boat drills were run, harpoons and lances sharpened, boats repaired, canvas sails mended, the decks scrubbed clean. And when all these big and small chores had been completed, they were done over again.

There wasn't much to do in the cramped, airless forecastle. Smoking, resting, and roughhousing were a few ways to pass off-duty time.

When a sailor was not on watch, however, his time was his own, and he had to fill it up any way possible. This was before the invention of radio, television, or portable disc and cassette players. Nor did a whaler have a gym, a comfortable lounge, a library, or any other area specifically designed to help a sailor relax or work off pent-up energy.

Most free time was spent belowdecks in the forecastle sleeping, eating, smoking, playing cards, or cleaning and mending clothing. Since many captains did not allow sailors on deck unless they were on watch, the forecastle, a tiny space to begin with, must have come to seem like the tiniest of prison cells.

Sailors did everything possible to distract themselves. Those who had some education might haul out a book, a magazine, or the most recent news-paper available (which could be several months old). Because each sailor's storage space was limited to a single sea chest, he had room for only two or three books and a few magazines or newspapers, in addition to clothes, shoes, and other personal items. Reading matter was passed from sailor to sailor until it became tattered and fell apart.

Keeping a diary or journal was another free-time activity, especially for greenies. Peleg Folger had just turned eighteen when his ship, the *Grumpus*, left Nantucket in 1751. Peleg began a journal, one he would maintain for nearly nine years, which begins on a rather pompous note: "Most People who keep Journals at Sea fill them up with some trifles or other. My part I purpose in the following sheets, not to keep overstrick history of every tri-fling occurrence that happens, only now and then of Some particular affair; and to fill up the rest with subjects either mathematical, theological, Historical, Philosophical, or poetical, or anything else that best suits my incli-nation. P.F."

Fortunately, Peleg did not hold fast to his rules, and proceeded to detail the life and work of a typical whaleman. During the first days and weeks, when everything about the ship and shipboard life was new, he spent hours scribbling down the many details of the strange world he had entered—everything from standing watch to the taking and trying out of the first few whales was covered in long, excited passages. After several months had passed, the novelty wore thin and the entries usually grew shorter and less descriptive: "Nothing remarkable these 24 hours only 'tis very hot and no whales to be seen." Then again, "Nothing Remarkable this Day—only here we are in lat't 39—0', all alone by ourselves. . . . No whales nor no Whalemen to be seen—what a Strange uneven sort of life a man lives!"

Letter writing was another common activity. A letter allowed a sailor to "talk" directly to those at home, to recall their faces and personalities, and to reminisce about pleasant times from the past. It gave him an opportunity to discuss his experiences and adventures or to complain about the hard work, food, or fellow crew members. Others talked about their loneliness and expressed love for those at home.

Sailors who did not know how to write usually found someone—such as Enoch Carter Cloud or William Fish Williams—with schooling enough to put their thoughts down on paper. And a sailor might write three or five or ten letters to the same people at home while waiting for his ship to reach a port where he could post them to the United States.

Receiving a letter was one of the greatest joys a sailor could experience. A letter was a physical link to home and family. It provided news about parents, relatives, friends, and town, told the sailor that people still cared for him and were waiting for his return. Sailors read their letters over and over, stored them away, and read them again weeks and months after receiving them.

But getting letters was not a common occurrence. Friends and relatives on land had to send their letters to the ship's scheduled ports of call. If the ship followed its planned course exactly, there was a chance—and only a chance—a sailor would find one or more letters waiting for him a month or two later. Since ships changed course frequently to pursue elusive whales, the likelihood of this happening was rare. One wife remembered sending her husband over one hundred letters during his three-year voyage. He received just six of them.

The crushing pain of not getting a letter is evident in Enoch Cloud's journal entry for October 20, 1852. He had been at sea fourteen long months when his ship anchored to take on supplies and pick up accumulated mail. "No letters for me!!!" he moaned. "One, and another of the crew receive their letter & the kindling eye & heaving breast betoken good news from friends at home!! But for me, no information from those most dear to me comes, and I feel myself, emphatically alone!!"

The ship must have seemed especially tiny to Enoch just then. Everywhere he turned, shipmates read their letters or shared news about home with those nearby. "Listen to this," one would blurt out excitedly, then

Blue Whale

OTHER COMMON NAMES: sulfur-bottom,
Sibbald's rorqual, great northern rorqual

FAMILY: *Balaenopteridae*
SPECIES: *Balaenoptera musculus*

Blue whales are the giants of the
whale family. Two centuries ago, it was
common for adult blues to attain a length of
100 feet and weigh 150 tons. This makes
them the largest creature to have ever lived
on earth, bigger than even the biggest dinosaurs! Today, because of overhunting,
most blues are smaller on average, measuring between 75 and 82 feet and weighing
100 to 120 tons.

proceed to read a passage about a family member's humorous exploit.
Enoch was able to escape to his journal, where he unleashed his emotions.
Other sailors could only curl up in their bunks and try to fall asleep, all the
while wondering if anyone at home still cared about them.

Physically, there was even less a sailor could do aboard ship. A wrestling
match might provide some distraction, but because these often turned into
full-fledged brawls, they were generally discouraged by the officers. Another
curious sport was referred to as "a scramble for the salt junk." The cook
would place a bucket of cooked whale meat on deck while most of the crew

This bluish-gray whale has a gentle and shy disposition and likes to travel alone or in small groups. In the summer, a blue whale can consume 1 to 4 tons of krill per day, preparing for the time it is forced to head south by colder weather. It is a leisurely swimmer but can attain a speed of 30 miles per hour when chased. While adults rarely breach clear of the water, a blue can be spotted from miles away by its spectacular spout. A blue can send a spout 20 to 40 feet into the air in a thin, vertical column.

As the steam and then diesel chaser became faster, blues became a favorite target for whalers. The population of 225,000 in the southern hemisphere, for instance, was reduced to a mere 200 to 400 individuals by the time its hunting was outlawed in 1966. Since it is impossible to get an accurate count of such a wide-ranging animal, the estimates of the present population worldwide vary from a generous 6,000 to a pessimistic 1,000. What is clear is that there may be so few blue whales alive that they may travel the same route as the dinosaurs in our lifetimes—into extinction.

BIRTH SIZE AND WEIGHT: 23 feet, 5,000 pounds
ADULT SIZE AND WEIGHT: 75 to 82 feet, 200,000 to 240,000 pounds
SWIMMING SPEEDS: 3 to 20 mph cruising or migrating, 24 to 30 mph fleeing
GROUP SIZE: 1 to 2; sometimes larger gatherings at feeding grounds

was below in the forecastle. Then he would shout, "Meat! Fall to," and the crew—always eager for something to eat—battled to see who could get the biggest pieces.

Most sailors chose less physical but more involved hobbies to kill time. Clifford Ashley remembered that "another fruitful field of interest was ornamental knot-work, a handicraft at which the whaleman excelled. He made elaborate beckets for his sea-chest and lanyards for his clothes-bags. At his officers' behest, he fashioned deck-fittings for the ship, bell ropes, fringes for line-tub covers, man-ropes and decorative draw-buckets."

Twelve crew members jockey and wrestle for a treat of cooked whale-meat chunks.

And despite their harsh work and living conditions, whalemen are best remembered for a hobby that is amazingly detailed and delicate: the art of scrimshaw. Whalemen were able to take the teeth of whales, pieces of bone, scraps of wood, tortoiseshell, and virtually any other fragments of material they could find and carve them into a variety of useful or ornamental items. They are most noted for the intricate designs and scenes etched into a whale's tooth, but their art went far beyond this. They could fashion water dippers, forks and spoons, rolling pins, pie crimps, walking canes, boxes, and mortars and pestles.

These objects were meant to be gifts to friends or loved ones, so sailors often carved in some sort of sentiment. One man fashioned a busk, or stay, for his girlfriend that would be used for a support in her corset, then added this verse to it:

> In many a gale,
> Has been the Whale,
>> In which this bone did rest,
> His time is past,
> His bone at last
>> Must now support thy brest.

Without doubt scrimshaw was the most widely practiced hobby among whalemen. "It is recorded," Clifford Ashley added, "that on some ships every man from the captain down to the cabin-boy had some article of Scrimshaw under way, and it once was a fiercely debated point among New Bedford

Extracting Ivory

Before any scrimshawing could be done, the teeth (ivory) had to be removed from the jaw. Robert Weir's drawing shows how the teeth and gums were ripped from the jawbone. After this, all flesh was cut from the teeth.

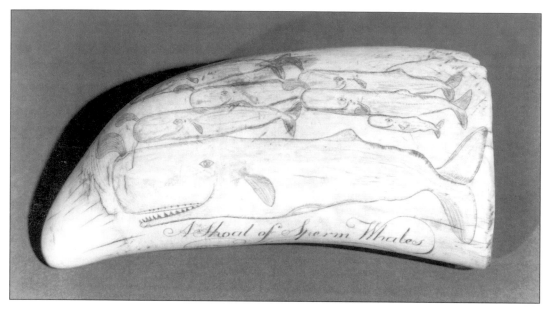

A typical piece of scrimshaw, this one depicting a shoal of smiling sperm whales.

owners whether the engrossing interest of the whalemen in their Scrimshaw was not seriously detrimental to the success of the voyages. It was even alleged that on occasion men had sighted whales, and rather than be interrupted at some particularly fascinating point in the practice of their Art, had failed to announce them! Certain captains forbade Scrimshaw altogether; on some ships its practice was limited to the forecastle, and the man who brought his work on deck was liable to have it confiscated."

The one thing certain to stop even the most avid scrimshawer was sighting another whaleship. With very few exceptions, the two ships would alter course in order to meet, then sail along side by side. When such a meeting happened, the ships were said to "speak" to each other, and sailors' journals and logs are filled with such encounters. In fact, it was considered downright rude to *not* speak to another ship. Peleg Folger was absolutely incensed when he observed: "In the morning we Spyed a Sail and Drew up with her but the Clown would not Speak with us. Steering off about SE."

Such unfriendliness was rare among whalers, and it was common to see ships bobbing along side by side, while the captains called to each other through speaking horns. During these conversations, they told each other how long they had been at sea, how much oil or bone they had taken, and even the location of whale herds. News from home was shared, everything from who the new president of the United States was to a bit of gossip about a fellow captain. Sailors would gather at the rails to drink in these bits of information, sometimes shouting out juicy details their captain might have forgotten.

Very often, such encounters would turn into actual visits between members of the ships. Such socializing was called a "gam" and was a unique feature of the whaling industry. Unlike merchant ships, whalers were not on tight schedules, and if there were no whales in the area, there was no need to rush off. A gam might last a day, a week, or even longer.

During the gam, the captain and as many as half a watch would leave one ship and row across to the other. At the same time, the other ship's first mate and an equal number of its men would also pay a visit. In this way, if whales were spotted, neither ship would have an advantage in the number of men available to hunt. To avoid a mad and potentially dangerous race to a whale, captains often came to a peaceful arrangement.

"When whales were sighted," Clifford Ashley recalled, "they were frequently hunted in common, in which case the ships were said to be 'mating.' The amount of the catch was equally credited between the two ships."

Joining forces for a hunt was not the purpose of gamming, and Ashley was quick to add: "As the gam continued, other groups of men were transferred, until every hand of the two ships had the benefits of a change of scene and a change of cookery, and met all the men on the other ship."

The men and boys swapped stories about their various encounters and near escapes with whales, talked about home, traded tobacco for pieces of scrimshaw, soap, needle and thread, or whatever item might be needed. A gam was also a good time to exchange twice- and thrice-read books and mag-

Two whaleships bob in the rolling sea as a whaleboat crew heads off for a gam.

azines. If one ship had a large supply of fresh vegetables, fruit, or fresh water, a sale could be arranged, using either cash or casks of oil for payment.

When the gam was over and all the men were back aboard, the ships would part and each head off in its own direction. As for the sailors, they "generally had an opportunity to readjust [their] viewpoint," Ashley concluded. "It made a break, and the men were left more contented."

Peleg Folger's recollection of one particular gam is brief but gives a clear sense of how his spirits had been raised. "We had a good breakfast upon meat and Doboys [biscuits] & we are all merry together."

The only other nonhunting event that might rival a gam in excitement would be a chance to take shore leave. Generally, a captain scheduled a port stop every two months or so. This was not out of kindness to the crew. He stopped to take on fresh water, meat, fruit, and vegetables. He might, if he felt the cruise was going well, allow some or all of the crew to step on dry land.

Here then was one of the reasons many boys had signed on for a whaling cruise—to see exotic places and people. Judging from the lengthy descriptions of many of these places, boys on whaling ships took every advantage of exploring the islands they were lucky enough to visit. William Fish Williams began his description of one of the Caroline Islands in the Pacific by citing its exact location: "The island of Ponape is in Latitude 6:45 North and Longitude 158:15 East."

William's tone changed, became more excited and delighted, as his whaleship approached the island. "As we passed out of the intense blue of the deep water, the bottom was suddenly so clear and distinct that it did not seem there was depth enough to float the ship, but it was probably fifty feet deep. We turned to the south and ran parallel to the shore as we approached. . . . We passed a few native houses on our way to the anchorage, low thatched structures near the shore, and numerous coconut trees with a dense background of foliage including many large trees. It was a beautiful prospect, intensely green and cool-looking."

William's discussion of his visit continues for another 4,000 words, in which he talks excitedly about the many types of plants and trees found on the island, the nature of the volcanic soil, the dimensions of a series of ancient ruins, and even an unusual native drink: "The Kanaka makes a concoction from the kava root . . . which produces a physical effect that would seem to be partly narcotic and the drinker's legs get badly tangled while his brain remains fairly clear. In the day of my experience, the liquor was produced by old women masticating the root and expectorating the juice into a coconut shell or a calabash. After fermenting sufficiently, the clear liquor was decanted into another vessel which was then passed around the gathering with the highest in authority drinking first."

The overwhelmingly positive feelings expressed for the landscape and many new experiences encountered on these islands usually did not extend to the local people. The prejudices that shaped these boys' views of fellow crew members was extended to include anyone with different skin color or lifestyle.

Generally, the stereotyping took two forms. If the local people were not happy to see the whalers or did not rush to help or trade with them, they were viewed as hostile and potentially violent. Make no mistake about it, some islanders viewed all sailors as invaders and did attack them when possible. And a number of island cultures practiced ritualistic cannibalism (much as prehistoric Europeans did). The rumors that various islands were home to man-eating tribes were out of all proportion to the actual situation but still managed to be passed from ship to ship as fact. The result was that whalemen never fully trusted these people, as an encounter Enoch Cloud had demonstrates.

One day, Enoch and some shipmates were strolling through an island forest when they came upon "a gang of Natives" trying to get some sleep near a small fire. The startled sleepers jumped to their feet, obviously annoyed by the intrusion. Instead of taking some blame for the situation, Enoch interpreted their glares as meaning something else: "Some of them," he said, "looked as though they were 'hungry!'"

Natives who were friendly and helpful were usually described as childlike and primitive. Of the people he encountered on Ponape, William Fish Williams said, "The present Kanaka of these islands is not the immediate descendant of a highly developed and vigorous race. He is the product of conditions that do not make such qualities and is just what one might expect of any people who never had to struggle for anything essential to life. . . . The Kanaka is soft and indolent."

While attacks by the inhabitants of Pacific islands were rare, the reporting and illustrating of them was frequent and usually very lurid.

Like most Americans in the nineteenth century, William could not understand why these people had not built brick or wood houses, why they did not wear western-style clothes, or why they weren't hustling off to work every day. And why hadn't they taken their abundant natural resources and turned them into successful, profit-making businesses? Such failures, for that is how they were viewed, were considered a sure sign of moral weakness and mental inferiority.

His attitudes, of course, flowed directly from those around him, those of his parents, fellow crew members, ministers—in short, anyone who spoke with authority. The Reverend J. G. Wood, for example, stated emphatically in his discussion of human beings that the Caucasian race is "considered the most beautiful specimen of the human form. From this race all ancient and modern civilized nations are descended and they have always been distinguished for superior intellectual and moral qualities." Reverend Wood then went on to find inferior every other ethnic group in the world. In describing the islanders encountered by whaling men, he even managed to condemn two groups of people in one sentence. They are, he stated, "as crafty and fierce on the waters as the American Indians in their woods."

Such racist statements went unchallenged for the most part back then, so the majority of boys rarely questioned their validity. These beliefs clouded their view of everyone they considered "different." William Fish Williams was a remarkably kind-spirited boy, and genuinely liked most of the native people he met. Still, he wasn't able to express a compliment without revealing his own prejudices. "The Kanakas were a good-natured, likeable people for all of their weaknesses."

Eventually, the gam or shore leave would end, and a boy would find himself on board again looking at the same faces, reading the same books and letters. The only thing left for the sailors to do was talk. And they talked a lot! "It doesn't cost a penny to talk," a young sailor named Gerald wrote home, "so there are always two or more of the men in earnest discussion on some topic, serious and silly. When no one is inclined to talk, then Isaac is willing to carry on a perfectly civilized discussion with himself."

Sailors discussed whales and whaling every day. They talked about the sizes of whales and which kind contained the most oil. They compared the habits and personalities of various whales, told tales about the meanest one they had ever encountered, speculated on the origins of the mysterious substance ambergris, argued about the best hunting grounds or how long a whale could stay underwater. Even the tiniest detail about whales or hunting them—such as the best shape for a harpoon iron—could be cause for a lengthy and heated debate.

Many of the "facts" cited in these discussions were the product of guess-

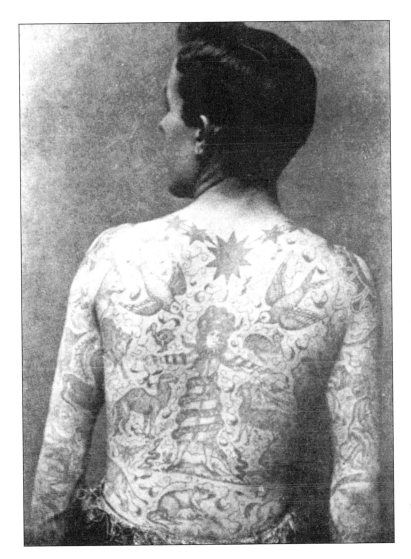

Shore leave was often a time when boys experimented with new things, among them drinking alcoholic beverages and getting tattoos. This boy has had his body transformed into a field of exotic animals, birds, and snakes.

work and imagination, but delivered with the passion and authority of an expert. "This is the Gospel truth," George Fred Tilton declared. "Hardly any whaler . . . can tell you anything very definite about [whales]. They handled them like a stevedore handles freight on a dock. . . . All the stevedore knows is that he has to rassel [the whales] that are dirty and cussed heavy."

Whether the stories were accurate or not, boys loved hearing the older men tell them. To be included in a storytelling session made the boys feel grown up and a part of a special club. Some boys would go to any length to hear these stories.

When William Fish Williams was still a little boy and living in his parents' quarters, he violated his father's direct order to stay clear of the forecastle. Instead, William would stroll casually along the deck and, when his father was distracted by some ship duty, the boy would dart down the steps to the forecastle. He wanted to learn the secrets of whales and whale hunting, but was often frustrated because "the few real sailors [on board] were interesting as they had experiences worth listening to but they would talk only when in the mood."

William probably didn't realize it, but his complaining was also a time-honored tradition among whalers. Complaining was an activity that most sailors perfected to a fine art. And everything came in for criticism—a shipmate's loud snoring, the harshness of the discipline or the lack of it, the sameness of the work. Some sailors seemed to focus their displeasure on one person or situation. Enoch Cloud was constantly complaining about his captain because he allowed Sunday to be violated by lowering for whales.

By far, the item that came in for the most criticism was the food. Ships almost always started off with fairly decent provisions—casks of beef, flour, rice, pork hams, preserved mackerel, coffee, bread, and even chocolate. However, several months of ocean sailing usually produced stale, wet, mildewing food, and a torrent of complaints.

"The beef was saltier than Lot's wife, and had to be soaked . . . overnight before it could be cooked," grumped Harty Bodfish. "Saltpetre would eat all the fat off it, and it was pretty tough eating. . . . The coffee was called 'bootleg'—I suppose it was made from old boots parched and ground. It came in four and five pound packages that smelled musty before they were ever opened. The tea looked as if it had been used, dried out and rolled up again, and where they got the molasses from, God only knows! It was the poorest to be found, black and sour, and mixed with salt water besides, to make it go further. That is what we had to sweeten our tea and coffee with."

Whether a whaleman was talking about the whales, complaining about the food, writing letters, reading, or working on some intricate piece of scrimshaw, the purpose of each was all the same: to distract him from the fact that he was trapped on a ship thousands of miles from home.

Back on watch, the men and boys would be refreshed but edgy. They'd scan the surface of the water for the telltale signs of whales, but it was no longer an exciting game. "Where are the whales?" a young whaleman wondered, almost trying to will them to appear. He knew that the ship would head for home only when it was filled with whale oil or bone. "Where are the whales?"

A slap of a sperm whale's tail has split this whaleboat in two and catapulted its crew into the water.

CHAPTER EIGHT
We Have Been Stove by a Whale

The Cachalot [sperm whale] is not only better armed than the True Whale [right whale] in possessing a formidable weapon at either extremity of its body, but also more frequently displays a disposition to employ these weapons offensively, and in a manner at once so artful, bold and mischievous, as to lead to its being regarded as the most dangerous to attack of all known species of the whale tribe.

Frederick Debell Bennett, Narrative of a Whaling Voyage
Around the Globe from the Year 1833 to 1836

IT WAS JUST AFTER BREAKFAST on a clear, calm day when the lookouts on Frank Bullen's ship sighted sperm whales, and the whaleboats set off. "Our prospective victim . . . was, in his leisurely enjoyment of life, calmly lolling on the surface, occasionally lifting his enormous tail out of the water and letting it fall flat upon the surface with a boom audible for miles."

The whale had no idea they were closing in on it. If anything, its slapping the water was actually helping cover any noise the men might make.

The harpooneer from another boat struck first, while Frank's approached from the other side. The whale struggled to rid itself of the initial harpoon, churning the water into yeasty foam, but Frank still felt "the proceedings were quite of the usual character." As if resigned to its fate, the whale stopped thrashing and sat still on the water's surface. Frank's boat moved in closer.

The first mate raised his arm high, lance ready, when the animal's tail flukes lifted from the water. "Before I had time to think, the mighty mass of gristle lept into the sunshine, curved back from us like a huge bow. Then with a roar [the tail] came at us from its tension of Heaven knows how many tons. Full on the broadside it struck us, sending every soul but me flying out of the wreckage as if fired from catapults. I did not go because my foot was jammed somehow in the [bottom] of the boat."

Frank struggled to free his injured foot, which he managed to do after a few moments. When he was finally clear of the wreckage and was able to look around, he discovered something horrifying. "Towering above me, came the colossal head of the great creature, as he ploughed through the bundle of debris that had just been a boat. There was an appalling roar of water in my ears, and darkness that might be felt all around. Yet, in the midst of it all, one thought predominated as clearly as if I had been turning it over in my mind in the quiet of my bunk aboard—'what if he should swallow me?'"

The next few minutes were a nightmarish blur to Frank—him flailing wildly to get out of the whale's path, the water sucking him under deeper and deeper, his lungs beginning to burn from lack of oxygen. Then "just as something was going to snap inside my head I rose to the surface. I was surrounded by a welter of bloody froth, which made it impossible for me to see; but, oh, the air was sweet!"

Frank survived, not just to hunt another day, but to write about it. Many other sailors were not so lucky. Peleg Folger recalled in graphic detail one chilling encounter with an angry whale. After putting four harpoons into the whale "she gave a flank and went down & coming up again she bolted her head out of the water . . . and then pitched the whole weight of her head on the Boat—stove ye boat & ruined her and killed the midshipman (an Indian named Sam Lamson) outwright a Sad & Awful Providence."

Such a sad and awful providence befell scores of sailors each year. Just about every ship returned to port with one or two such incidents to report. Early on in his voyage, Enoch Cloud seemed acutely aware of the precarious nature of life at sea. "I was thinking this morning of all the dangers incident

The thought of dying at sea troubled many boys, especially since they were thousands of miles from their families. This drawing from a nineteenth-century sea novel portrays this feeling in a melodramatic way: Utterly alone except for some passing sea birds, this boy awaits his fate.

to a whaleman and curiosity led me to sum them up. 22 forms of death (and those of the worst form) constantly stare me in the face!"

Sailors died from many causes other than whales—food poisoning, illness, shipboard accidents, fighting, infected wounds. And since most of the sick and injured had to rely on the "doctoring" of the captain or a bunkmate, the medical attention itself could prove fatal.

Whalemen rarely lingered long on the less dramatic dangers of their profession. Talk almost always focused on the whale that nearly killed them or that took the life of a friend. One amazing incident in particular seemed to haunt sailors more than most and was often cited when the talk turned to the harshness of their profession. This was the story of the whaleship *Essex*.

The *Essex* was in the Pacific on November 20, 1820, and only a few casks shy of a full cargo. That morning, a herd of sperm whales was spotted and the boats lowered.

During the hunt, first mate Owen Chase's boat was struck by a whale's tail and severely damaged. Chase stuffed four jackets into the hole to stem the water, then hurried back to the ship to make repairs.

A half hour later, he and the others of his boat were on deck of the *Essex* hammering boards over the hole when a large whale surfaced three hundred feet away. "His appearance and attitude gave us at first no alarm," Chase recalled.

Suddenly, the eighty-five-foot-long whale shot forward at ramming speed. Chase shouted out orders to turn the ship to avoid the collision, but "the words were scarcely out of my mouth, before he . . . struck the ship with his head, just forward of the fore-chains; he gave us such an appalling and tremendous jar, as nearly threw us all on our faces."

The whale continued under the ship and swam off some distance. Meanwhile, the bow of the ship was gradually settling down in the water. "I of course concluded that he had stove a hole in the ship, and that it would be necessary to set the pumps going." Chase also had a signal flag hoisted to get the other two whaleboats back to the ship as quickly as possible.

It was at that moment a man on deck screamed a warning that would freeze the men in place. "Here he is—he is making for us again!"

"I turned around," said a stunned Chase, "[and] saw him about one hundred rods [about sixteen hundred feet] directly ahead of us, coming down apparently with twice his ordinary speed, and to me at that moment, it appeared with tenfold fury and vengeance in his aspect. . . . He struck [the ship] to windward, directly under the cat-head, and completely stove in her bows."

An enraged sperm whale has rammed this whaleboat and made kindling out of it. The painter, Louis Garneray, has given the whale a cold, calculating eye and a spout that looks like smoke.

The whale passed under the boat again, swimming off casually and apparently unhurt, and, Chase reported, "we never saw him again."

As for the ship, it took on water so rapidly that it began to lean over dangerously. Chase knew they were over a thousand miles from land and had no time to waste, so he ordered the pumping stopped and got his boat into the water, along with some navigational gear. They had barely pushed clear of the ship when "she fell over to windward and settled down in the water."

From the initial attack to the relaunching of his whaleboat, Chase guessed that ten minutes had elapsed. "Amazement and despair now wholly took possession of us. . . . Not a word was spoken for several minutes by any of us."

Sometime later, the other two whaleboats drew near. Captain George

This dramatic pencil drawing shows a sperm whale biting a whaleboat in half. The harpooneer is nowhere in sight, and viewers are left to conclude that the enraged whale has swallowed his attacker.

Pollard stared at his ship, which was floating on its side, temporarily held afloat by the buoyant casks of whale oil in the hold. The captain's first words were, "My God, Mr. Chase, what is the matter?"

"I answered, 'We have been stove by a whale.' I then briefly told him the story."

The situation was dire. Twenty sailors were crammed into three small boats, with no land in sight, and no provisions. The first order of business was to get as much food and water from the ship as possible before it sank from sight.

Using small hatchets from the whaleboats, the men chopped through the ship's planking and managed to save six hundred pounds of hard biscuits and "as much fresh water as we dared to take in the boats, so that each was supplied with about sixty-five gallons."

They stayed next to the stricken ship for three days, hoping another whaler might chance upon them. None came. Since the ship was beginning to break apart, the captain and officers decided to leave the scene of the disaster.

The Marquesas Islands were approximately fifteen hundred miles away, with the Society Islands next closest, but they did not set sail for them. The captain believed it was hurricane season in that area. More important, as Chase explained, "these islands we were entirely ignorant of; if inhabited, we presumed they were by savages, from whom we had as much to fear, as from the elements, or even death itself." Captain Pollard added, "We feared we should be devoured by cannibals."

With their reasoning clouded by such wild rumors, they sailed for the coast of South America—a journey of well over three thousand miles. They left the *Essex* behind on November 22, and "many were the lingering and sorrowful looks we cast behind us."

Almost immediately, the sea made it clear that it would not cooperate with them. That first night, the waves grew high and rough, and the three boats were tossed about and battered until the sun came up. "We were obliged to keep one man constantly bailing," Chase recalled.

Careful calculations were made to preserve the meager provisions for as long as possible. If each man had one biscuit and a half pint of water per day, they could last exactly sixty days at sea. Once again, events conspired to upset this delicate plan.

A day later, a very strong wave hit Chase's boat and split it along the seam. Water poured in and ruined some of the biscuits before repairs could be made. On another night a twelve-foot-long fish "of the killer-fish species" literally took several bites out of Captain Pollard's boat. More precious biscuits were damaged. "The night was spissy darkness itself," Chase moaned, "the

If you wanted to keep your sewing machine humming along noiselessly, the Nye Oil Company suggested that you use their brand of sperm oil. The whale, as always, is depicted as a dangerous brute.

sky was completely overcast, and it seemed to us as if fate was wholly relentless, in pursuing us with such cruel complication of disasters."

Days went by with the broiling sun and never-ending bailing sapping the men of energy and spirit. The already meager rations were cut in half. The men were so hungry that they ate the barnacles off the bottom of the boat and devoured some flying fish that landed in the boats, bones, scales, innards and all.

As if their journey were not hard enough, the wind that was supposed to carry them to safety abandoned them. After drifting backward ten miles,

Captain Pollard ordered that all three boats be rowed. But, a weary Chase explained, "we made but a very sorry progress. Hunger and thirst . . . had so weakened us, that in three hours every man gave out, and we abandoned the further prosecution of the plan."

They struggled along like this for thirty days. Every man and boy was, according to Chase, "dispirited, silent & dejected." Some stared out at the water around their boat, others were slumped forward, exhausted. Then at around seven o'clock one morning "one of our companions suddenly and loudly called out, 'there is land!'"

Those three simple words charged the sailors with energy. The other two boat crews had heard the cry and also leaped into action. Several stood up, hands shielding their eyes from the already bright sun, while they searched to make sure they weren't responding to a trick of the light. "There indeed was the blessed vision before us."

They had chanced upon Elizabeth Island, a bit of land that was roughly six miles long and three miles wide. The shore was extremely high and rugged and surrounded by rocks, while the interior "mountains were bare, but on the tops it looked fresh and green with vegetation." They hesitated only a moment, wondering if the island were inhabited "by beasts or savages," but soon realized they had little choice and landed.

It turned out that no one lived on Elizabeth Island. Very few living things—plant, animal, or insect—called it home. A small number of crabs scuttled near the shore, and tropical birds had nests in the side of a mountain. The reason for this paucity of life became clear after an initial search of the island. Aside from a mere trickle of fresh water found in the shore rocks, there was no other source of this precious commodity.

The men and boys fell to eating anything they could, which included the leaves of the shrubs and the tough peppergrass that grew between the rocks. Within days they had stripped the island of just about every edible plant and most of the birds. They sailed on, leaving behind three men who did not want to venture out onto the water again.

It probably didn't take very long for the three on the island to wish they'd gone with the others. Their water supply dried up, and an attempt to dig a well failed to produce even a drop. The only water they had after this came from puddles of water that collected after chance showers.

The three scoured the island for food, picking berries and leaves by day and stalking the dwindling supply of birds at night. One day they came across several caves and looked in each. An unidentified writer relates what they found: "In one of these caves they found eight human skeletons . . . the remains of some poor mariners who had been shipwrecked on the isle, & perished for want of food and water. They were side by side, as if they had laid down, and died together! This sight deeply affected the [three men]; their case was similar, and they had every reason to expect ere long the same fate." These three sailors would have been startled to learn that they were the lucky ones.

For while they hunted for food and water, the tiny fleet sailed into more and more trouble. Eight days after leaving the island, they were blown far off course by heavy squalls accompanied by thunder and lightning. They had no other choice but to head for the Juan Fernandez Islands, some fifteen hundred miles away. Chase was a realist. "We must abandon altogether the hopes of reaching the land, and rely wholly on the chance of being taken up by a vessel."

One week after this, the first man died. Second mate Matthew Joy "had suffered from debility, and the privations we had experienced, much beyond any of the rest of us, and . . . he died very suddenly."

They sewed Joy in his clothes, tied a weight to his feet, and "consigned him in a solemn manner to the ocean." The sixteen survivors watched as their friend was swallowed by the ocean, probably wondering if they would be the next. "It was an incident," Chase adds, "which threw a gloom over our feelings for many days."

The gloom deepened when torrents of rain fell, accompanied by mighty flashes of lightning. In the darkness and confusion, the boats became separated and, a saddened Chase said, "we saw no more of them afterwards. . . . We had lost the cheering of each other's faces, that . . . we so much required in both our mental and bodily distress."

By the middle of January, the men on Chase's boat were barely able to move. "We would lie down in the bottom of the boat, cover ourselves over with the sails, and abandon her to the mercy of the waves. Upon attempting to rise again, the blood would rush into the head, and an intoxicating blindness came over us."

Their biscuits and water were almost gone, and the men took to gnawing on pieces of leather out of sheer desperation. On one particularly bad night, as if to chastise them for their past hunting, a herd of whales appeared. Two months before this, the nearness of whales would have been cause for celebration and action. Now, it produced only fear and panic. "The terrible noise of whale-spouts near us sounded in our ears; we could distinctly hear the furious thrashing of their tails in the water, and our weak minds pictured out their appalling and hideous aspects."

No doubt the men recalled the sperm whale that had so effortlessly sunk the *Essex* and wondered if he and his friends had come to finish off the job. "Two or three of the whales came down near us, and went swiftly across our stern, blowing and spouting at a terrible rate." The whales swam off, but the men's luck only worsened.

Two days later, one of the men, Richard Peterson, "made up his mind to die rather than endure further misery." He died before the day was out, and his body was committed to the sea. Next, Isaac Cole gave up hope. "All was dark he said in his mind, not a single ray of hope was left for him to dwell upon." Cole died shortly after this.

Normally, Cole's body would be dumped overboard like the others, but the desperate situation led Chase to propose an equally desperate solution. "I addressed them on the painful subject of keeping the body for food!!"

No objections were made, and they set about their grisly work.

"We separated his limbs from his body, and cut all the flesh from the bones; after which, we opened the body, took out the heart, and then closed it again—sewed it up as decently as we could, and committed it to the sea. We now first commenced to satisfy the immediate cravings of nature from the heart, which we eagerly devoured, and then ate sparingly of a few pieces of the flesh; after which, we hung up the remainder, cut in thin strips about the boat, to dry in the sun." The rest of the flesh was roasted and provided sustenance for seven days.

Only three were left now: Chase, a seaman named Benjamin Lawrence, and a seventeen-year-old boy, Thomas Nicholson. "We knew not then, to whose lot it would fall next, either to die or be shot, and eaten like the poor wretch we had just dispatched."

They were, by Chase's reckoning, only three hundred miles from land. With just a little effort, they could set a course and reach land in a matter of days. Unfortunately, the three were too weak and disoriented to do much at all. In fact, Thomas Nicholson lost all hope, "drew a piece of canvas over him, and cried out, that he then wished to die immediately."

Thomas Nicholson was still alive when Chase settled himself down to pray and sleep. The next morning his sleep was shattered by Benjamin Lawrence's sudden, loud scream of "There's a Sail!"

Chase bolted to his feet. Even the boy "took a sudden & animated start from his despondency."

They altered the course of their little boat to intercept the ship and this time luck was with them. They actually traveled faster than the ship and were soon spotted. "I do not believe it is possible to form a just conception of the pure, strong feelings, and the unmingled emotions of joy and gratitude, that took possession of my mind on this occasion."

Chase and his two companions were so weak that they had to be lifted aboard the rescuing ship, which immediately took them to the nearest port. A ship was dispatched to Elizabeth Island for the three men left there.

As for the fate of the two other boats, it was, if possible, worse than that of Chase's. Several days after Chase's boat disappeared in the storm, the boat

Owen Chase as he looked later in life. He has the eyes of a person haunted by the all-too-clear recollection of what he did in order to survive.

the second mate had commanded ran out of supplies. The captain's boat ran out a week later. Then, within the space of six days, four sailors—Lawson Thomas, Charles Shorter, Isaac Shepherd, and Samuel Reed—all died from dehydration and starvation. "The bodies of these men constituted [the] only food while it lasted."

One dark night, these boats became separated, and the second mate's boat was never seen again. As for the remaining boat, it contained Captain Pollard, a sailor named Brazilla Ray, a seventeen-year-old sailor named Charles Ramsdale, and the cabin boy, fourteen-year-old Owen Coffin. Very quickly, their supply of flesh ran out.

"We looked at each other with horrid thoughts in our minds," Captain Pollard recalled. "I am sure that we loved one another as brothers all the time; and yet our looks told plainly what must be done."

They cast lots to see which one of them would die so the others would live, and they cast lots to see who would do the killing. Fourteen-year-old Owen Coffin drew the fatal straw; his executioner would be seventeen-year-old Charles Ramsdale. Two boys who had eagerly gone to sea to seek adventure now found themselves in a situation of unspeakable horror.

Captain Pollard told young Coffin, "'*If you don't like your lot,* I'll shoot the first man that touches you.' The poor emaciated boy hesitated a moment or two; then quietly laying his head down upon the gunnel of the boat, he said, 'I like it as well as any other.'" One can only imagine the scene that followed involving the two terrified boys; Captain Pollard wrapped his description up efficiently and coldly: "He was soon despatched, and nothing of him left."

Several days later, Brazilla Ray died, and he shared the fate of Owen Coffin and the others. Days later, a ship spotted the boat and came to the two survivors' rescue. Out of a crew of twenty, eight survived. Of the twelve who had died, seven had been eaten.

The *Essex* was not the only whaleship attacked and sunk by the animal it hunted. Several other ships, most notably the *Union* (1807), the *Ann Alexander* (1851), and the *Kathleen* (1906), were all sent to the bottom of the oceans by enraged whales. Since all the crews from these other ships were rescued and did not spend a great deal of time at sea, none of them entered the history of whaling the way the story of the *Essex* did.

Of course, the whale did not participate in the shaping of the written record of this incident. As a result, the sailors are always presented as the only victims. This could not be just a random accident, one to be expected when hunting a large creature; no, this had to be the work of an evil force. Chase himself referred to the attack as "premeditated violence" by an animal whose "aspect was most horrible."

Giving the whale a malevolent personality created instant sympathy for the victims and survivors of the *Essex*. Like Jonah in the Bible, they had faced the terrible wrath of the whale. Whatever they did to survive was considered understandable (even if it included an adult, Captain Pollard, assisting in the murder of one boy by another so that he and the others could feast upon the flesh).

If the whale could argue its case, it would have insisted it was doing nothing more than defending itself and the rest of the herd against attack. A passionate defense of the whale's character is made by Jacques-Yves Cousteau: "There is not one bona fide report of any whale charging a boat that did not mean it harm. When it comes to the human race, whales are accommodating to a fault, unfailingly peaceful and forebearing."

There was no Cousteau around to argue the whale's position in the nineteenth century, and the picture of the whale as monster stuck. The story of the *Essex* and the fate of her crew was told and retold in every forecastle, giving each green hand a clear understanding of the enemy he faced and had to kill. One such greenie was a young man by the name of Herman Melville.

Melville was not a boy when he stepped on board his first whaler. He was twenty-two when his ship, the *Acushnet*, left New Bedford for a Pacific whaling cruise in 1841. Melville not only heard stories of the *Essex*, he had his own copy of Chase's narrative. Melville would explain, "The reading of this wondrous story [while on] the landless sea, and so close to the very latitude of the shipwreck, had a surprising effect upon me."

Melville would borrow elements from Chase's narrative, as well as from accounts of a rogue white whale called Mocha Dick that was rumored to stalk ships in the Pacific after 1834. He combined them with his own whaling experiences and rich imagination to create one of the most powerful American novels ever, *Moby-Dick*. This great white whale—and with it all whales—comes down to us as little more than an agent of the devil: "Retribution, swift vengeance, eternal malice were his whole aspect, and spite of all that mortal man could do, the solid white buttress of his forehead smote the ship's starboard bow, till men and timbers reeled."

The Sunday wash adorns the California *in 1903 while a young man
(center) coils a line.*

CHAPTER NINE
Homeward Bound!!!!!

I am growing weary of this long voyage, one season more than
we expected, but everything has an end. I suppose this will too.

From a letter written by Susan Folger
while aboard the Cowper

FRANK BULLEN'S SHIP HAD BEEN three and a half years out of New Bedford, and the officers and crew were all eager to get home. A check belowdecks showed there were still a good number of casks to be filled.

The captain pondered the situation. On the one hand, he had his sailing orders from the owners, which clearly stipulated "we mean for you to cruise . . . until you have filled your casks." If he arrived in New Bedford with anything less than a full cargo, the owners of his ship (or any other shipowners in the town, for that matter) would probably never employ him again. On the other hand, he had a tense and tired crew who might mutiny if pushed too far.

As always in whaling, commerce won out over compassion and the captain insisted that they take two more whales before turning the ship around. To Frank's frustration, the wind died out that same day and they sat, unable to fill their quota.

"Our patience was sorely tested," Frank said angrily. Only two whales separated them from the end of the voyage, but they were helpless. One day, then another and another, went by with no change in the situation. "In vain we tried all the old amusements [to pass the time]; they had lost their 'bite;' we wanted to go home."

These must have been painful times for everyone, even for the captain. They had had a reasonably good voyage and taken whales at a steady pace. But with each passing day, they knew their luck might turn sour, and the whales might disappear. It could take weeks, even months, to find and kill those two additional whales.

Frank's voice nearly explodes with joy when he announces, "At last the longed-for shift of wind came and set us free." Imagine his feelings when, a day later, they not only spotted whales but managed to kill two of them.

The Sunbeam *cruising slowly in a gentle sea.*

"Behold us, then, in the gathering dusk with a whale on either side [of the ship]. . . . They represented so much to us. Very little was said, but all hearts were filled with a deep content, a sense of a long season of toil fitly crowned with complete success."

Time and again, boys reacted with the same kind of delirious joy when the voyage was officially termed over and a course set for home. For many, it was as if a prison door had been thrown open. Enoch Cloud's response to the news makes most other reports seem calm indeed. "Homeward Bound!!!!!! No dream, no fiction, no romance, no supposition,—but candid, self evident, sound, sober, fact!!!! A glance aloft, exhibits the glistening studding sails, bellying full to the breeze, and the roaring of the water at her bows seems to say—Homeward bound!!—indeed, 'homeward bound' is seen, felt, tasted, smelled, heard, eat & drank, by all hands!"

Even with the voyage declared over, it would be months before a ship would reach its home port. The last whales had to be cut in and boiled. Frank's two whales would take up nearly eight full days. And sailing home could be plagued with the same problems that had struck on the way out—storms, a lack of wind, a leaking hull. Enoch Cloud was even outraged when his captain slowed to speak other ships. "How long in the name of . . . common sense, will we be humbugged, speaking the *Dartmouth*! We lose just about one day in each week, hauling back and speaking!"

Even if nothing interfered with the progress of the ship, sailing home was a slow process. When they left port, most whalers could attain a top speed of only eight knots. Two years out and the speed had slowed to two or three knots, due to the hundreds of full oil casks below deck and a huge collection of barnacles and weeds on the hull. Finally, if whales were spotted, the boats would be lowered to hunt them. A good captain simply never missed a chance to add to his cargo and profits.

As they traveled, the men were kept as busy as possible. The spars, masts, and woodwork were scraped and painted, as was the hull down to the waterline. The lookout posts were dismantled, and the brick and mortar of the try-

Fin Whale

OTHER COMMON NAMES: finback, finner, common rorqual, razorback, herring whale

FAMILY: *Balaenopteridae*
SPECIES: *Balaenoptera physalus*

Fin whales are the second-largest creatures in the world, measuring up to 85 feet and weighing 80 tons. They are also among the fastest marine mammals and have been called "the greyhound of the sea." A fin whale can attain a speed of 33 miles per hour when pursued by an enemy—and it has only two: humans and orcas.

works was broken up and tossed overboard (though not until they were very close to port). Scrimshaw pieces were now given great attention so they would be finished by the time the ship reached home. If any in the crew liked to sing, he might serenade his shipmates with a tune, such as:

> Our yards we'll swing and our sails we'll set,
> Good-bye, fare ye well,
> Good-bye, fare ye well:
> The whales we are leaving, we leave with regret,
> Hurrah, my bullies, we're homeward bound!

The fin whale gets its common name from its prominent dorsal fin. This and its unique asymmetrical coloration (it is black on one side and white on the other), plus a spout of 20 feet, make it easy to identify.

Fins are aggressive feeders, diving 750 to 1,000 feet to gather in krill, herring, squid, mackerel, and anchovies. They will also breach, and typically land on their bellies with a tremendous splash.

The fin whale was one of the most common of the large whales before being hunted, with a worldwide population of over 450,000. In 1976, scientists estimated that around 100,000 of them were alive.

BIRTH SIZE AND WEIGHT: 19¾ to 21½ feet, 4,000 pounds
ADULT SIZE AND WEIGHT: 59 to 85 feet, 60,000 to 160,000 pounds
SWIMMING SPEEDS: 3 to 22 mph cruising or migrating, 25 to 33 mph fleeing
GROUP SIZE: 3 to 7; 100 or more sometimes gather at good feeding areas

Across the Pacific they would toil, around Cape Horn, and up the coast of South America. After the east-coast whaling ports closed, the trip home would be only as far as San Francisco, though even this meant covering thousands of miles of ocean. Old letters were reread during the long days and nights, old stories retold.

"Steadily we battled northward," Frank Bullen reported, "until at last, with full hearts, we made Cape Navesink, and on the next day took a tug and towed into New Bedford with every flag we could scare up flying, the center of admiration—a full whale-ship safe back from her long, long fishing round the world."

An 1870 view of anchored whaleships in New Bedford, the wharf crowded with the fruits of their long voyages.

On shore, the sighting of a sail on the horizon created an instant buzz around town. "Every hill-top and house-top was occupied to see the welcome ship as most families in town had near or distant relatives in the fleet," an eyewitness wrote about the return of a ship in 1793. "A great suspense pervaded the minds of the people for several hours, not knowing which [ship] it could be, as no signal colors were on board. . . . At length, Thaddeus

Joy . . . announced from his look-out the ship *Beaver*, Captain Worth. The boys were eager to carry the glad tidings to the wives and families of the officers, for which it was customary to pay $1 to him who first imparted the first news."

Most arriving ships received a warm welcome from relatives and friends, dockworkers, and even the ship's owners. There were exceptions. One boy recalled sailing all the way from whaling grounds off Japan to Martha's Vineyard with a full cargo and a badly leaking hull. The manually operated pumps had to be kept going day and night in order to keep the ship afloat and save the valuable oil. "The *Aurora* arrived at [Martha's Vineyard] on Christmas Day, 1826, after an absence of three years and two months, with 1800 barrels of oil. And neither the captain, officers, nor crew received so much as 'I thank you,' from the owners and underwriters, although the ship's bottom was eaten to a honeycomb."

A few boys—such as Harty Bodfish and George Fred Tilton—would set out on other whaling trips and eventually become masters of their own ships. Most boys knew long before seeing their home port that they would never set foot in another ship, let alone a whaler. William Fish Williams' feelings at this time capture what the majority must have felt. "So, we sailed through the beautiful Golden Gate into our home port on November 12, 1874. This was the end of my ambitions, if ever very serious, to be a whaleman. . . . I decided that I had enough of the sea."

If the experience of being on a whaler had not altered a boy's romantic image of the business, receiving his hard earned pay would.

No one on a whaleship received regular wages during the trip, not even the captain. The chances that a ship would be lost at sea or that it would return without much oil and bone were simply too great. In 1853, for instance, 44 of the 58 ships that set sail from New Bedford failed to turn a profit. Since the entire venture was really a game of chance, owners decided that everyone would share in the gamble. Thus the lay, or share, system was devised.

In general, owners were not very trusting. Before any money was paid to the captain or crew, they had every cask measured and weighed so they knew precisely how much oil had been taken, then had samples examined to determine the kind and quality of the oil.

Quite simply, everyone received a portion of the profits from the oil and bone taken, with the captain receiving the most and the cabin boy the least. A captain's share was expressed as $\frac{1}{15}$, which meant that he received the value of one barrel of whale oil for every fifteen taken. A green hand's share was usually around $\frac{1}{180}$, while cabin boys received the smallest share, only $\frac{1}{240}$.

Naturally, expenses had to be figured before a profit could be calculated. Owners deducted the price of the ship and the cost of outfitting it from the total amount of cash from the sale of the oil and bone. They also took out the cost of feeding the crew for the entire voyage, any medical expenses incurred, and any money advanced to a sailor along the way. If a green hand had been given clothes at the beginning of the voyage, he was usually charged $75, plus 25 percent interest. Some owners even charged crew members for insurance on the ship (though if the ship went down, it was the owner who collected the money).

A California processing plant for baleen. Here the plates will be cut into uniform sizes, wrapped, and sent to various manufacturers.

When George Dodge stepped off the *Baltic* after forty-four months of backbreaking work, he received a total of $125. This came out to around $2.85 per month. At the time, an inexperienced boy could get around $8 per month on a merchant ship and not be subjected to the dangers of facing angry whales.

One of the reasons Harty Bodfish had gone whaling was to make his fortune. "But the wealth I had hoped for had failed to materialize," he confessed. "When I came ashore . . . they paid me just one dollar for eleven months' work. One of my mates was in an ambulance bound for the hospital, and I gave him half of the money."

These boys were lucky. They actually got some money. If a ship did not kill enough whales to turn a profit, no one on board received a penny. George Fred Tilton put in his time and risked his life as much as any of the men he worked alongside, including the captain. "I left the ship considerable bigger and stronger than I was when I went aboard. I also was richer in experience, and darned little else, for I owed the ship thirty-five dollars."

With cash in pocket or not, the boys headed for home. They had grown during their years away, their faces and arms had become deeply tanned, their hands callused and scarred as a result of the hard work. Some arrived home sporting mustaches and beards, or even tattoos. All of them had stories to tell.

At first, some might express bitterness at the treatment they had received. One young sailor from the *Izette* was so frustrated, he complained: "This whaling business is not all it is cracked up to be, let me tell you, and not half so profitable as some have been foolish enough to suppose. . . . I often think it wonderful how a man can exile himself so long from friends and from home and knock about the ocean for so greasy an object. It is a life of trouble and toil at the best."

With time, the anger would fade for most boys, and their view of their whaling experience would soften and take on a romantic glow. Yes, the work and discipline had been hard, and the food had been awful. But they had

Shipowner (center) and his workers stand proudly beside bundles of twelve-foot-long pieces of baleen.

also been places and seen things that few in the world would ever have a chance to experience. Maybe even more important, they had been a part of a team—a kind of rough and greasy family—that hunted the world's largest animal.

And when asked why they had signed on for such a dangerous job, they would shrug and give the standard answers—the money, the adventure, something to do besides walking behind a plow all day. Deep down, they probably knew these answers fell short of the truth: They had been drawn to whaling by a stronger force, one that Henry Wadsworth Longfellow spoke of in his poem "My Lost Youth."

As prices for oil and baleen dropped in the beginning of the twentieth century, other whale-body parts were collected for sale. This pile of whale bones will be ground up, bagged, and shipped to farmers as fertilizer.

I remember the black wharves and the slips,
      And the sea-tides tossing free;
And the Spanish sailors with bearded lips,
And the beauty and mystery of the ships,
      And the magic of the sea.
            And the voice of the wayward song
            Is singing and saying still:
            "A boy's will is the wind's will,
And the thoughts of youth are long, long thoughts. . . ."

An 1890 German drawing of a steam chaser's whale gun firing and striking a whale. The insert drawing shows the harpoon in closeup, complete with hinged barbs.

CHAPTER TEN
The Great Killing

Whaling represents a series of near-extinctions, from species to species and ocean area to ocean area, each destruction proceeding faster than the one before it.

Robert McNally, So Remorseless a Havoc

THE NORWEGIAN STEAM CHASER SLICED through the choppy northern Atlantic seas, bounced on the water, then cut through another wave. The boy aloft in the crow's nest clung tightly to the sides, his eyes never leaving the object of the pursuit—the white plume spouts of three sei whales.

A new course was set to head off the whales, and the steam engines belowdecks chugged painfully to maintain a top speed of nine knots. Each time the whales surfaced, the course was adjusted. Thirty minutes after the initial sighting, the engine was slowed and the boat hovered, waiting for the reappearance of the whales.

They surfaced four hundred yards from the boat, unaware of the danger. The boat shot forward, the engines throbbing into high gear. There was no need for quiet now; the seis were exhausted and would not be able to sound again for four or five minutes.

The boat was less than fifty yards from the fleeing animals when an ear-splitting explosion erupted as the harpoon gun was fired. The concussion of the gun sent a shudder throughout the ship's beams, an eerie quiver felt by all nine crew members. The boy in the crow's nest clutched the railing firmly to steady himself and followed the curving arc of the harpoon and whale line as they sailed toward the target.

Seconds later, the harpoon struck with a dull, hollow thud and ripped into the side of a whale. Before the startled animal had a chance to react, an explosive charge in the point of the harpoon went off, forcing four sharp prongs to snap open, anchoring the harpoon firmly in the guts of the whale. The explosion also shredded flesh, arteries, and organs in the terrified creature.

The injured animal swam forward as quickly as it could, but the massive loss of blood was already beginning to slow it. The engine was tossed into reverse, and the weight of the boat began to tug at the whale. Still, the whale's immeasurable power was able to drag the boat along, even if the pace was barely noticeable. A half hour later, the shadow of the bow crossed the exhausted body of the sei. A second shot rang out and a killing lance bomb entered the animal and brought its suffering to a merciful end.

Following the kill, air was pumped into the whale to keep it from sinking. Another boat would tow the carcass to a shore station, where the cutting in and processing would be done. Meanwhile, the steam chaser continued its deadly search.

By the mid-1880s, this kind of scene was becoming more and more typical in waters around the world. The harpoon gun (perfected by a Norwegian named Svend Foyn in 1864) and the steam chaser (another Norwegian creation, this time in 1875) revolutionized the whaling business. The combination made the killing of whales easier, faster, safer, and—most important—cheaper. A single chaser could take over forty whales in a single summer, making it almost four times more efficient than an old-style whaler.

What's more, refinements in the steam chaser and later in the diesel chaser meant these boats would eventually reach speeds of fifteen knots—fast enough for the hunters to go after the very speedy rorqual whales. From this time on, the sei, minke, fin, humpback, and blue whales would have no rest.

The new method of whale hunting had another consequence: It spelled the end of the old style of whaling, and of whaling in America. Norway would be the dominant whaling country in the world, though others, notably Great Britain, Russia, and Japan, eagerly joined the hunt, too.

Old-fashioned American whalers would continue to go out into the twentieth century, but in ever-dwindling numbers. Whaling ports gradually disappeared on the east coast of the United States, leaving only San Francisco on the west coast as a major staging center for Arctic and northern Pacific whaling grounds. This decline was hastened along by the way the American people took to the use of petroleum and its by-products, which drove the price of spermaceti and whale oil down. Meanwhile, whalebone, once prized for its elasticity, was superseded by the steel spring later in the century.

As returns on costly whaling expeditions slowly evaporated, American owners chose to get out of the business altogether. Even so, some ships did manage to make immense amounts of money. In 1905, Harty Bodfish was the forty-one-year old captain of the *William Baylies*, and mighty proud to announce: "My share of that voyage was about $13,000."

Such lucky voyages kept a few owners in the business—always hoping the prices of oil and bone would go up, always hoping a new source of whales would be discovered, always hoping that luck would be with their ship's captain and crew. Eventually, even the most optimistic whaleman had to admit the truth. Just six years after his 1905 cruise, Harty Bodfish's tone would be somber and melancholy.

"We had taken . . . considerable trade bone, making a total of around 30,000 pounds for the voyage, which was very good under normal conditions. But I didn't get a penny for my share, and I don't even know that the bone was ever sold." Quite literally, while Bodfish was out collecting baleen, the demand for it dried up and the price offered dropped to below what it cost to get. "The end of whaling had arrived, that was all, and I saw it plainly. For my part I went ashore . . . with my mind definitely made up to quit whaling, and this I did."

A Vanity Fair *cartoon entitled "Grand Ball by the Whales in Honor of the Discovery of the Oil Wells in Pennsylvania." A banner (top right) proclaims: "Oils well that ends well." Unfortunately, this turned out to be a premature celebration. It would be over sixty years before oil from the ground replaced whale oil in America, and another sixty before the killing of whales was banned.*

One year later, it was George Fred Tilton's turn to face reality. He was the captain and part owner of a ship at this time, and remembered having "just as good a voyage as I did the year before . . . but when I got back to Frisco the bone market had gone to pieces and you couldn't give it away. I was eighteen thousand five hundred dollars in the hole."

As the American whaling industry faded away, whaling stations continued to spread beyond the Atlantic. After 1905, the Pacific Ocean had stations from Alaska down to Australia. Each day, chasers went out, hunted down whales, and dragged them back to the stations where they were processed. Everywhere in the Atlantic and Pacific, chasers poked into bays and inlets searching for prey. It seemed a perfect setup to many, except for an obvious flaw. The supplies of whales began to run out.

In 1890, for instance, 160 whales were killed off Iceland. The number increased steadily, year after year, until a high of 1,257 were taken in 1903. Then the numbers declined sharply, so that only 54 were harpooned in 1915, and most of these were not very big. The same thing was happening at all the stations—a dramatic and very profitable surge in killings was followed by a sudden disappearance of whales. One by one the stations were forced to close.

The killing of whales might have ended at this point except for one sad fact: There was still great profit to be made. The market for baleen and oil was gone in the United States, but it was still very strong in the rest of the world. This was especially true after a way was perfected to use whale oil to make margarine. To satisfy the demand, whale hunters were poking around a new and as yet unexploited hunting ground: the waters surrounding the Antarctic.

The Antarctic waters are among the most treacherous in the world—strong currents, shifting, unpredictable ice pushed around by fierce winds. Sail-powered whaling ships had steered clear of the area, and so the whales that made their home there had been safe. Chasers, though, had little trouble maneuvering in the Antarctic waters.

When Carl Anton Larsen, a Norwegian sea captain, chugged into this sanctuary in 1905, he found the sea alive with spouts. There were hundreds and hundreds of them in close proximity. Unfortunately, most of the whales would be killed off before an accurate count could be made of their populations. Estimates based on the amount of oil and bone taken place the original population of fin whales at 350,000 to 400,000, blue whales at 150,000, sei whales at 150,000, and humpbacks at over 100,000.

Larsen wasn't there to count whales. Such a notion would have been laughed off the deck. No, he was there to hunt. Larsen established a shore station on the island of South Georgia and soon had the waters frothing with the blood of 195 whales. Following his success, shore stations popped up all over the region, and with them the number of whales killed: 10,000 in 1910, 20,270 in 1912. Whaling had entered a new era, one that many people refer to as the Great Killing.

During these early years in the Antarctic, whales were so plentiful that only the thickest parts of the back and belly blubber were cut off and processed. The rest of the carcass was cast away to rot. Such reckless waste had the expected result—whales became scarce in the areas hunted, so the operations had to be moved to other parts of the Antarctic. The waste was so obvious that Great Britain even passed a number of regulations to control and limit hunting in its waters. One rule forbade the killing of female whales with calves, in order to allow the herd to be replenished.

Whalers—including those from Great Britain—ignored these rules completely. They also began experimenting with an idea to reduce the cost of dismantling shore stations when whales became scarce. This was the floating factory ship.

The factory ship did the same work as a shore station—cutting up the whale and processing it—only it could follow the catchers into the hunting grounds. This twentieth-century version of whaling was dubbed pelagic (or seaborne) whaling.

The factory ship was the hub of the activity from which a small flotilla of vessels consisting of catchers, buoy boats, and corvettes went out to get whales. R. B. Robertson, the doctor on a factory ship that sailed in 1951, was impressed by the efficiency of the system. "When we reached the whales in any quantity, the thirteen catchers, assisted by their superior speed of fifteen knots, would draw ahead of [the factory ship] and fan out over an arc of ocean that in the beginning would be about fifty miles across. Within this arc, between us and the catchers, would steam the two buoy boats, vessels almost identical with the catchers and armed like them. Their job would be

This British drawing of the factory ship Balaena *shows it in full, smoke-belching* operation. Spotting planes covered hundreds of miles every day in search of whales, while two 500 ton catcher ships hunted their prey. Dead whales on line await their turn to be hauled up the slipway to the flensers' knives.

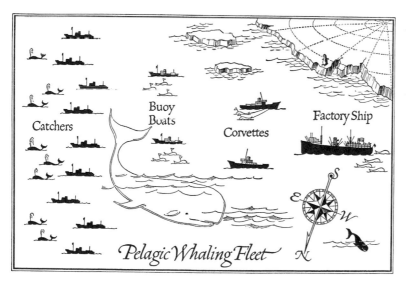

For such a grisly business, this drawing is a little too cute. A penguin in Antarctica (top right) watches as catchers stalk some merrily spouting whales. At lower right, a lone whale makes its escape, a sadly accurate comment on the number of whales that avoided death.

to [inflate] and collect such whales as the catchers killed, and do a bit of hunting themselves if circumstances permitted. Also in the arc would be the two unarmed corvettes, which would . . . tow in to us the dead whales."

In the old style of whaling, a ship's crew might, on a very lucky day, have to contend with cutting in and cooking two or possibly three whales. The factory system meant that twenty or more whales might be brought in *every day!* And when the dead whales arrived, there was immediate action on deck. The men knew that they had to get every whale aboard and cooking before the flesh and oil began to go bad, and this required round-the-clock work, with three crews working eight-hour shifts. Besides, each whale added to the ship's quota and the men's pay.

The whales were tied to the stern of the ship to await their turn in processing. A pair of giant tongs, called the *hval kla*, or whale claw, was lowered and positioned to pounce on a dead whale's tail. Next, the one-hundred-ton whale was hauled up the slipway onto the main deck of the ship, where flensers leaped on the body and went to work using long knives and large tackles to strip the blubber off in long sheets.

Robertson was astonished by the pace of the action: "They hurried; they rushed; they appeared to be in a state of complete confusion throughout the blubber-stripping process." After watching for some time, he realized the men moved with astonishing care and precision. "I began to see that every man among them was being extremely methodical and careful. None of the curved hockey-stick blades was ever turned in the direction of a fellow flenser in the melee; every wire rope on deck was walked around as carefully as a man will walk around a rattlesnake; and no flenser would signal to his winch to haul away until he ascertained that his mates were standing clear."

When one side of the whale was done, the whale was turned over and the other side's blubber attacked. Once the blubber was all off, the jaw and its baleen were ripped out by a winch and dumped overboard. The ton of baleen, once an important product, was now considered garbage. After this, the blubber was sliced up into long, narrow strips and tossed down large

A giant rorqual whale is hauled up the slipway of a factory ship to the waiting flensers.

holes in the deck that led to the choppers and giant cookers. Hauling the blubber about was left to the "blubber boys," who, Robertson noted, were "a motley collection of ages ranging from eighteen to eighty."

As soon as the blubber and baleen had been removed, the whale's naked carcass was dragged to the forward part of the deck. At the same time, the whale claw was grabbing another animal from the water and hauling it up the slipway to the flensers' knives.

Meanwhile, the first whale passed through a narrow opening (usually known as "hell's gate") between the fore- and afterdecks. There another group of workmen called lemmers cut off the meat, removed the viscera, and broke up the skeleton with huge steam saws. If anything, these men worked at an even more intense pace, in Robertson's opinion. "The steam and noise and variety of lethal objects flying about were tenfold greater than on the flensing deck, and the diabolic tempo at which the lemmers worked made the flensers seem slow and awkward." Soon whale number two would be pulled through "hell's gate," and they didn't want to have whale carcasses backing up on the deck.

The flensers and lemmers have done their work, and the deck of this ship is littered with body parts ready to be dumped into the steam cookers.

Chunks of meat were fed into one pressure cooker, the bones into another; even the blood and any bits of body on deck were washed down into a cooker. The liver, which might weigh as much as a ton, was hacked into manageable pieces and fed into its own cooker to extract liver oil. All these cookers, plus those with the blubber in them, were monitored by a small army of technicians belowdecks. When every last ounce of oil had been wrung out of these body parts, it was piped to giant tanks for storage. The chunky goop that remained in the cookers was then dried, pulverized, and bagged as bonemeal for sale to farmers as fertilizer.

Abovedecks the last bit of work was done to the stomach and guts. These were considered useless, unless they came from a sperm whale. In that case, they were checked for the ever-valuable ambergris. Then a winch hauled this mountain of smelly matter, referred to by whalers as "grax," to an opening in the side of the ship and dropped it into the sea for the sharks and Cape pigeons to feast upon.

The factory system sounds as modern and efficient as an automobile assembly plant, and in one unfortunate way it was. It meant that more and more whales could be taken every year. In 1913, 25,673 whales were killed; by 1938, that number had more than doubled to 54,835. The record killing season came in 1961–62, when 66,090 whales went into the cookers. Cetologists and environmentalists are quick to add that these numbers don't fully reflect the extent of the carnage. "Remember," says Robert McNally, "these figures refer only to processed and reported kills. At least one whale out of every five harpooned was lost to bad seas, sinking, or spoilage."

Despite the use of modern technology, there were still elements of whale hunting reminiscent of the old days. Even though the hunters never got very close to a live whale, accidents continued to be a part of the work. Wire cables snapped taut; men with sharp blades and screaming saws stepped through the oil and blood and bits of slippery intestines to get at the whale. A sudden roll of the ship could send fifty tons of whale sliding along the deck.

On one ship, for instance, the flensers were working on the jaw of an eighty-five-foot blue whale when a simple miscommunication occurred. Ivan T. Sanderson relates what happened: "Either the winchman jumped the gun in his eagerness and ripped the great mass free before the chief flenser had completed his last cut, or the flenser did not give early enough warning, or the boy was just not listening. More than a ton of flesh, with eight hundred-odd baleen plates attached, literally catapulted out of the whale's gaping mouth at the same moment that a heavy steel pulley and grappling hook swung across its path. This was flipped aside like a flying steel ball, caught the boy behind the ear, and smacked him to the scuppers. He was quite dead before he hit the bulwark."

There was a brief pause in the frenzied work, and some men shouted for the ship's doctor. A man near the boy's body bent to see the extent of the damage, then shook his head solemnly. A good quantity of the boy's blood had already begun mixing with the whale's. No one else left his position to see to the boy or to find out how the accident had happened. This was an assembly line, and work had to go on. "The chief flenser just looked at the winchman," Sanderson continued. "Neither spoke. The work did not stop even when the medicos hurried on deck."

This nonstop pattern of work had the expected results. Whales, especially the largest ones, began to disappear. In the past, this dilemma had been easily solved: The hunters would sail to another part of the ocean and locate a fresh herd. The situation was different in the twentieth century.

The world's oceans had been completely explored, and no new collection of whales had been found. Whalers could not fall back on the old logic—that the whales had swum off to a safer part of the ocean. It was obvious that the massive killing had done in the older and bigger whales, and that continued hunting of the smaller survivors would mean an end to whales in the Antarctic. The same held true for all the other places around the world where fleets were stalking a dwindling supply of whales.

What is more, the pace of the killings had escalated alarmingly. "It took about 400 years to reduce the [northern] rights to a few thousand survivors," Robert McNally said. "The sperm whales of the Atlantic absorbed about a century of abuse; those in the Pacific, somewhat less. The bowheads of the western Arctic were hunted into near-nothingness in only fifty years. All this destruction occurred without the cannon and the steam catcher. With them, the whalers took most of Antarctica's humpbacks in two decades and shifted their attention to the blue whale. In only fifteen years catches of blue whales had declined to half what they once had been. Each season was a quantum jump toward commercial extinction." It was clear to anyone who wanted to see that time was running out for the whales, and running out quickly.

"Experts published the facts," the thoroughly exasperated Jacques-Yves Cousteau and Yves Paccalet explain, "but whalemen refused to acknowledge the significance of them; still dreaming of immense herds of fin and blue whales, they greedily hunted the survivors of those species. When that fishery did not suffice, they turned their attention once again to sperm whales (which, by and large, had been left in peace since the end of the nineteenth century) and to sei, minke and Bryde's whales." How could they do this despite the mounting body of evidence? For Cousteau and Paccalet, the answer is sadly simple: "Mankind kills first and counts later."

Others did take note of the evidence and began to act. To put brakes on the destruction of whales, the Norwegian legislature took control of their country's whaling fleets and passed a series of rules in 1929. Among other things, it prohibited the killing of right whales, of calves, and of females with calves. It set a minimum size requirement for each type of whale (to allow the animals to grow larger and reproduce at a steady rate), and required that each factory ship keep accurate records of its kills. A government inspector was placed on each ship to enforce these rules (and later, two were placed aboard to ensure round-the-clock surveillance).

Two years later, other countries joined Norway in an international agreement based on their 1929 rules. The countries would meet every so often over the years and eventually, in 1946, form the International Whaling

Commission. Each meeting brought adjustments to the existing rules, while the IWC sponsored scientific research on whales to insure that these restrictions and limitations were truly protecting the survival of whales.

Many scientists and conservation organizations felt that the early rules, and even the IWC itself, were nothing more than a giant sham. In many ways they were correct. Each member country sent one commissioner to the annual meeting, as well as experts and advisors. Almost universally, these representatives were in some way or another closely associated with whaling companies. It's no wonder that the IWC's guiding principle was not so much to protect whales but, in the words of the preamble to the 1946 convention, to safeguard the "great natural resources represented by the whale stocks."

What about the various rules passed? The toughest ones protected species that were already so reduced in numbers that whalers no longer hunted them. "Again and again," a frustrated Robert McNally makes clear, "the regulations [were] form without substance, legal creations that [gave] the appearance of conservation while in fact conserving nothing."

One of the most telling examples of "form without substance" was the minimum size limitation on blue whales. The stated purpose of the limit was to allow blues to grow to a certain length so that they would be mature enough to reproduce. This would not just ensure the survival of the whales, but mean that there would always be large animals available to hunt. The size put in place for blue whales was seventy feet.

Unfortunately, seventy feet was far short of the size required. McNally points out that if the IWC had really wanted a proper minimum size regulation, the information was readily available to them in a 1942 publication of *International Whaling Statistics.* In it, the results of a study of 15,000 pregnant blue whales killed showed that most were between eighty-three and eighty-seven feet long, with only a small fraction under seventy-eight feet. Obviously, a seventy-foot limit was not enough; an eighty-five-foot limit was needed to allow this whale to survive.

Such a limit would have reduced the kills of blue whales by almost 75 percent. "The whalers would never have agreed to such reductions," McNally concluded, adding, "The 70-foot limit was a mockery." Truly tough regulations would be put in place only when the world population of blue whales was so low that their survival was threatened.

While the IWC failed to protect most whales, they did manage to protect another valuable resource—very young boys. With governments now actively involved in regulating the industry, the IWC decided to follow child labor laws for the first time. When R. B. Robertson sailed in 1951, no one under the age of seventeen was allowed aboard a whaler, and no one under the age of nineteen could participate in the killing, chopping up, or cooking of the whales. Boys were assigned to the mess hall, where they served food and cleared tables.

Needless to say, Robertson was a bit surprised when he visited the twenty mess boys and was greeted by some very young faces. "Their ages ranged, in my medical opinion, from thirteen to sixteen—although on the ship's articles all were listed as in their seventeenth year." Still, with government inspectors on duty twenty-four hours a day, owners and captains were careful to keep these kids safely belowdecks at all times.

And so it went through the 1940s, 1950s, and 1960s. The factory ships went out each year and filled up their cookers with little regard for the consequences. Only profound changes in economic, social, and political conditions would save the whales, changes that finally came toward the end of the 1960s.

First, inflation drove the price of outfitting a factory fleet and taking care of the 420 sailors involved to over $24 million. Diminishing whale populations meant there was little chance a company could make enough money to turn a profit. Adding to pressure on whalers was the fact that cheaper substitutes for whale oil drove its price down.

Next, a growing worldwide concern for environmental issues resulted in the publication of more and more information about the plight of whales. For the first time, cetologists were able to tell a large number of people how overhunting was destroying whale populations and present a fair view of cetacean life. One scientist, Roger Payne, managed to record the unique sounds of whale calls, which later became a hit record album. Accenting scientific concern and adding pressure to politicians for change, scores of independent groups, such as the Cousteau and Save the Whales societies, used their voices to protest the senseless destruction of whales and other animals. A group called Greenpeace even went out to confront whalers on the open sea.

All this changed the way the average person viewed whales. Gone was the idea that every whale was a killer in the image of Moby-Dick; instead, whales were increasingly viewed as harmless, intelligent, very social animals that had been ruthlessly hunted, sometimes to the verge of extinction. And since there was absolutely no real need to kill whales anymore, the hunting was seen as senseless slaughter.

This awareness eventually translated into political action. By the end of the 1960s, the United States (along with Great Britain, France, Canada, Mexico, and Argentina) began calling for severe cuts in the number of whales being killed each year. A decade later, this request was changed to a demand for a moratorium—a complete end to the hunting.

Despite stubborn resistance from countries that still had fleets in the water, the number of whales killed gradually—very gradually—began to fall. The years 1970–71 saw 38,771 go into the cookers; five years later the number was down to 29,961. By 1980, the political and social pressure to stop whaling had brought the kill down to 2,928.

"1982 marked the great turning point for the protection of whales," a jubilant Cousteau and Paccalet announced. "At its annual meeting . . . the IWC adopted a resolution banning all commercial whaling, effective 1986. The organization's membership had doubled, and includes [both large and small countries], for whom the protection of marine life is a highly important issue."

Japan, the Soviet Union, Norway, and Iceland were the only countries to object to the moratorium, and they continued to send out their factory ships.

These Greenpeace protesters know exactly what it feels like to have a diesel catcher closing in on them. They have placed their inflatable raft between a whale and the Japanese catcher Kyo Maru No. 1 to disrupt the hunting.

The ban also contains two specific loopholes, which result in several hundred whales being killed each year. One allows for certain native populations, which historically have relied on whales for subsistence and raw materials, to kill a limited number of whales every year. The other is for "scientific research" purposes.

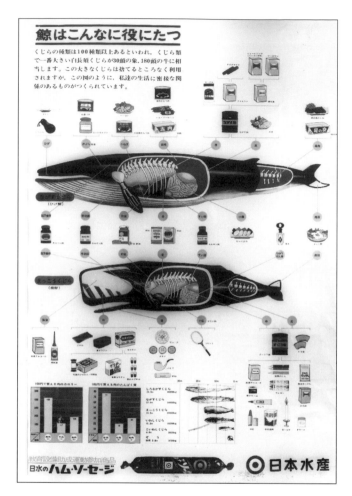

This Japanese chart shows the many types of products that can be made from whales, including food, medicines, and lubricating oils.

Despite the loopholes in the international moratorium, the killing of whales has dropped to around 600 a year. After a thousand years of commercial hunting, the Great Killing has nearly come to an end and whale populations are beginning to grow again. It is a painfully slow process, and a number of whale species—the northern right, the bowhead, the blue, and the humpback—are still considered rare or endangered. The northern right whale is down to between 300 and 600 individuals, a number so small that the species may not be able to survive.

What would it mean to lose the northern right, or any other whale, forever? Some would say not much at all, especially since we no longer need whales as a source of food, oil, or baleen. For many others, even those who live hundreds of miles inland, an ocean without whales would be incomplete and indescribably sad.

Roger Payne has some idea of what the world would be like without whales. For many years, Payne has lived near a bay in Argentina frequented by whales "spouting, swimming, courting, sailing, breathing, pushing and shoving—all at their majestic, glacial pace. . . ." Then, around mid-December, the whales leave the area and begin their winter migration.

Payne has been studying these whales for over twenty-five years, so their departure does not come as a complete surprise to him. Even so, when he looks out across the bay and sees nothing, it comes as a shock. "They are gone—have departed in the night—leaving me behind. The bay returns to silence, loses its mystery and allure. It is no longer unique, but just like any other body of water. My mind, which only hours before was free and gliding with the whales, is reoccupied with annoying details. I feel peevish and irritable—symptoms, I suppose, of loneliness of spirit."

I SUPPORT PACIFIC WHALE FOUNDATION

In the past, most of our knowledge about whales came from whalemen. Over the past fifty years, more and more organizations have been founded for the purpose of studying and preserving whales, among them the Pacific Whale Foundation.

CHAPTER ELEVEN
The New Whale Hunters

*Some of my happiest hours have been spent at night lying back
in the cockpit of a sailboat, . . . gazing at the mast sweeping
across fields of stars, while the songs of humpback whales poured
up out of the sea, to fill my head, my heart,
and finally my soul as well.*

Roger Payne, Among Whales

THE ENGINES OF THE *DOLPHIN VII* throbbed gently as the boat eased away from MacMillan Wharf, turned, and headed for the open waters of Massachusetts Bay. It was the end of October, unusually warm for the time of the year, and the water was flat calm.

Loudspeakers crackled, and a naturalist from Provincetown's Center for Coastal Studies welcomed us on board and gave us some statistical information about the boat: its length, tonnage, speed, and the number of passengers it could carry. As we rounded Long Point and Provincetown grew smaller and smaller, he added, "There's a good chance we'll see whales today. We've seen a lot of minkes this week, as well as a few humpbacks and right whales. The big ones can be shy around large boats, but you never know—we might get lucky."

Since the lower deck of the ship was crowded, I went to the upper observation deck and stationed myself near the back of the boat. It didn't take long to realize that a lot of the veteran whale watchers had assembled here.

I ♥ WHALES

Whales are still big business, though now they are more valuable alive than dead. Every year, hundreds of thousands of people venture out to see whales (bringing with them millions of tourist dollars).

Almost everyone up there either had seriously powerful binoculars or was fitting cameras with giant zoom lenses. I had neither, so I found a spot at the railing and leaned over to stare at the water.

By this time, we were several miles out, and the expanse of water seemed endless. Not only that; it seemed absolutely empty as well. No flukes, no spouts, no long, dark shapes breaking the water's surface. Nothing.

The *Dolphin's* engines slowed, and the naturalist informed us that we had arrived. If there were whales, they would be somewhere within our sight. "The most obvious thing to look for is the whale's spout," the naturalist explained. "Each breed of whale has a unique size and shape of spout, and with practice, you can tell which kind of whale you're looking at even without seeing its body, just as the old-time whalemen did."

I squinted to block the glare of reflected light and forced myself to scan the water from left to right very slowly, very carefully. I had never been on a whale-watching trip before, and like any one of the thousands of greenies before me, I wanted to be the first to spot a whale.

Left to right. Right to left. I never let my eyes leave the surface of the water even though they were already beginning to feel strained. How long have we been here? I wondered. Just ten minutes, it turned out, though it felt much longer. Imagine what it would be like to be ninety feet up in wildly swaying rigging and not spotting a whale for weeks on end.

Then it happened. "We've spotted something breaking the water's surface approximately a thousand yards off the bow," the naturalist said. The engines of the *Dolphin* revved slightly, and the boat began plowing ahead. "We're going over for a little closer inspection."

There was an immediate sense of excited tension and expectation on board as everyone crowded the rail and looked for the whales. My disappointment at not being the first to spot whales gave way to another feeling, one of being left behind. All around me I heard people murmuring, "There . . . there they are," or "Yes, I see 'em. Two of them swimming together." I, on the other hand, still hadn't seen a thing. For me, the bay was just as empty now as five minutes ago.

"Judging by the speed at which they're swimming," the naturalist explained, "we're probably following minke whales, the smallest of the baleen whales and very common in the waters off the northeast coast of the United States. They can grow to be thirty feet long and weigh up to ten tons."

Nice, I thought, but where are they? Obviously, I would never have made one of those eagle-eyed whalers. Matters got even worse when a second and then a third group of minkes were sighted. They were all around us, but all I could see was glittering water.

Fortunately, I wasn't alone. Someone nearby asked out loud the position of the second group of whales, and a helpful man with binoculars pointed to them. I followed the direction of his finger to the water and quickly saw the long, slim, black bodies and distinctive dorsal fins barely breaking the surface as they swam along.

We were two hundred feet away when the naturalist explained that we would try to maintain this distance so we wouldn't alarm the whales. Since the minkes were going at what the naturalist termed a moderate rate, we established a parallel course and tried to stay with them.

We ran along like this for several minutes when the whales veered to the left and picked up speed. We did not try to keep up with them, the naturalist explained, because we did not want to frighten them. I had been able by

Minke Whale

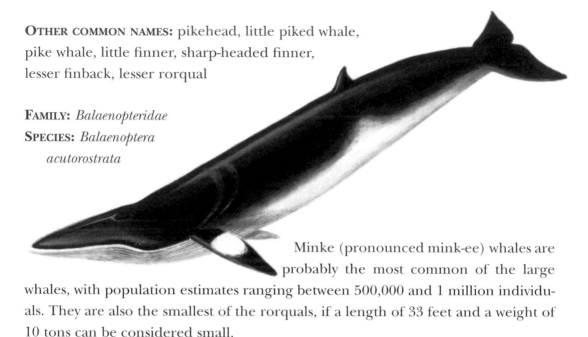

OTHER COMMON NAMES: pikehead, little piked whale, pike whale, little finner, sharp-headed finner, lesser finback, lesser rorqual

FAMILY: *Balaenopteridae*
SPECIES: *Balaenoptera*
    acutorostrata

Minke (pronounced mink-ee) whales are probably the most common of the large whales, with population estimates ranging between 500,000 and 1 million individuals. They are also the smallest of the rorquals, if a length of 33 feet and a weight of 10 tons can be considered small.

this time to find the other two groups of minkes, both moving very swiftly away from us.

"We may have something farther out," our naturalist said as the boat's speed decreased. "I'd say it's about—"

He didn't have a chance to finish his sentence before a large humpback whale burst from the water, arched its back, and came down, creating a watery splash. On board, everyone seemed to gasp at once and stiffen to rapt attention, binoculars and cameras ready. We were the new whale hunters, ready to sight, not slaughter, the great creatures.

A second, slightly smaller humpback surfaced near the first. This was a young adult, we were told, probably two or three years old. The younger

Like the other rorquals, minkes are found worldwide, gobbling up krill and small fish and straining seawater through very short baleen bristles. The minke is the only rorqual that leaps completely out of the water when breaching, reentering headfirst in a graceful dive that looks remarkably similar to a dolphin's.

Most minkes swim alone or in very small groups, and they are hard to approach in a boat. When a minke dives, it moves without much predictability and may vanish without a trace.

As long as supplies of blues, fins, and seis were plentiful, whalers ignored the minke. But as the bigger whales grew scarce or were placed on protected lists, the minke became a more and more popular target. At present, it is the only whale still being hunted commercially.

BIRTH SIZE AND WEIGHT: 8 to 9¼ feet, 770 pounds
ADULT SIZE AND WEIGHT: 23 to 33 feet, 10,000 to 20,000 pounds
SWIMMING SPEEDS: 3 to 15½ mph cruising or migrating, 18 to 21 mph fleeing
GROUP SIZE: 1 to 3; up to 100 at good feeding grounds

humpback swam a little distance; then in a graceful, almost slow-motion rhythm, its head rose out of the water, pitched forward, and reentered the water, the rest of the body following. Before it disappeared, the youngster's tail flipped up in a playful wave.

The older humpback, which the naturalist speculated was the youngster's mother, reappeared and did the same as her child. All this activity was accompanied by the clicking of cameras and excited chatter on the boat. The minkes were impressive in size, but these humpbacks were something else. The bigger one was probably fifty or fifty-five feet long and could have weighed as much as forty-five tons.

Minutes later, the two whales surfaced, swam a bit, then began what can

In this amazing photograph, a humpback whale leaps gracefully from the water directly in front of some excited whale watchers.

only be described as a water ballet. One would do a half dive and stop abruptly, so that its tail was high out of the water. It would hover in this position for a long time before submerging and popping its head out of the water. Meanwhile, the other might do a small backward roll out of the water, or slap the surface several times with its tail. Every so often, one or the other whale would disappear for a minute or two, then erupt from the calm sea in a powerful, awesome leap.

The boat got to within two hundred feet of the humpbacks, close enough for us to clearly see the long grooves that run down their undersides and the colonies of barnacles that attach themselves there. The amazing show went on for ten or twenty minutes, the whales frolicking and dancing, the humans clicking away. After a while, I moved to the other, empty, side of the boat to let someone else get to the railing.

Up to this point, my attention had been riveted on our whales. But standing alone, looking away from them, I was aware that there were at least three other large whale-watching boats in the bay. They were a small part of the new American whaling fleet that now numbers more than 400 craft leaving from over two hundred locations on the east and west coasts, plus Alaska and Hawaii. Over 3.5 million people in the United States went whale watching in 1992 alone. It's possible to view gray whales off Long Beach, California, in a three-tiered boat capable of carrying 700 passengers, or get an up-close, sea-level view of humpbacks from a small, inflatable raft in Hawaii. Wherever whales come close to shore in substantial numbers, people go out to meet them in friendly, nonviolent encounters.

Unfortunately, even today, not all whale hunting is done with cameras. Hundreds are still being killed every year. In addition to native populations, which are allowed to hunt whales for survival, three countries—Japan, Norway, and Iceland—continue to kill whales, claiming they do so for "scientific research" purposes.

The entire notion of scientific whaling upsets and disgusts most cetologists and environmentalists. Roger Payne's anger is very evident on the subject. "When the moratorium came in and Japan, Norway, and Iceland decided to go for science, the difference between scientific whaling and commercial whaling was a little difficult to see. Scientific whaling was done by the same people in the same boats hunting the same whales in the same areas and selling the same products to the same markets. . . . It occurred to me that if these people subverted science in this way there was no limit to what they might do—and no end to the kind of destruction that such a precedent might wreak."

Recently, Norway defied the international moratorium on whale hunting and set its own limit on minke whales at 250; in another part of the world,

According to the Japanese, this minke whale was killed for "scientific research" purposes in 1989.

Japan announced that it would sell the meat from twenty-one "research" minke whales (a total of 65 tons) as food. Both countries claim that minke whale populations are sufficient to tolerate commercial hunting to a limited degree.

Whales are threatened in other ways as well. Pollution from sludge dumped at sea contaminates their waters, power plants located on bays and inlets change the water temperature of rare breeding areas, and even the noise from industrial underwater explosions, ocean drilling, ship engines, and other sources can disorient whales, whose primary sense for spatial orientation is hearing. Over the past twelve years an unusually high number of beluga whales in the Gulf of St. Lawrence have been dying of intestinal cancer. Scientists from Canada's National Institute for Scientific Oceanic Research have concluded that the cause is pollution, either in the water or in the food they eat.

There is even some concern that as whale watching becomes more and more popular, the armada of boats required to carry people to the whales may disrupt these creatures' lives. This is especially true when boats enter the whales' breeding areas, as happens along Peninsula Valdes in Argentina.

Happily, the majority of cetologists and environmentalists feel that viewing migrating whales causes few problems. "In these areas," Cousteau and Paccalet agree, "whales are just 'passing through,' and human curiosity causes little disturbance. This is especially true for near-shore species, such as right whales, grays, and humpbacks."

As I stood there on the upper deck of the *Dolphin*, this certainly seemed to be true. Behind me, our humpbacks were still frolicking. In the distance, I could see another large humpback entertaining two tour boats. Minke whales—to my count at least fifteen of them—were swimming along in groups of two or three. In fact, it seemed to be the perfect way for humans to get to know and respect these creatures as gentle giants.

It was then that I noticed the bubbles, directly below me, only a few feet from the side of the boat. One, then another and another floated lazily to the surface. I leaned over the railing, counting the bubbles and wondering where they were coming from. They were small at first, but seemed to be growing larger and larger. Probably from the engines, I told myself. Or maybe they're from—

Just then, I saw an eye, at first only a murky suggestion, but getting clearer and bigger as the whale neared the surface.

A second later, her nose emerged, followed by her eyes, and fins, and body. Without a sound and very gently, she rose out of the water and came right up toward me, her powerful tail flukes lifting her forty-five tons with no effort at all. Up and up and up she came, until half or more of her body was out of the water and we were eye-to-eye.

She had turned her body as she emerged, so now only one huge, black eye was staring at me from not more than ten feet away. It would take the rest of the passengers five or more seconds to realize what was happening and come pouring over to my side of the boat. In those brief moments, I was able to look into an eye filled with ancient wisdom, curiosity, wonder, and mischief. How could anyone drive a harpoon into a gentle creature like this and not feel shame and guilt?

A humpback whale shows flukes before disappearing below the water's surface. While most of the killing has stopped, these gentle giants of the sea are still waiting for a truly happy ending.

By this time, the rails on this side of the boat were filled with people, cameras clicking away. The female humpback edged away from the boat, all the time slowly sinking into the water. Just before her flippers went under, she twisted and dove below the water's surface. She rejoined her calf; then with a few quick flicks of their tails, they sped away from the boat and across the bay.

My immediate reaction to this encounter was anything but inspired. Wow! I thought, then I remembered how close I'd been to the whale. *Wow!*

Later, when I'd had a chance to read about whales, I found a quote that seemed to fit that moment. Fittingly, it came from Étienne Lacépède, one of the first lone voices to plead the case of one of the earth's most unusual creatures way back in 1804. "Curiosity gets the better of us; we draw near to learn what we can. They live in the midst of the sea, like fish; yet they breathe like land species. They dwell in cold-water regions; yet they are warm-blooded and quick to react to the world around them. . . . They are huge; yet they can move about at great speed, even though they have only forelimbs and no feet as such. . . . Of all animals, none holds sway over so vast a dominion; their watery realm extends from the surface to the bottommost depths of the sea."

GLOSSARY

Aft or **after:** at, in, toward, or near the stern of a vessel.

Aftermast: the mast nearest the stern of a ship.

Aftermost: nearest the stern of the ship. It refers to an officer of the ship when used in connection with an individual.

Aloft: at or toward the upper rigging.

Ambergris: a substance found in the digestive system of a sperm whale that is used in the making of perfume.

Articles of agreement, also **ship's papers** or **papers:** a contract signed by each sailor before boarding a vessel, stating his legal obligation to the company, as well as his pay and the length of the voyage.

Backstay: a rope running from the top of the aft mast to the side or back of the ship to help support the mast.

Baleen, also **whalebone** or **bone:** flexible, comblike plates that grow in the mouths of toothless whales. A baleen whale takes large quantities of water into its mouth, then presses the water out through the baleen plates with its tongue. After the water is gone, the only thing left in its mouth is food, which is chiefly a tiny shrimplike creature called krill.

Barnacle: a marine crustacean that forms a hard shell and attaches itself to the bottom of submerged surfaces.

Barrel: on a whaleship, a unit of measurement. Each "barrel" contained 3½ gallons. *See also* Cask.

Beach, to: to come up on land, said of a whale.

Beam: a timber that crosses the widest part of a ship, used to support and brace the ship's sides.

Beam end: the outermost part of the beam. When water is at the ship's beam end, it means the water is at deck level.

Becket: a device, such as a looped rope, strap, or grommet, used to hold ropes, spars, or oars in position.

Bilgewater: water that collects in the very lowest part of a ship and is often stagnant and foul.

Blanket, also **blanket piece** or **piece:** a long strip of blubber ripped from the whale by using a block and tackle. The blanket is then cut into progressively smaller chunks before being cooked in the try-pots.

Blubber: the thick oily layer of fat just below the skin of a whale that serves as protection against pressure and cold.

Boatheader: the man who steered the whaleboat as it approached a whale for harpooning, and who afterward killed it with a lance. Usually one of the mates handled this job, but sometimes a ship's captain headed a boat.

Boatsteerer or **harpooneer:** this man had three tasks in a whaleboat—he pulled the foremost oar (called the harpoon oar); then he struck the whale with a harpoon; then, after making fast to a whale, he took over the rudder from the boatheader. Clifford Ashley insists that the term harpooner was "not used by whalemen," though many personal accounts spell the word with one e.

Bobstays: ropes or chains used to steady the bowsprit.

Boil, to: to cook or try out the oil from a whale's blubber.

Book, to: to sign articles of agreement for a whaling voyage.

Boom: a long pole or spar used to hold the bottom part of a sail.

Bow: the front section of a ship or boat.

Bowsprit: a long wooden pole that projects out from the front of the ship.

Breach, to: to leap completely (or nearly completely) out of the water and land with a splash. Humpback whales have been known to breach two hundred times in a single display.

Brine: water containing large amounts of salt.

Bulwark: the part of a ship's side that is above the deck.

Bunk: a sailor's bed. A bunk on a whaleship was nothing more than a wooden shelf made somewhat softer by a thin mattress. *See also* Donkey's Breakfast.

Buoy boat: vessel used in pelagic whaling to inflate dead whales so they float on the water's surface and can be found by a corvette. *See also* Corvette.

Cachalot (pronounced cash-a-lot): the French word for a sperm whale; sometimes used by English-speaking whalemen.

Captain, also **skipper** or **master of the ship:** the man in command of the ship and ultimately responsible for the ship, crew, and officers, as well as for locating and killing whales and bringing the oil and baleen to port for sale.

Case: the forehead of a sperm whale. It is outside the skull, and is composed almost entirely of spermaceti.

Cask: a barrel-like container used on a whaler. Everything from whale oil to spare sails was stored in casks. Whale oil was usually stored in large casks that held between five and seven barrels (157½ to 220½ gallons) each. Some ships went out with casks that could hold fourteen barrels of oil and weighed about two tons when full. A ship could hold anywhere from four hundred to six hundred casks, depending on the size of the hold, as well as the size of the casks.

Cathead: a short beam located to the side of the bowsprit, used as a support to lift the anchor.

Cetologist: a scientist who studies whales and related animals and their behavior.

Chaser: a steam- or diesel-powered vessel designed for the high-speed chase of whales.

Chest or **sea chest:** a small, sturdy container in which a sailor's personal items were stored. Because space was so limited on a whaler, the sea chest was also used as a seat or table.

Cicatrix: scar tissue that forms as a result of a wound.

Clipper ship: a sharp-bowed ship built for great speed and used to transport passengers and important items, such as mail.

Coaming: a raised curb around an opening in the deck, designed to keep out water.

Compass, to box the: to memorize the various points of the compass in proper order.

Cooper: a maker of wooden casks and tubs. Because virtually everything was stored in some sort of cask, especially the valuable whale oil, the cooper's job was vital for a successful voyage and a reliable cooper was a highly valued member of the crew.

Corvette: a small, unarmed boat used in pelagic whaling to haul dead whales to the factory ship.

Cowfish: another name for the bottlenose dolphin. An adult cowfish can be 6 to 12 feet in length and weigh 330 to 1,450 pounds. Cowfish were often hunted by whalers as sport or for food.

Cut in, to: to remove blubber from a whale. The process was known as cutting in.

Cutting spade: a long-handled chisel-shaped implement used for cutting blubber.

Cutting stage: a wooden platform with a low railing that was lowered when cutting in a whale. The cutting stage allowed the men to get very close to the whale and meant they did not have to stop working when a blanket piece was hoisted onto the deck.

Deckspade: a tool used on deck for cutting blubber, similar to a cutting spade but with a shorter handle.

Dock the rations, to: to withhold some portion of each meal as punishment.

Donkey's breakfast: a thin, straw- or cornhusk-filled mattress. New hands were usually issued one of these when they got their outfits before sailing.

Drop whaleboats, to: to lower the whaleboats into the water.

Drug, also **drogue** or **druge:** a wooden plank or block that was fastened to a whale-line and intended to slow a harpooned whale's dive and tire the animal.

Eye of the ship: a place belowdecks at the very front of a ship under the forecastle.

Factory ship: a large vessel that functions as the command center for a pelagic whaling fleet, where whales are cut up, cooked, packaged, and stored while at sea.

Fat: a whale's blubber.

Fin: an appendage extending from the body of a whale and used for locomotion, steering, and maintaining balance.

Fitting or **fitting out:** getting a ship ready and supplied for a whaling voyage.

Flenser: the man who makes the initial cut to a whale's body.

Flipper: the paddle-shaped front fin of a whale, used for locomotion, steering, and maintaining balance. Whales will often use their flipper to slap the surface of the water, called flipper-slapping.

Flukes: the two halves of a whale's tail, which is horizontally flattened. Whales are said to be fluking when they raise their flukes in the air upon diving. Whales also slap the surface of the water with their flukes, which is called tail-slapping or lobtailing.

Flurry: the dying struggle of a whale. After a whale weakens due to injuries, it will list to one side and swim in progressively smaller circles. Very often, it dies after thrashing the water wildly with its flukes.

Forecastle or **fo'c'sle:** a tiny, unventilated space belowdecks at the front of a ship where common seamen slept, ate, and stored personal belongings.

Forechains: chains used to secure an anchor to the front of the ship while at sea.

Foremost: nearest the bow or front of a vessel. A foremost hand was a common seaman.

Fore-topsail: the sail at the very top of the foremost mast.

Forward: at, toward, or near the bow of the ship. A forward hand was a common seaman who slept in the forecastle.

Foxes: small ropes made by twisting together two or more strands of tarred yarn.

Gam: a visit between whaleships at sea. When whaleships visit they are said to be gamming.

Gilding the trucks: painting the metal or wooden devices used to hold the flags or banners at the very top of the uppermost mast.

Glass or **spyglass:** a small telescope.

Go aloft, to: to climb the ropes to the masthead.

Goose-pen: a water tank under the tryworks that prevented the ship from catching fire.

Grampus: a small member of the whale family, possibly the Risso's dolphin, frequently found close to a ship. Grampuses puff or grunt very loudly.

Grax: the stomach and intestines of a whale; the term is used chiefly on factory ships.

Green hand or **greenie:** an inexperienced man or boy on his first voyage.

Grub: food served aboard a ship.

Gullet: the throat.

Gunnel: a variant spelling of gunwale: the upper edge of a ship's side.

Gurry: a stinky sort of stew that consisted of brackish water, sewage, decayed bits of whale meat, and rancid whale oil.

Hand: any worker, such as a seaman.

Harpoon, also harping iron or iron: barbed implement used to fasten onto a whale. The best and most commonly used harpoon was the Temple Toggle-Iron, invented in 1848 by Lewis Temple, a black craftsman from New Bedford.

Harpoon gun: a deck-mounted cannon that can fire an explosive harpoon into a whale. Various kinds of cannon and shoulder guns were experimented with during the seventeenth and early eighteenth centuries, but none proved reliable until Norwegian Svend Foyn developed his in 1864.

Hatchway or hatch: an opening from the deck leading to any lower area of a ship.

Helm: the tiller or, later, the wheel used in steering the ship.

Hitches: the knot and loop securing the whaleline to the harpoon.

Hold: a space belowdecks to store equipment, supplies, and cargo, such as whale oil or baleen.

Hook chain: a heavy chain used to lower and raise the anchor.

Hove: past tense of heave; to raise or lift with great effort.

Hull: the main body of a ship, not including the mast, sails, yards, and rigging.

Iron: a harpoon.

Irons: shackles.

Junk: the wedge-shaped lower half of a sperm whale's forehead. It is composed of equal parts of white meat and oily matter, both regular whale oil and spermaceti. There is no blood in this section, which is why the flesh is white.

Knot: a unit of speed, approximately 1.15 miles per hour.

Lanyard: a short rope used to secure ladders, rigging, or other pieces of equipment.

Larboard: the left-hand or port side of a ship facing forward.

Lay: a whaleman's proportionate share of the profit of a voyage. The principle by which the shares were allocated was known as the lay system.

Learn the ropes, to: to memorize the name and function of every rope, chain, and tackle used to support and control the sails and yards.

Lemmer: a man stationed in the aft section of a factory ship whose job is to saw and cut up whatever is left of a whale once the flensers have done their work.

Leviathan: from the Bible (Job 14:1), referring to a monstrous sea creature and commonly applied to large whales, especially sperm whales.

Line: *See* Whaleline.

Log or **logbook:** a book in which the speed and position of the ship as well as events of importance were recorded daily.

Lookout: a man aloft who searched the water for whales, other ships, and land.

Lower, to: to put a whaleboat into the water.

Main cabin: a large space just forward of the captain's quarters used by the officers of a ship for meals and recreation.

Mainmast: the tallest mast of a ship. In a three-masted ship, this is usually the middle one.

Make fast, to, also **to fasten to** or **to get fast:** to lodge a harpoon firmly in a whale so that it will not come loose.

Man: to join in the operation of a piece of equipment, as in "man the pumps."

Mast: a tall, vertical pole used to support the sails and riggings. Many whaleships carried three masts— the fore (at the front of the ship), the main (in the middle), and the mizzen (at the back). Each mast is erected in sections, one attached to the other. For instance, the mainmast would be topped by the main-topmast, which would be topped by the main-topgallant mast, which would be topped by the main-royalmast.

Master of a ship: the captain.

Masthead: the top of a mast.

Mate: an officer of the ship. Whalers always had at least three mates. The first mate was just below the captain in authority and was generally in charge of running the ship when the captain was belowdecks or ill. The second and third mates were ranked below the first mate. In addition to shipboard duties, each mate was the boatheader for a whaleboat. When a ship had four whaleboats, a fourth mate would often be added to the crew. A fourth mate was a highly skilled seaman and whaleman, but he did not have officer status.

Mate, to: said of two whaling ships; to agree to hunt whales together with the resulting oil and baleen being divided up equally.

Merchant ship: a ship used to haul goods.

Midship or **waist:** the middle of the vessel.

Mince: to cut blubber into small pieces.

Navigator: the person responsible for figuring out the location of the ship and plotting its course. Most captains acted as their own navigators, with help from one or more mates. Oddly enough, most sailors were not navigators and would have become lost at sea.

Oil: whale oil.

Poop deck or **quarterdeck:** the raised aftermost deck of a ship, which was usually reserved for officers only.

Port: the left side of a ship facing forward.

Ports of call: the various places where a ship stops, whether scheduled or not.

Rigging: the system of ropes, chains, and tackle used to control the sails.

Royalmast: a small pole or mast and its sail and rigging positioned at the top of a mast.

School, also **pod, herd,** or **shoal:** a group of whales that travel together. School and schoal can also be used in connection with fish, as in "a school of fish."

Schooner: a ship with two or more masts with the rear mast the tallest of all.

Scrimshaw: useful and decorative objects made from the bone and teeth of a sperm whale. The exact origins of this art form are unclear. Some believe that Eskimo carvings on walrus tusks inspired whalemen to begin creating these objects; others maintain that it was first practiced on board whaling ships.

Scupper: an opening in the side of the ship at deck level that allows water to run off.

Ship, to: to sign articles for a voyage.

Ship an oar, to: to take an oar out of the water and secure it on board.

Ship's agent: the person responsible for hiring a ship's crew. Agents often held part ownership in one or more ships.

Shoal: a large group, generally of fish or marine mammals.

Shore station: an area on land where whales are cut in and the blubber boiled.

Skipper: the captain of a ship.

Sound, to: to dive deep underwater.

Spar: any pole used as a mast, boom, yard, or bowsprit, or used to support the rigging.

Speak, to: to pause during a voyage in order to communicate with another ship.

Spermaceti: a high-quality oil taken from the case of a sperm whale and used chiefly to make candles and in the manufacture of cosmetics.

Spout or **blow:** the moisture-laden air exhaled by whales. Spout can also be used as a verb, as in "the whale spouted."

Spout hole or **blowhole:** the external opening to a whale's nasal passage located on or near the top of the head (except in the sperm whale, where it is located on the left side near the snout). Baleen whales have two spout holes side by side; toothed whales have just one.

Spyglass or **glass:** a small telescope.

Starboard: the right side of a ship as you face forward.

Stern: the rear portion of a ship or boat.

Stew, to: to boil or cook blubber.

Stove, to: smashed; said of a whaleboat or ship. Usually this refers to damage by a whale, but can also apply to holes, cracks, and splits caused by hoisting or lowering boats.

Strike, to: to harpoon a whale.

Stroke, to: to pull an oar through the water.

Stroke oar: the shortest and lightest oar in a whaleboat.

Tail fluke: *See* Flukes.

Tank: container used to cool and store whale oil.

"There blows": the common call when a whale was sighted, repeated each time it spouts. There seem to be many variations of the call, including "Ah, blows!" "Blows!" "There she blows" "There she breaches!" and "There go flukes!" The call was drawn out to last many seconds, so as to attract the attention of everyone on board. The officer of the deck would then ask, "Where away?" to determine the direction of the whale in relation to the ship.

Tiller: a lever controlling the ship's rudder, used to steer the ship.

Trick, to take a: to take a turn at some duty, such as steering the ship.

Try out, to: to extract oil by boiling, said of blubber. The process was known as trying out.

Try-pots: large containers in which blubber is cooked.

Tryworks: a large, brick structure holding the try-pots.

Tub: a container that holds whaleline.

Tug: a small but powerful vessel used to pull or push a larger ship out of a harbor and into open water.

Waist: *See* Midship.

Watch: a work shift. At all times during a voyage, at least half the crew would be "on watch" to take in or let out sails, steer the ship, help with repairs, move items around, and, in general, be available to do any sort of work required. The other half of the men would be off-duty and belowdecks. Each watch was four hours long, though a turn at the wheel usually lasted just two hours. Between four in the afternoon and eight at night, all hands were on duty; this was called the dog-watch.

Well: an enclosure inside a ship's hold.

Whale-fisher: a whale hunter. Even though whalers knew that whales were mammals, they often referred to them as fishes.

Whaleline or **line:** the rope attached to a harpoon. Whalemen would often fasten wooden planks or blocks (called drugs, drogues, or druges) to the line in order to slow down and tire a fleeing whale.

Wharf: a landing where a ship can tie up and unload cargo.

Wheel: the rudder control used to steer a ship.

Yard: a long tapering pole hung at right angles to a mast used to support a sail. A yardarm is the outermost end of this pole.

BIBLIOGRAPHY AND SOURCES

In order to conserve space, I have taken the liberty of combining the bibliography and sources in as compact a form as possible. The opening two sections are general reference books, the first dealing with whales, the second focusing on the whaling industry. After this, the list is divided up by chapters. A number of individuals are quoted extensively throughout the text, but I have chosen to list the sources of their quotes only in the chapter where they make their initial appearance. An asterisk (*) indicates a personal account by someone who has been on a whale ship.

GENERAL REFERENCE BOOKS ON WHALES

Baker, Mary L. *Whales, Dolphins, and Porpoises of the World.* Garden City, NY: Doubleday, 1987.

Carwardine, Mark. *Whales, Dolphins and Porpoises.* New York: Dorling Kindersley, 1995.

Cousteau, Jacques-Yves. *The Whale: Mighty Monarch of the Sea.* Garden City, NY: Doubleday, 1981.

———— and Yves Paccalet. *Whales.* New York: Abrams, 1986.

Ellis, Richard. *The Book of Whales.* New York: Knopf, 1980.

————. *Men and Whales.* New York: Knopf, 1991.

Fichter, George S. *Whales and Other Marine Mammals.* New York: Golden Press, 1990.

Friends of the Earth. *The Whale Manual.* San Francisco: Friends of the Earth, 1978.

Harrison, Richard, ed. *Whales, Dolphins & Porpoises.* New York and London: Facts on File, 1988.

Leatherwood, Stephen, Randall R. Reeves, William F. Perrin, and William E. Evans. *Whales, Dolphins, and Porpoises of the Eastern North Pacific and Adjacent Arctic Waters: A Guide to Their Identification.* New York: Dover, 1988.

McNulty, Faith. *The Great Whales.* Garden City, NY: Doubleday, 1974.

Scammon, Charles Melville. *The Marine Mammals of the Northeastern Coast of North America.* New York: Dover, 1968.

Small, George L. *The Blue Whale.* New York: Columbia University Press, 1971.

GENERAL REFERENCE BOOKS ON THE WHALING INDUSTRY

Brewington, Dorothy E. R. *Marine Paintings and Drawings in Mystic Seaport Museum.* Mystic, CT: Mystic Seaport Museum, 1982.

Brewington, M. V., and D. Brewington. *Kendall Museum Paintings.* Salem, MA: Kendall Whaling Museum, 1965.

———. *Kendall Whaling Museum Prints.* Salem, MA: Kendall Whaling Museum, 1969.

Dow, George Francis. *Whale Ships and Whaling: A Pictorial History.* Salem, MA: The Marine Research Society, 1925.

Hawes, Charles Beardman. *Whaling.* New York: Doubleday, 1924.

Irvin, Shapiro, and Edouard A. Stackpole. *The Story of Yankee Whaling.* New York: American Heritage, 1959.

Robotti, Frances Diane. *Whaling and Old Salem.* New York: Bonanza, 1963.

Sanderson, Ivan T. *A History of Whaling.* New York: Barnes & Noble, 1993.

Stackpole, Edouard A. *The Sea-Hunters: The Great Age of Whaling.* New York: Bonanza, 1953.

Starbuck, Alexander. *History of the American Whale Fishery: From Its Earliest Inception to the Year 1876.* New York: Argosy-Antiquarian, 1964.

Verrill, A. Hyatt. *The Real Story of the Whaler.* New York: Appleton, 1916.

CHAPTER 1: ENTICED BY THE RICHES

*Browne, J. Ross. *Etchings of a Whale Cruise, with Notes of a Sojourn on the Island of Zanzibar. To Which Is Appended a Brief History of the Whale Fishery, Its Past and Present Condition.* New York: Harper, 1846.

Clark, Grahame. "Whales as an Economic Factor in Prehistoric Europe." *Antiquity*, Vol. XXI, No. 82, June 1947, Gloucester, England.

Crevecoeur, J. Hector St. John de. *Letters from an American Farmer*. London: Dent, 1782.

Edwards, Everett Joshua, and Jeannette Edwards Rattray. *"Whale Off!" The Story of American Shore Whaling*. New York: Frederick A. Stokes, 1932.

Greeley, Horace, et al. *The Great Industries of the United States Being an Historical Summary of the Origin, Growth, and Perfection of the Chief Industrial Arts of This Country*. Hartford, CT: J. B. Burr & Hyde, 1873.

Leary, Warren E. "Fossils Point to a Walking Ancestor of Whales." *The New York Times*, Friday, January 14, 1994, Sec. A, p. 25.

Lacépède, comte de. *Histoire naturelle de cétacés*. Paris, 1804.

Morison, Samuel Eliot. *The Maritime History of Massachusetts: 1783–1860*. Boston and New York: Houghton Mifflin, 1921.

———. *The European Discovery of America: The Northern Voyages A.D. 500–1600*. New York: Oxford University Press, 1971.

Mount. *Purchas: His Pilgrims*. London: Hakluyt Society, n.d.

*Scoresby, William, Jr. *Journal of a Voyage to the Northern Whale-Fishery; Including Researches and Discoveries on the Eastern Coast of West Greenland, Made in the Summer of 1822, in the Ship* Baffin *of Liverpool*. Edinburgh, Scotland: Constable, 1823.

Weiss, Harry B. *Whaling in New Jersey*. Trenton, NJ: New Jersey Agricultural Society, 1972.

Wilford, John Noble. "How the Whale Lost Its Legs and Returned to the Sea." *The New York Times*, Tuesday, May 3, 1994, Sec. C, p. 1.

(For more information on prehistoric and early commercial whaling, see both Cousteau titles, both Ellis books, and Robotti, Sanderson, and Stackpole from General References.)

CHAPTER 2: SO WE WERE ALL SOON ABOARD

*Ashley, Clifford W. *The Yankee Whaler*. Garden City, NY: Halcyon House, 1942.

Beale, Charles E., and M. R. Gately, eds. *Gately's Universal Educator*. Boston: M. R. Gately & Co., 1883.

*Bennett, Frederick Debell. *Narrative of a Whaling Voyage Around the Globe from the Year 1833 to 1836*. London: Richard Bentley, 1840.

*Bodfish, Hartson H., and Joseph C. Allen. *Chasing the Bowhead*. Cambridge, MA: Harvard University Press, 1936.

*Bullen, Frank T. *The Cruise of the Cachalot*. New York: Appleton, 1926. (This book was originally published as a novel, but whaling historians feel it is an accurate and not overly dramatized account of Bullen's actual voyage on the whaleship *Splendid*.)

*Cloud, Enoch Carter. *Enoch's Voyage: Life on a Whale Ship 1851–1854*. Wakefield, RI: Moyer Bell, 1994.

Davis, Charles G. *Ships of the Past*. Salem, MA: The Marine Research Society, 1929.

*Dodge, George A. *A Whaling Voyage in the Pacific Ocean*. Salem, MA: Salem Gazette Press, 1882.

Durant, John and Alice. *Pictorial History of American Ships: On the High Seas and Inland Waters*. New York: A. S. Barnes, 1953.

*Erskine, Charles. *Twenty Years Before the Mast*. Washington: Smithsonian Institution Press, 1985.

Gemming, Elizabeth. *Blow Ye Winds Westerly: The Seaports & Sailing Ships of Old New England*. New York: Crowell, 1971.

Lancaster, Clay. *Nantucket in the Nineteenth Century*. New York: Dover, 1979.

*Tilton, George Fred. *Cap'n George Fred*. Garden City, NY: Doubleday, 1927.

Wood, J. G. *Illustrated Natural History Comprising Descriptions of Animals, Birds, Fishes, Reptiles, Insects, etc., with Sketches of Their Peculiar Habits and Characteristics*. Boston: DeWolfe, Fiske & Co., 1887.

(For more on recruitment practices by whaling companies, see Robotti, Sanderson, and Stackpole.)

CHAPTER 3: WORK LIKE HORSES AND LIVE LIKE PIGS

*Allen, Harry (Capt.). *Sails and Whales*. Boston: Houghton Mifflin, 1951.

McNally, Robert. *So Remorseless a Havoc: Of Dolphins, Whales, and Men*. Boston: Little, Brown, 1981.

*Morrell, Moses E. "Whim-Whams & Opinions" Journal. Private collection.

*Samuels, S. *From the Forecastle to the Cabin*. New York: Harper, 1887.

*Weir, Robert. Personal diary from the collection of the G. W. Blunt White Library, Mystic Seaport Maritime Museum.

*Williams, Harold, ed. *One Whaling Family*. Boston: Houghton Mifflin, 1964.

CHAPTER 4: IT ALL SEEMS SO STRANGE

Church, Albert Cook. *Whale Ships and Whaling*. New York: Bonanza, 1938.

DePauw, Linda Grant. *Seafaring Women*. Boston: Houghton Mifflin, 1982.

Garner, Stanton, ed. *The Captain's Best Mate*. Providence, RI, 1966.

Putney, Martha S. *Black Sailors: Afro-American Merchant Seamen and Whalemen*. New York: Greenwood, 1987.

Riggs, Dionis Coffin. *Far Off Island: The Story of My Grandmother*. New York: McGraw-Hill, 1948.

*Russell, Mary Hayden. Journal kept on board ship *Emily*, 1823–1825. Private collection.

Whipple, A. B. C. *The Whalers*. Alexandria, VA: Time-Life Books, 1979.

Whiting, Emma Mayhew, and Henry Beetle Hough. *Whaling Wives*. Boston: Houghton Mifflin, 1953.

CHAPTER 5: NOTHING SO ELECTRIFYING

Bales, Ernest Sutherland, ed. *The Bible* (King James Version). New York: Simon & Schuster, 1951.

*Bell, J. J. *The Whale Hunters*. London: Nelson, 1929.

Dulles, Foster Rhea. *Lowered Boats: A Chronicle of American Whaling*. New York: Harcourt, 1933.

*Ferguson, Robert. *Harpooner: A Four-Year Voyage on the Barque* Kathleen *1880–1884*. Philadelphia: University of Pennsylvania Press, 1936.

Murphy, Robert Cushman. *A Dead Whale or a Stove Boat*. Boston: Houghton Mifflin, 1967.

Tripp, William Henry. *There Goes Flukes*. New Bedford, MA: Reynolds, 1938.

Watson, Arthur C. *The Long Harpoon*. New Bedford, MA: Reynolds, 1929.

(Almost every personal account cited in the bibliography contains a detailed account of harpooning and lancing a whale. Also see Robotti, Sanderson, Stackpole, and Verrill.)

CHAPTER 6: A FOOT OF OIL ON DECK

Melville, Herman. *Moby-Dick or the Whale*. New York: Barnes & Noble, 1994.

(This is a highly dramatized novel of the search for the white whale, but the actual whaling scenes are accurate and reflect Melville's own experience on the whaler *Acushnet*.)

(Almost every personal account listed describes the cutting up and boiling of a whale in detail. Also see Ashley and Bullen from Chapter 2, and Robotti, Sanderson, and Stackpole from General References.)

CHAPTER 7: A STRANGE UNEVEN SORT OF LIFE

Doerflinger, William Main. *Shantymen & Shantyboys*. New York: Macmillan, 1951.

Raban, Jonathan, ed. *The Oxford Book of the Sea*. New York: Oxford University Press, 1992.

(Almost every personal account cited describes the leisure time activities aboard a whaler. Ashley from Chapter 2 has a particularly good section on the art of scrimshaw. Also see Bullen, Cloud, and Dodge from Chapter 2, Weir from Chapter 3, Russell from Chapter 4, and Melville from Chapter 6, plus Robotti, Sanderson, and Stackpole from General References.)

CHAPTER 8: WE HAVE BEEN STOVE BY A WHALE

Arvin, A. *Herman Melville*. New York: Sloane, 1950.

*Beale, Thomas. *The Natural History of the Sperm Whale, to Which Is Added a Sketch of a South-Sea Whaling Voyage*. London: John van Voorst, 1839.

*Chase, Owen. *Narrative of the Most Extraordinary and Distressing Shipwreck of the Whale-Ship* Essex *of Nantucket*. New York: W. B. Gilley, 1821.

Chappel, Thomas. *An Account of the Loss of the* Essex *from Having Been Struck by a Whale in the South Seas with Some Interesting Particulars of the Sufferings of Her Crew on a Desert Island and in Their Boats at Sea*. London: Religious Tract Society, 1830.

Ellis, Richard. *Monsters of the Sea*. New York: Bantam Doubleday Dell, 1991.

Reynolds, J. E. "Mocha Dick, or the White Whale of the Pacific." *Knickerbocker Magazine*, No. 13, May 1839.

Tyerman, D., and G. Bennet. *Narrative of the Loss of the Whale-Ship* Essex. London: London Missionary Society, 1831.

(For more information on the nature of whales, see both Cousteau and both Ellis books in General Reference.)

CHAPTER 9: HOMEWARD BOUND!!!!!!

(Almost every personal account listed deals with the journey home, though Ashley, Cloud, and Bullen are particularly good.)

Chapter 10: The Great Killing

Ackerman, Diane. *The Moon by Whale Light.* New York: Vintage, 1992.

*Andrews, Roy Chapman. *Whale Hunting with Gun and Camera.* New York: Appleton, 1916.

*Ash, Christopher. *Whaler's Eye.* New York: Macmillan, 1962.

Baky, John S., ed. *Humans and Animals.* New York: H. W. Wilson, 1980.

*Bennett, A. G. *Whaling in the Antarctic.* New York: Holt, 1932.

Brower, Kenneth, and William Curtsinger. *Wake of the Whale.* San Francisco: Friends of the Earth, 1979.

Carringhar, Sally. *The Twilight Seas: A Blue Whale's Journey.* New York: Weybright and Talley, 1975.

Hunter, Robert. *Warriors of the Rainbow: A Chronicle of the Greenpeace Movement.* New York: Holt, 1979.

———— and Rex Wyler. *To Save a Whale: The Voyages of Greenpeace.* San Francisco: Chronicle Books, 1978.

Liversidge, Douglas. *The Whale Killers.* New York: Rand McNally, 1963.

McClung, Robert M. *Hunted Mammals of the Sea.* New York: Morrow, 1978.

*Robertson, R. B. *Of Whales and Men.* New York: Knopf, 1954.

Scheffer, Victor B. *The Year of the Whale.* New York: Scribner, 1969.

Singer, Peter. *Animal Liberation: A New Ethics for Our Treatment of Animals.* New York: Random House, 1975.

Udall, Stewart L. "Hope for Earth's Fragile Wildlife." International Union for Conservation of Nature and Natural Resources, IUCN Bulletin (Morges, Switzerland), 1966, Vol. 2, p. 2.

Villiers, A. J. *Whaling in the Frozen South.* Indianapolis, IN: Bobbs-Merrill, 1925.

(For more information on pelagic whaling, see both Cousteau and both Ellis books, Robotti, Sanderson, and Small, plus McNally from Chapter 3.)

Chapter 11: The New Whale Hunters

Angier, Natalie. "DNA Tests Find Meat of Endangered Whales for Sale in Japan." *The New York Times,* Tuesday, September 13, 1994, Sec. C, p. 4.

Associated Press. "Japanese Rally for Hunting of Whales." *The New York Times,* Tuesday, April 20, 1993, Sec. C, p. 4.

————. "Norwegians Harpoon 50 Whales." *The New York Times*, Tuesday, June 29, 1994, Sec. A, p. 20.

Broad, William J. "Calving of Right Whales Faces New Threats." *The New York Times*, Tuesday, April 9, 1996, Sec. C, p. 1.

Browne, Malcolm B. "Human Noises in Ocean Held to Threaten Marine Mammals." *The New York Times*, Tuesday, October 19, 1993, Sec. C, p. 1.

Carwardine, Mark. *On the Trail of the Whale.* Guildford, England: Thunder Bay Publishing Co., 1994.

Coerr, E., and W. E. Evans. *Gigi: A Baby Whale Borrowed for Science and Returned to the Sea.* New York: Putnam, 1980.

Corrigan, Patricia. *Where the Whales Are: Your Guide to Whale-Watching Trips in North America.* Chester, CT: Globe Pequot Press, 1991.

Darnton, John. "Norwegians Claim Their Whaling Rights." *The New York Times*, Saturday, August 7, 1993, Sec. A, p. 1.

Delatiner, Barbara. "On the Water with Dr. Arthur Kopelman: 'See, I Promised You Whales, and Whales You've Got.'" *The New York Times*, Sunday, July 31, 1994, Long Island Section, p. 1.

Farnsworth, Clyde H. "Scientists Are Puzzled over the Deaths of Whales in the St. Lawrence." *The New York Times*, Tuesday, August 22, 1995, Sec. C, p. 12.

Fullam, Anne C. "The Humpback Whale Is Making a Comeback" and "Effects of Whaling." *The New York Times*, Sunday, April 24, 1994, New Jersey Section, p. 7C.

Hoyt, Erich. *The Whale Watcher's Handbook.* New York: Doubleday, 1984.

McIntyre, J. *The Delicate Art of Whale Watching.* San Francisco: Sierra Club Books, 1982.

Mowat, Farley. *A Whale for the Killing.* Boston: Little, Brown, 1972.

Payne, Roger. *Among Whales.* New York: Scribner, 1995.

Pollack, Andrew. "Commission to Save Whales Endangered, Too." *The New York Times*, Tuesday, May 18, 1993, Sec. C, p. 4.

Reuters. "Japan to Sell Meat from 'Research' Whales." *The New York Times*, Saturday, November 12, 1994, World News Briefs, Sec. 1, p. 7.

Sherman, Paul. "The Friends of the Whales Fight a Salt Factory." *The New York Times*, Thursday, April 27, 1995, Sec. A, p. 24.

(For more on the present-day threats to whales and the effects of whale watching, see both Cousteau and both Ellis books.)

WHALE CONSERVATION
& RESEARCH ORGANIZATIONS

If you are interested in knowing more about whales and how you can help ensure their survival, you might want to write to one of the following groups for more information.

Allied Whale
College of the Atlantic
Bar Harbor, ME 04609

American Cetacean Society
P.O. Box 2639
San Pedro, CA 90731

California Marine Mammal Center
Marin Headlands Ranger Station
Fort Cronkhite, CA 94965

Center for Whale Research
1359 Smuggler's Cove
Friday Harbor, WA 98250

Cetacean Research Unit
P.O. Box 159
Gloucester, MA 01930

Cetacean Society International
P.O. Box 9145
Wethersfield, CT 06109

Cousteau Society
930 West 21st Street
Norfolk, VA 23517

Greenpeace USA
1436 U Street NW
Washington, DC 20009

International Wildlife Coalition
634 North Falmouth Highway
P.O. Box 388
North Falmouth, MA 02556

Marine Mammal Fund
Fort Mason Center
Building E
San Francisco, CA 94123

Marine Mammal Stranding Center
P.O. Box 773
3625 Brigantine Boulevard
Brigantine, NJ 08203

Pacific Whale Foundation
Kealia Beach Plaza, Suite 21
101 North Kihei Road
Kihei Maui, HI 96753

Save the Whales
P.O. Box 3650
Washington, DC 20007

Society for Marine Mammalogy
c/o Robert L. Brownell, Jr.
U.S. Fish and Wildlife Service
P.O. Box 70
San Simeon, CA 93452

Whale and Dolphin Conservation
Society
191 Weston Road
Lincoln, MA 01773

Whale Center
411 Campbell Street
Tofino, British Columbia VOR 2ZO
Canada

ACKNOWLEDGMENTS & PICTURE CREDITS

This book could not have been researched and written, nor the photographs assembled, without the generous help of many individuals and organizations. Among those who have shared their knowledge and skills, I especially want to thank Mary Jean Blasdale of the Old Dartmouth Historical Society/New Bedford Whaling Museum; Philip L. Budlong of Mystic Seaport Museum; Arthur Cohen; D. Louise Dembrowsky of the Kendall Whaling Museum; Diane Goloff; Mark Kessler of Editions Robert Laffont; Calvin Lane, Interpretation Staff, Mystic Seaport Museum; and Sally A. Mizroch of the National Marine Mammal Laboratory.

Author's collection: 11 (top & bottom), 14, 20, 23, 32, 39 (bottom), 40, 50, 68, 84, 87, 89, 100, 103, 108, 115, 117, 123, 144, 147, 157 (bottom)

Editions Robert Laffont: 12, 24, 44, 52, 74, 94, 106, 140, 174

Greenpeace/Culley: 167

Greenpeace/Morgan: 178

Kendall Whaling Museum: 83, 98, 120, 125, 150, 157 (top), 168

Kingston-upon-Hull Museums: 7

Mary Anne Stets Photo/Mystic Seaport Museum: 37, 92

Mystic Seaport Museum: 27, 88 (bottom), 109, 110, 136

Nantucket Historical Society: 2, 34, 42, 58, 126, 133

National Marine Mammal Laboratory/Sally A. Mizroch: 8, 180

New Bedford Whaling Museum: 55, 112, 138

Old Dartmouth Historical Society/New Bedford Whaling Museum: 22, 39 (top), 43, 47, 49, 57, 61, 62, 64, 65, 71, 73, 77, 79, 88 (top), 90, 91, 128, 142, 145, 154

Pacific Whale Foundation: 170, 172, 176

San Francisco Maritime National Historic Park: 30, 148, 159, 160

INDEX

Italics indicate illustration or caption